NINE PARTS WATER, ONE PART SAND.

KIM SALMON AND THE FORMULA FOR GRUNGE

Published by Melbourne Books
Level 9, 100 Collins Street,
Melbourne, VIC 3000
Australia
www.melbournebooks.com.au
info@melbournebooks.com.au

Title: Nine Parts Water, One Part Sand.
Kim Salmon and the Formula for Grunge
Author: Douglas Galbraith
ISBN: 9781925556964
Publisher: David Tenenbaum
Cover design: Sean Hogan

A catalogue record for this book is available from the National Library of Australia

NINE PARTS WATER, ONE PART SAND.

KIM SALMON AND THE FORMULA FOR GRUNGE

DOUGLAS GALBRAITH
WITH KIM SALMON

M
MELBOURNE BOOKS

To Sharon and Hannah.
Thank you for your enthusiasm about this book,
for your encouragement and for sharing the music.

Foreword

People are surprised that I'm not telling this story and that I would entrust it to someone else.

'My' story certainly wasn't writing itself and the couple of attempts I'd made had failed due to my 'poverty of time'.

I had been urged by an editor to have a crack at my memoirs, not once but twice.

One attempt was to take the form of a guide to being 'semi famous'.

How to deal with the anomalies associated with that strata of 'celebrity' in which I found myself. I was told by the publisher that they liked the idea but I wasn't famous enough for them to pay me an advance. My other attempt was to be called 'You're Not Kim Salmon' a phrase that, oddly perhaps, I've heard a lot in my time. My friend and fellow Sandgroper Rob Snarski, completely unaware of my attempt, went on to use the very similar 'You're Not Rob Snarski' as the title to his book. The irony in all this is that he's very much at the equivalent level of fame to me and he seems to have made a very good go of his book.

However, this is the writer, Doug Galbraith's story.

A story *about* me, to be sure, but Doug's story none the less.

What could I possibly say about such a thing?

Well let's start with Douglas Galbraith.

I got to know Doug as a guitar student of mine and found him to be a quick learner and an intelligent, articulate person who enjoyed a conversation.

We indulged in many a yarn after our lessons.

The little ironies and quirks of fate that peppered my 'rock stories' were never lost on him. He was quick to take up the threads and dangle baits for me which would keep me guilelessly talking on.

After maybe a term or two of lessons, and more yarns, he was prompted to see if there was a biography out there. Finding a gap, he one night summoned up the chutzpah to put it to me that he might be the one to rectify this imbalance and write my story.

'Well' … I thought.

If he had the time and the inclination I would, based on what I knew of him, be more than happy to give his enterprise my blessing.

Doug's account cuts a swathe through the details that I and others have provided in accounts of what we think happened to get to the narrative he presents.

It's not just a case of 'if a tree falls in the forest and there's no one to observe it does the tree fall at all?' It's a matter of what colour was the tree, was it a tree, was it a concept or construct?

It's down to the observer, or lack of, their state of mind, or lack of and a whole range of factors.

I actually don't believe there's any one objective truth out there.

For example, I have a memory of kicking down a hotel door following a night of indulgence after my 'last' Beasts Of Bourbon show in Perth 1994.

Not a malicious act, I stress.

There are several accounts of this that I've heard and they all differ wildly.

I definitely kicked someone's hotel door down.

Beasts mixer Matt Crosby says it was his door but I remember he was accompanying me looking for a party when I did the deed.

But what would I know?

It was like four in the morning and my 'intake' had been steady since the end of the gig.

Something happened and there were indeed a few witnesses.

Every perception here was very subjective … filtered.

One of the eerie things about reading through this book has been encountering the poignant memories of close friends who have died.

Before this book they were still here and there were only our shared memories.

Now I read their stories and they tell a different story to mine.

There are overlapping details that don't quite match up to how I remember.

Good stories, but different ones — ones that I will never again get to discuss with them. I enjoy them regardless.

Now that Doug's book is written I'd like to acknowledge my respect to him for going to all of the bother to go out and find all of the stories. Having found them, then sifting through with a fine-tooth comb, using all of his imagination and intelligence to fashion a cohesive and compelling narrative. Finally for all the legwork of finding a suitable publisher to put that story out into the world.

I'd also like to thank everyone who gave generously of their time to provide Doug with the fuel for this story. It is them and not me that give the tale credibility.

I want to thank Doug's daughter Hannah and his wife Sharon for giving up so much of their time with him, and for their support and encouragement in the frankly nebulous project of finding enough of the loose ends and threads shed by my random journey through time and space to fashion something that people might want to read.

Doug cared enough to do this and he wrote the story so I'm pleased to have you all read it!

Memphis, 1996

The Oldsmobile drifted to the edge of Riverside Drive, Memphis Tennessee and stopped, engine running. An early morning mist was draped over the town, and the Mississippi River was dappled with rain drops. Kim Salmon held the steering wheel tightly and stared ahead, bleary from the night before. As if in a dream, he opened the car door and stood up, looking through the misty rain punctured with the first rays of sun. His eyes fixed on an enormous, unearthly pyramid of mirror and glass shimmering on the Memphis skyline.

Bewildered, it appeared to him not as a building but a vestige from outer space. An iridescent shrine to a far-flung lifeform. He took a step back and rubbed his eyes. His momentary alarm faded as the Memphis Pyramid sports arena swam into focus. But an echo of the unworldly apparition remained.

Kim Salmon doesn't always see the world through earthly eyes.

Collecting himself, he returned to the driver's seat and pulled back onto the still empty road. He had a record to make.

Introduction

Kim Salmon. Art School dropout, seminal punk rocker, and living legend. Born into the isolation of the semi-industrial wastelands of 1950s outer suburban Perth, Kim Salmon clawed his way out of the swamp and onto the world stage in his bands the Scientists, the Surrealists, and the Beasts of Bourbon.

Conjuring the nascent snarls of antipodean punk rock in the late 70s, Salmon formed the Cheap Nasties, simultaneously making seminal punk music in far flung Perth as the Saints were in Brisbane, Radio Birdman in Sydney and Nick Cave with the Boys Next Door in Melbourne.

As the 80s dawned, Salmon rematerialised with the Scientists and a new sound was born. Dark, primitive, swampy, demented — this was punk, rock 'n' roll, psychobilly and blues all at once — but it was something new too. In the early 90s, Seattle based Grunge would sell millions of records worldwide. In Australia, a decade earlier, Grunge was simply the noise of the Scientists.

Internationally acclaimed and pronounced a 'national treasure', Kim Salmon has earned his reputation as an authentic artist incapable of choosing the safe road. For over forty years, he has performed on the world's biggest stages and with the most remote punk bands, marauding the most subversive corners of music and art. Kim Salmon's journey is a triumph of the persistent search for substance — in everything he does, Salmon is endlessly creative, restlessly intelligent and uncompromisingly original.

Kim Salmon's artistic legacy is assured and his story begs the telling.

1

'So, you written my book yet?'

Beechworth, North East Victoria. When I was growing up, the town was all county football, bad beer and public service institutions — the gaol, the aged care home, and the psych hospital. Music was strictly square, the outside world unknown.

One weekend, at age 16, I took a pilgrimage to Melbourne, 300 kilometres away. Sitting on the shabby carpet of my sister's Camberwell rental house, an epiphany in the shape of her wannabe-punk boyfriend's record collection shone out of the suburban night. I scrambled frantically through the vinyl — Howlin' Wolf, John Lee Hooker and Muddy Waters. Radio Birdman, the Stooges, the Cramps, the Ramones. Intoxica, Cosmic Pyschos, Corpse Grinders and X. It was an epiphany, as though a new universe had been revealed. I was in awe.

In amongst all this gold, was Kim Salmon. Scientists, the Surrealists, and the Beasts of Bourbon. Sinister looking albums — a dark, blood red theatre with the band lying indolently amongst the empty seats; a ghostly monochromed half-impression of the band with the suggestion that there was much, much more to see.

On one album, 'The Axeman's Jazz', the gang of miscreant Beasts slunk back in the darkness, glowering, looking like cats you'd want to know, but not get on the wrong side of. The vinyl quickly found its way onto the turntable. Mumbled studio chatter and a faint count in gives way to guitars, scratchy, lackadaisical rhythm and demented cowboy licks that thread their way throughout the song. From the very first sounds, I was sold.

•••

It's a Sunday afternoon in Brunswick Street Fitzroy when, still underage, I walk into the front bar of the Punters Club Hotel. The sunlight quickly loses penetration in the comfortably shadowy bar, where the barkeeper is immersed in cleaning beer glasses.

I'm still green, and mistakenly think Kim's surname is pronounced SALmon with a hard L. I say to the taciturn barman, 'is Kim SAL-mon playing here?' He barely looks up as he sneers with contempt, 'It's *Salmon*'.

I am chastened and retreat, but see a poster saying, 'Kim Salmon Solo Residency'. And there, in the band room, is Kim Salmon with his Fender Thinline and a huge can of European beer. Kim tilts to the side with left leg stuck out slightly off kilter as he leans into the microphone. His shirt is a stranger to its buttons, and his sharp boot taps out the song's heartbeat as he conjures its body from the guitar. There's only one of him, but the Punters sounds like it's hosting a band as the bass notes run their own lines, joining the melody which lurks somewhere above.

'The unknown remains unknowable, until you finally know it. The un-thought remains unthinkable, until you happen to think it,' he intones. 'And the obvious is always obvious, except of course, when it isn't … obvious'. These intriguing word plays hold the audience hushed, and the heavy musical mood draws us into the murky landscapes.

I purchase the cassette *Hook Line and Singer* with a hand drawn Kim Salmon on the cover and listen to it relentlessly. The songs on the tape, and from that Sunday afternoon gig, remain just as potent today.

•••

The night before we'd seen Fugazi & Magic Dirt and tonight here we are standing on the hallowed turf of the MCG. The biggest band in the world, U2, are posturing on stage, all sunglasses and leather pants and beanies and TV screens. Earlier, Kim Salmon and the Surrealists had delivered a blistering opening set, Salmon screaming 'I declare myself a GOD' to the assembled U2 fans as the sun faded over the colosseum.

How many of the 50,000 crowd had come to watch the opening, rather than the main, act? Maybe just us … Standing on a seat in the midst of the screaming crowd, I scan the scene gazing slowly from left to right. And there, standing only meters away, alone and contemplative in a yellow velvet jacket, is Kim Salmon. '50,000 people', I think, 'and he stands next to us. It's gotta be fate …'

•••

Many years later, I see Kim at the IGA Supermarket on Station Street, Fairfield. How odd to see the Godfather of Grunge doing such a mundane thing as buying groceries — and at my local!

Then, I read an article in the Age, a journo relating a tale of guitar lessons with Kim. Wouldn't that be cool …[1]

So, late at night, a bottle of wine directing traffic, I hit send on the email link to the Salmon webpage. 'Do you still do private guitar lessons …?' The next day, Kim Salmon replied, 'Sure. How about Wednesdays?'

And so, every Wednesday evening I decamped to the front room of Kim's house, my Epiphone Hummingbird sounding like an imposter amongst the Fenders and Col Clarkes. We played — he taught, I learnt.

And always, we talked. An idea grew and itched and refused to go away. Until one night at 2:27am, I hit send on this email:

'Hey Kim. An idea to run by you, triggered by some comments you've made, a gap in the market and a bottle of Sangiovese. When I started lessons with you I did a search for a biography and couldn't find one. I thought that was outrageous and a missing part of Australian music history. So, I wanted to let you know that in the unlikely event you wanted an untried unknown non author to write your book, then I'd jump at the chance. No harm asking right?'

Kim's reply was positive but guarded, concluding 'Let me think about it.' Next week at our guitar lesson, I was more nervous than usual. I played badly and felt the weight of this question about the book hanging between us. Finally, as I packed up my guitar, almost red with the embarrassment of not talking about it, Kim switched off his amp and said casually, 'So, you written my book yet?'

•••

The book starts with breakfast. I arrive first, awash with nerves. I stare at the menu from which endless breakfast options cascade in a torrent. Kim Salmon walks in, sits down and promptly orders fruit toast and a long black with milk on the side. Already three coffees in, I follow with a strong flat white and in a train wreck of cognition, order waffles. What arrives is a monolithic tower of berries, cream cheese, waffles and sugar. It's an abomination, a screeching banshee soaking up the oxygen, an aberration next to the understated fruit toast sitting calmly on the small plate. 'Wow,' observes Salmon. 'You win. That's not breakfast, that's dessert.'

We start talking, and this is how it goes — a crooked pathway back and forth through Kim's life, journeys through songs, bands, artists, movies, politics, clothes, hair, people and places. We talk at great length on small fragments of life. Breakfasts turn into lists, phone numbers, emails and before long, I'm on a plane.

I land in Perth. It's like a foreign city — sunny, calm and at ease. I drive up Wade Street where the swamps have given way to housing but still look untamed, holding the echo of a young Kim Salmon riding his bike and catching gilgees. Kim's mother, Joy, is sitting on the step of the house at the end of a long driveway to meet me. She is small, sharp and instantly welcoming. We step inside. This was the house where a teenage Kim Salmon would soak up valuable bathroom time, practicing rock moves in front of the mirror and tweaking his hair. Joy introduces me to Kim's father, Owen. He is neat, upright — a proud man with a firm handshake.

Joy makes coffee before we retire to the lounge room, and I set up the Zoom recorder on the carpet.

2

The end of the perfect marriage

On a summer's day in 1953, a young Joy Hill travelled from Perth to Bunbury to attend the Bunbury Rowing Club's Coronation Weekend Dance. Joy was, by her own estimation, 'always a dancer', and she trod the boards with gusto. It was just before the interval as she lined up for the barn dance, her hair a little tousled and her face flushed, that Joy looked across the dance floor and saw a handsome young man talking to a group of friends.

'He looks alright,' she thought.

His name was Owen Salmon, and suddenly the Coronation Dance seemed a lot more interesting. In the months that followed, Joy spent more and more time in Bunbury with Owen, and before long, they were dancing at their wedding reception.

In 1956, Joy fell pregnant. 'And that', she says delicately, 'was the end of the perfect marriage.'

•••

When anything went wrong with electricity in Western Australia, Owen was dispatched to fix it. Joy was ten days overdue with the apparently reticent Kim Salmon, sick of the sight of herself and everybody else, when the call came in to the Depot for Owen to head out — now. As Owen jumped in the truck the news reached him that Joy was to be induced. He drove hard for 160 miles north, knowing that Joy was heading for hospital in the opposite direction.

After a lengthy hospital stay, Joy was enduring a horrendous thirty hour labour, unable to get word to Owen on her slow, painful progress to delivering the future Godfather of Grunge. Owen was beside himself, worried about Joy, berating himself for being so far away, and juggling the 66,000 volts of power coursing around him as he worked.

Eventually the news reached him. His son, Kim Leith Salmon, was born. It was, almost literally, electrifying news. Owen turned his truck south and made for Bunbury.

3

C'est Ce Soir!

It's May 2017, and only a few months ago Kim Salmon turned 60. The Volkswagen tour van hurtles through France towards tonight's gig at Les Toques, Perigueux. Nuclear power stations expelling thick columns of smoke loom beside the road, connected by an endless parade of power line towers that bear a surprising resemblance to cartoon cats. Inside the van, guitar cases, drums, suitcases and other flotsam bounce around, moving together like cogs in a machine. Kim Salmon has a sketch pad on his knee, capturing scraps of scenery in watercolour and ink.

A dozen shows in as many days through Switzerland, Germany and France have Kim invigorated. The entourage is congenial; his partner Maxine delights in the company, food and surroundings. Tour Manager Gary is pretty and unflappable, and Laura is archetypically French. Parisian drummer Dimi is tall and good looking and oozes a gentle cool, while musical co-conspirator Michael Stranges provides comic foil.

Banquets of oysters, baguettes, cheese, wine and beer are typical of the touring party. Locals insist on proving their hospitality and the nights of song are accompanied by days of affable indulgence. Only one café offers resistance through an inscrutable girl with an ambiguous haircut, thick rimmed glasses and a *chambray onesie* — either perfectly hipster cool or hopelessly out of step. Icily rejecting Kim's overtures to the small garden salad, she intimidates with her cool demeanour and command of the menu.

As darkness falls in each town, Kim Salmon occupies the stage. Le Volume in Nice, Sonic Ballroom in Cologne, the Sedel Club in Lucerne … each show is scorching, and Kim Salmon like a dervish. Bent over his guitar, he performs a wild exorcism of noise and the refrains of *Swampland* pour out for perhaps the millionth time. The audiences are euphoric and they stand up close, circling the stage and shouting like they're watching an illegal cock fight. Dimi, Mike and sometimes Delphine form a tight gang behind Kim, and as the set lists get longer the band gets sharper.

Undeterred by lost passports, relentless driving, wrenched guts and long nights, the tour reaches its crescendo at Tek Rock Zen in Evreux before a final scramble to Charles de Gaulle for the flight home. Just twenty-four hours later, Kim is back teaching guitar at JMC Academy in South Melbourne. Age does not weary him.

4

Swampland

Kim's earliest recollection of childhood is walking down the front steps of his parent's Bunbury home and becoming aware of his knee joints, his skin and bones. 'God this is really hopeless, how flimsy is this? I became aware of my body, I had this idea of flesh and bones and it seemed disappointing. It felt very squishy and frail. I had to accept my mortality. I guess I was expecting to be some kind of metallic alien, but I was just a plain old human.'

His first few years were spent alone with Owen and Joy, embarking on long walking expeditions around Bunbury. Exploring the wasted spaces along the railway line, nosing around the rusting wheat silos, scarpering along the jetties, and messing about in the estuarine mud. An observant and interested Kim quietly accompanied his parents, listening but not talking much as the world was introduced to him.

His brother Brad arrived when Kim was 3 years old, breaking the quiet. 'Brad was a pretty good baby for about a fortnight. And then he started to scream', says Joy. As Joy tried to soothe the crying Brad,

Kim would disappear into drawing, blocks, or Meccano constructions and generally keep a safe distance from this noisy new thing. 'It was like the party was over when Brad came. We moved to Perth, and Bunbury seemed like a lost haven, green and full of adventure with ships, lighthouses — the whole thing.'

Transplanted to Embleton in North Perth, Kim adapted to his new surrounds. It was semi-industrial wasteland; part rural, part sandpit, part swamp. The Salmons landed in a state housing district: 'lots of housing blocks with nothing on them, lots of T junctions and L shaped streets going nowhere.' Embleton's local mythologies were soon woven into Kim's psyche — missing children crushed in the sandpits, swallowed by the ravening grit, never to be seen again. He trod carefully.

As the empty streets gradually filled with houses, a gang of kids emerged for Kim to consort with. They'd ride up the deserted streets to the nature reserve beyond Irwin Road, and hunt insects or catch gilgees and tadpoles in the muddy waters of Mahogany Creek. In the rain, the dirt roads would flood and transform into misshapen canals of gushing, sludgy water. The boys made boats out of sheets of rusty corrugated iron and rowed down the tracks using broom sticks as oars.

On infrequent incursions to Bunbury, Kim and his cousin David would manufacture tin can bombs, hang out amongst the mechanical relics in the railway yards, and swim at the rugged back beach. On occasions he would accompany his grandmother Sammy to her job cleaning doctors' surgeries where Kim was entranced by the gleaming tangles of laboratory test tubes and science equipment.

To a young Kim Salmon, it was all his very own sci-fi drama or jungle adventure.

•••

When Kim was 7, his sister Megan appeared, and the Salmon family was complete. Good at drawing and music, Megan's artistic temperament was aligned to Kim's, and she adored her older brother. Brad, meanwhile, was gorgeous, with movie star looks and a beguiling twinkle in his eye. But he was larger than life, and just didn't fit into the normal picture. The swamps of Embleton held enough cruel kids to make life uncomfortable for him. Observing the unwanted attention drawn by Brad's antics, Kim learned to be invisible. 'As a child I wanted to be left alone and left to do my own thing. I saw attention as a danger and hoped people wouldn't notice me; stick your head up and you'll get it sliced off...'

The conclusions drawn from watching his errant younger brother confirmed Kim's inherent independent streak. He refused to go to Sunday school, scouts, play team sports or join clubs. 'I wasn't a joiner. I didn't want to join things.'

At primary school, Kim alternated between successful invisibility and revealing the first sparks of his talent. 'In primary school, I found that the odd years were good, and the even years were crap. Every second year I hated, and the teachers hated me. I didn't fit in, I was colouring outside the lines.' Kim's grade five teacher recognised him as not only a thinker, but an artist. She introduced him to De Vinci and Picasso, and under her tutorage he excelled. 'Then the next year, with another teacher, I was invisible again.'

With this on again, off again trajectory, Kim exited primary school having gravitated to science, art and free-thinking. His principle accomplishments outside of school revolved around making bombs, conducting chemistry set experiments, devouring Science Weekly magazines, and returning frozen mosquitos to thawed life. 'Like Frankenstein,' recalls Owen. Or perhaps, like a scientist.

•••

Kim's teenage years and the start of high school coincided with the end of the 60s. Music — while always present in the Salmon house through Joy's piano playing, Megan's singing or Owen's classical tapes

— did not impact Kim as a child. He didn't respond to the sounds of the 60s. For Kim, the decade was kind of like wallpaper, a backdrop of which he was aware, but which didn't make an impression. 'I was a science nerd. Hippy stuff didn't wash with me. But in 1970, at age 13, I heard pop music. I went into the 70s and became a teenager. It was the beginning.'

The first thing that made an impression was *Spirit in the Sky*. 'To my primitive mind, it sounded like electronic, space age music it was a combo of pop hooks and sci-fi, taking the piss out of the afterlife.'

Wandering around his new high school, Kim saw a group of girls dancing to Creedence Clearwater Revival's *Up Around the Bend*, their dresses hitching up as they moved. It was an inviting association. He later saw the band play at Perth's Subiaco Oval and the spell was cast.

He watched The Kinks play *Lola* on TV, and was enamoured of Ray Davies' flouncy hair, leather coat and lace up boots. He loved the humour and sharp intellect in Daddy Cool's *Eagle Rock*, and the Stones' *You Can't Always Get What You Want* shepherded him into the next era — 'the last of the innocent before all the cool stuff happened'.

With these discoveries came the need for cash. Kim took on chores and odd jobs, doing the dishes, shoving leaflets into letter boxes, working in factories and salvage yards and enduring pathetic rates of pay. But eventually, there it was in his possession, his first LP: Creedence Clearwater Revival's 'Cosmos Factory'. At $5.50, it was a major investment, roughly the same price as the concert ticket. Another few weeks of hard labour and Hawkwind's 'In Search of Space' joined the fledgling vinyl collection.

Music had arrived with force for the 13-year-old Kim Salmon, and out of the blue, he came home from school and announced that he wanted to learn the guitar. Soon, he had selected a $14 Audition acoustic guitar from Kmart. Joy remembers it as 'a cheap old thing; it was dreadful'.

Despite his early lack of interest, Kim had inherited an innate musical sensibility from his maternal grandmother, Jessie, who could play anything. Banjo, piano, mandolin, and guitar — she could play them all. Kim's great grandfather had been a travelling musician and Jessie had collected his tricks of the trade and adopted the spirit. When told that Kim was learning guitar she said, 'Oh I do hope it's an electric guitar!'

Unsure of how to tune the Audition, Kim adopted some esoteric tuning patterns, and as he really wanted a whammy bar (absent from the acoustic) he used the tuning keys for that purpose instead, turning the keys dramatically to bend the notes up and down. It took a sprinkling of lessons from his tobacco-stained, jazz-infused guitar teacher to eventually correct his unorthodox tuning habits.

The Audition made way for an electric Coronet. 'I didn't have an amp, and in the end I couldn't get it together. It had a whammy bar, which is what I wanted, but all I could do was break strings.' The Coronet found its way to Kim's friend Gary who loaned Kim his Yamaha G60 nylon string in return. 'We ended up doing a swap, and I got the Yamaha. That was where I explored music really, and where I experimented on some of my identity with the paint jobs!' Bowie-inspired sci-fi paintings adorned the guitar only to be replaced the next week with Cat Stevens themed art work and so on. The Yamaha, witness to the early formation of Kim Salmon's creative impulse, waits patiently at his parent's house still, stripped back to plain wood, ready to be called into action if needed.

•••

Kim's wit and sharp mind were quickly evident in high school. He was very good academically and by fourth year he'd progressed to the advanced work stream. It came easily and he succeeded without a stretch. The school was impressed, but inadvertently engineered the competition against which academic work had no chance. School sponsored music was drawing Kim away from his studies.

> *I grew up with* J'taime *blaring around the speakers in my high school. They used to have it going at recess. Whether it was the*

radio or some senior kid in there being a DJ, I was never quite sure. They played a lot of Philly soul and Motown. I remember hearing the Delfonics doing Didn't I Blow Your Mind this Time. *Eddie Holman's* Hey There Lonely Girl. *Old Elvis songs.* I Can't Stop Loving You, *but the Ray Charles version …* J'taime *just stuck in my mind. The B3 organ, that incredible melody, with the sound effects … it was a wonderful thing. Things like that had seeped through into my consciousness and stayed there.*

In fourth year, Joy got a call from the concerned headmaster. Kim had declared that he was changing from the top academic stream to go into the Arts course. The attraction of sketching, painting and playing music had overtaken his other school work. Joy says, 'Of course we knew that he'd always been able to draw and it was no great shock that he was good, but he'd never said anything. The school was concerned because they thought he was such a good student, but they didn't understand just how good he was with his art.'

Music, too, was becoming serious. Increasingly, Kim would be holed up in his room with the guitar, picking over riffs from the radio. Or when his musical friends dropped in it became full blown band rehearsal. Dragging mattresses up against the wall to block out the noise from the neighbours, and scattering cushions everywhere to dampen the acoustics, the bedroom morphed into a band room. What did it sound like when he was practicing in his bedroom? Says Joy, 'It was just very loud'.

•••

I get a tram to St Kilda, early 1990's, and the Prince of Wales chalkboard announces Kim Salmon and the Surrealists are playing. It's summer, and so hot the palm trees are drooping in the thick, still night.

Fitzroy Street is alive. Twelve-foot transvestite hookers, midget pimps, dealers in parachute tracksuits, girls in impossibly short skirts, rockers, punks and pre-grungers stagger, swagger and carousel up the street and down the laneways.

It's already midnight and there's no sign of the Surrealists. The Prince Piano Bar is heaving, sweating and cacophonous. It's friendly, but dangerous and menacing all at once. The hookers are holding court at the crowded bar, and on the squashed stage Fred Negro is riding a toy horse, wearing a cowboy hat, but no pants.

I take refuge in the band room. It looks like a cathedral: lights dim, sticky carpet scattered with plastic pots and the stage lying in wait at the front of the room. It's close to 1am when three of the coolest looking cats saunter onto stage. Kim Salmon and the Surrealists. Long hair, satin shirts wide open, pointy boots and tight black pants. Kim Salmon looks like a video clip, hair and smoke and shirt billowing around him, as he extracts shards of broken noise from nowhere. Twenty years away from the bedroom in Perth, it's still *very* loud.

•••

The quiet self-reliance and impulse for invisibility of Kim's childhood incurred debts that would become due as isolation and disconnection in adolescence. At 16, he was adrift without identity and with no place to fit.

> *Adolescence is like being a chrysalis stuck in a cocoon. I didn't have a single friend, I'd kind of ostracised myself. I remember before I even liked music, I saw David Bowie perform on a Grammy Awards on TV. I knew* Space Odyssey *the film, and when they announced 'David Bowie', in my mind I thought the guy from* Space Odyssey *had decided to write a song and start singing, because his name was David Bowman ... And there's this curly haired guy strumming a guitar saying 'ground control to Major Tom' ... and I remember that making a mark. And then later, when adolescence happened, sure enough, there I was in my bedroom, floating in my tin can.*

16 was miserable. Estranged from friends, nursing a broken heart, and dodging the school toughs, Kim retreated to his bedroom.

The post-war periods saw an influx of European immigration to Perth, and Hampton Senior High School in the early 70s hosted some pretty tough kids. There were the 'Rock Outs', dressed in satin purple shirts, black hipster jeans, black tee shirts and black tractor tread desert boots. Long hair was a pre-requisite, which they were forever flicking out of their eyes. Then there were the 'Surfs', with hair parted in the middle and more mundane clothes, thongs and drab looking jeans. They rarely surfed, but got the girls. These two main groups were rounded out by studious but tough Yugoslavians, razor sharp Italians, and embryonic British skinheads. 'Kids who had been mild in primary school seemed to have transformed over the holidays and were suddenly stealing cars.' It was a scary amalgam of cultures, which made for a menacing social environment. And anyone who didn't fit one of these cliques was singled out for derision.

The best way not to fit in was to look different. Kim successfully achieved this by happenstance. Owen was nuts about motorbikes and gifted one to Kim for his 16th birthday. Joy insisted he wear protective clothing and took Kim to the Army Disposals to buy a black leather jacket, foreshadowing the ones that would adorn the first Ramones album three years later. Kim would ride the bike to school each day wearing the jacket, often accompanied by large Sunaroid aviator shades to protect his light sensitive eyes from sun glare. And to combat persistent hay fever, Kim was taking polaramin tablets causing him to frequently doze off in class. 'So I looked like a pilled out cat in a leather jacket and sunnies doing badly at school.' Without trying, Kim had affected full punk rock regalia years before it arrived on Australian shores. He stood out. 'I got shit for it but I didn't care.'

If he had grown not to care about fitting in with other people, fitting in with himself was more troubling. 'It's almost like you're not really anybody, just a series of little scripts … It's not that I didn't fit in 'cos I was such a freak, although that would be a great thing to say. I just think I didn't know what I wanted.'

There were possibilities, but nothing was happening. He sensed potential and direction and went deeper into himself to find it. Like his earliest memory of his alien expectations needing stronger skin, Kim was reaching for the right identity to bind together the simmering concepts in his head. He was looking for the formula.

The conventional was not going to work. Kim was cultivating a framework for interpreting the world that was at once primitive and sophisticated; or sophisticated because it *was* primitive. Incapable of adopting the popular paradigms, Kim identified the more rudimentary angles, creating space for the concepts that would shape his music to grow.

The decision to pursue the arts against the school's guidance spoke of his determination not to be constrained by other's expectations. His refusal to join the pack or fit in had sharpened his independence, while his adventures in the Embleton everglades and Fremantle docks had instilled a freedom and wildness of heart. He was stripped back, self-reliant and resolute.

The final ingredient was music. The guitar became a refuge. Although isolated in his room, through the guitar and the vinyl records accumulating on his floor, Kim connected his interior existence with the world beyond the sandpits of Northern Perth. He knew that sometime, something would happen.

•••

As the end of school loomed, Kim had found some kind of social foothold, falling in with a group of older kids. Relative sophisticates, they were Kim's ticket into parties where he was able to encounter some of the hedonism he'd been reading about. A friend who worked at a record shop told Kim about a party, promising hash and live music. Kim went along to jam with his harmonica, smoked pot and killed it on the harp. His first performance was a success.

In the end, he got through high school and scraped in with his leaving certificate. The day before his art exam, Kim and a friend stumbled across a bottle of vodka and a case of Fosters and got smashed. After throwing up all over his parent's front yard, Kim fronted for his final exam in dusty shape, but made it through. Walking home, he paused at one of the L shaped streets that led to nowhere. He didn't know exactly what was next, but he wouldn't find it there.

5

Seein' Spots

1975 arrived for Kim with career plans undetermined and an identity still in formation. The Whitlam Government's fast-moving agenda of social reform and political miscalculations paraded towards the Dismissal. But while the social landscape in the Eastern States was twisting and shouting, Perth was still slow dancing to a more conservative tune.

Perth was really just a big country town and, like many country towns, reflected a white bread, mainstream culture with little diversity. The counter culture was corralled into an out of the way cinema, and music was dominated by 'Top 40' cover bands playing in suburban beer barns like the Scarborough Beach Hotel.

It was from this claustrophobic atmosphere that Kim escaped to the Art Faculty of the Western Australian Institute of Technology. 'I was thinking that by the time I get to art school it's all going to happen; free love, drugs, action, rock and roll. I imagined the whole Woodstock thing would be there in the art faculty.' He pictured holing up in a garret somewhere, walls splashed with paint, surrounded by a community of artists, and started his tertiary studies enthusiastically.

Kim's natural skills refined under the tuition of teacher Henry Hall — a skinny, aging, chain-smoking hipster in the mould of Keith Richards. 'I learned to draw properly then; I got my drawing chops down. Drawing was easy, they stuck a nude model in front of you … and you'd draw it.' But the students were older than Kim, rundown hippies who had already been 'round the block. The vibe was like *this isn't for you*, it's a burned-out scene … They weren't trying ideas other than the ones they already had.'

Outside art class, however, a troupe of likeminded accomplices had emerged, and Kim spent the year exploring Perth's nocturnal life. One night, his high school friend Ken Seymour introduced him to fellow student and keyboard player Dave Faulkner. Kim recognised Dave's sensibility straight away, 'and it became clear that maybe we should have a jam'.

Dave Faulkner would go on to be one of Australia's most successful musicians, selling hundreds of thousands of albums and his songs on constant radio play. But in 1975, he was just 'Dave Flick' and still working out his angle. Dave had gathered a strange conglomeration of players that loosely resembled a band, including Neil Fernandes, a laid-back guitarist with a beautiful voice who would, the following year, respond to Kim's punk call to arms. Into this mix arrived Kim Salmon. Epic art rock paroxysms, 'prog' explorations and blues jams followed, but it was the increasingly alcoholic drummer's suggestion to play atonal noise over an unlikely 7/4 beat that stuck in Kim's head.

Dave adorned the combo with the name Moulin Rouge. 'Nobody said anything, giving Dave carte blanche to be the boss you see. He was a keyboard player. He also played a little guitar but not that well. The embarrassing thing was you'd be playing and he'd say, "oh your B string's slightly sharp" and you'd tune it and he'd say "yeah but now your A's out" — it was off-putting! Even in those days he must have had an amazing ear, everything sounded ugly to him.' The band never got off the ground. Practice in the faculty rehearsal room at midday would blend into drinks at the uni tavern, 'and by 6 o'clock I'd be in the garden in fisticuffs with the bass player.'

In the wake of Moulin Rouge, Dave suggested joining a blues band. Perth was awash with stylised, holier-than-thou blues bands like The Elks, Beagle Boys or Duck Soup. The other choice was carbon copy, white-washed cover bands. Playing Beatles songs to huge crowds in awful beer barns was big business, and Neil Fernandes recalls stories of people earning house deposits from playing covers.

Kim was over it. 'God it was an awful time. Everything seemed to compound the idea that I wasn't meant for this world.' Hanging out with Ken, Dave and Neil was fun, but when Friday night came around and Dave rang up to say 'We're going out tonight,' the horizon opened up only as far as the Broadway Tavern to watch the Elks play more blues. Kim Salmon again was searching for something to happen.

'I'd done a year of art school but I still knew nothing. It seemed like art school was standing around drawing nudes while John Lennon's 'Imagine' was playing on a crappy turntable all day. So after a year, I dropped out.'

6

Cheap & Nasty

Free from art school, Kim attempted to enter conventional society by getting miserable, ill-fitting jobs in hospitals and banks. It was an uncomfortable accord. 'I just thought *fuck this*, I'm going to get into a band. I don't care what band it is, even if it's playing music I hate, at least I'll be playing music. If I'm going to make a living from music, that's what I should be doing.'

So he auditioned. For anything. But a mountain of cold calls to prospective cover bands didn't land him a gig. 'I just didn't have the right sound.' It wasn't until Joy answered the phone to a Fremantle bandleader John Farley that things looked up. John was singer, bass player and band leader of Troubled Waters, a covers outfit that played '50/50' — a repertoire of half hits, half 'oldies' — and on Joy's recommendation he invited Kim for an audition.

At the first jam, Kim was taken through *Walking the Dog*, *Honky Tonk Woman*, *Your Cheatin Heart* and a Decker song called *The Israelites*, songs he'd heard once or twice at best, but played well straight away. John said, 'Okay, we have a gig tonight, you're in. We play three sets a night from 11pm to 3am, six nights a week. And we don't play any heavy music, so no *Smoke on the Water* or *Black Magic Woman*.' Kim was in Troubled Waters.

That night he arrived at the venue, the Tarantella Tavern in Fremantle. Prickly with pre-gig nerves, Kim swiftly collided with the drinks menu and kept a safe distance from his new band mates. At show time, he stepped gingerly onto the sweaty, slightly too small stage of the Tarantella Tavern with John's advice fresh in his ears — 'If you don't know the song just turn your amp down.' Amid the darkness, smoke haze and low, shady murmuring of the Tavern's interior, Kim plugged his guitar into the small amp leaning against the dirty wall. Years later, he would capture his time at the Tarantella Tavern in the song *Shine*:

I look out across to the bar, as I hide behind my guitar
Given up on all that lies in between
Anyone who's worked this kinda shit pit is gonna know what I mean

The band got underway, punching out a sharp version of the Beatles *Birthday*, which, it turned out, bookended every single Troubled Waters set. The set list of curiously combined hits and oddities washed out onto the Tavern's only vaguely interested audience. As Kim and the other guitarist traded guitar duties, John sang raspy tenor with a cockney accent.

And the singer is crooning at some age-old song
Its meaning obliterated in time, but his voice is still strong
Though somewhat off key it kind of falls on deaf ears
This is the kinda place that could rise to anyone's fears

A refugee from the London Beat scene, John regaled the band with tall tales of his encounters with Charlie Watts and Mick Jagger and unveiled the old tricks of early 60s R&B music. John respected the grimy atmosphere and dangerous potential of the Tavern. His ethos was simple: work hard, always take requests and keep out of trouble.

But I've grown used to it and its denizens of the night
Learned how to keep my trap shut and stay out of fights
Only two songs til the end of the set
Johnny B Goode can sound a good deal better yet

The Tarantella Tavern was a strip club and hookup joint for prostitutes and drunken sailors; an underground haven for the crooked, transgendered and otherwise excluded. Patrons would compare the merits of local penitentiaries and make deals while hunkering shadily around the bar tables, watching the strippers out of the corner of their eyes. Each night, one of the prostitutes would climb to the highest point and sing *House of the Rising Sun*, the performance often descending into an all-in-brawl, with the singer and her sister — both big ladies and tough as — taking on all comers.

Then it's time for the stripper, and her dance of the seven veils
Here's John the Baptist and he's looking kind of pale
I look hopefully out as I see you walk in
Whoever you are, you don't belong in this stinking rotten bin

It was gruelling work. John drove the band hard, playing long sets with new songs each night from a repertoire that stretched to well over two hundred. It was a quick education for Kim. 'I saw a lot and I played a lot and we played new songs I'd hardly heard. I learned to make something up and play what suited the song, the beginning of the salvage operation.' The seedy environment and nefarious characters of the Tavern were always entertaining, but the grime was starting to rub off on Kim and before too long he was looking for the fire escape.

Show me the way, outa here with its strippers and hookers and
drunken old sailors
And over-dressed pimps in purple suits who could use a better tailor
And all the has beens and never were all destined to lose
Still trying to hang onto their dreams by feeding them with too
much booze

After a few months, Kim left Troubled Waters with a glowing reference from John, which, alongside the reputation Kim had built on stage, ensured a solid year's well-paid work as a gun for hire on the cabaret circuit. 'I had learned a trade and I could do it, so why not? I was like a carpenter — it was fun, but work. I was adaptable and played different styles; I was the casual relief guitarist. It was like session playing. No one ever asked me to play sessions thereafter, except years later I got $200 for playing Jews Harp on a Tex Don and Charlie record.'

The countless hours on the Tarantella Tavern stage had given Kim a super charged education in negotiating the darker laneways of the music business. It had elevated his playing, sharpened his eye for detail, and implanted a shrewd song-writing nous. And *Shine*, the song the Tavern produced, remains one of the finest moments of Kim's live solo shows.

You shine like a torch
You're so outta place
I bet you're just a dream
In fact, I suspect your appearance here
Has got a reason for being
You're here to shine.

•••

Punk. It discovered Kim through the *New Musical Express*. Still contemplating his unformed identity, Kim read an article in NME titled *Are you alive to the jive of 75?*, Charles Shaar Murray's grubby portrayal of the gloomy underworld of New York's CBGBs. Kim was electrified. 'That was the world that I belonged in. When I read that, I knew! I was looking for somewhere to land from my spaceship and it was CBGBs. I'd made connection with Ground Control; I wasn't floating in my tin can any more.'

Gulping in as much punk music as he could, Kim scoured Perth's record shops for anything that sounded right. 'The common factor was that people had exotic names — Blondie, Johnny Thunders, Richard Hell, Tom Verlaine. It was just like an enchanted world. It was all black, black and white and dark. It wasn't coloured. It was dingy. Pretty much then, my mind was made up that that was the direction I was going.' By hitching himself to the punk wagon so early, Kim was ahead of most and at the forefront of a new force in Australian music. Isolated in Perth, he didn't have any sense of who was doing what elsewhere in the country, but renowned musicologist Ian McFarlane recognised that Kim was one of the first Australians to 'embrace wholeheartedly the emergent punk phenomenon of the mid-to-late 70s.'[1]

Kim's friend Brian shared a copy of the Stooge's 'Raw Power', telling him it was 'the heaviest and worst thing I've ever heard'. Kim loved its extremity. He read fervently about the Clash and the Buzzcocks and discovered the Modern Lovers. 'I thought this *has* to be punk rock. If it isn't, I'm calling it! The first Modern Lovers album became my universe for a few weeks. Jonathan Richman's stance on the world was so unique, but something you could relate to. If you were having trouble finding your niche in the world, Jonathon Richman was a revelation.' And then 'there was the call from 78 Records (Perth's best record shop) to tell me the Ramones LP was finally in! Bringing it home and putting the needle in the groove and hearing that mix of bubble gum, buzzsaw guitar, tribal drums and Joey Ramone's *Hey Ho Let's Go* was one of the perfect moments of my life.'[2]

While Kim was playing cabaret and discovering punk, Dave Faulkner had been playing blues with the Beagle Boys or with Neil Fernandes in a duo called 'Dave & I'. The rest of the cast — assembled from the remnants of Moulin Rouge, the art faculty or Kim's high school — had yet to commit to a musical direction when Kim rushed in and announced that punk was where it was at! Dave wasn't going to be convinced, intoning loftily that he 'needed some evidence'. But Neil Fernandes was intrigued, and Ken Seymour (aka Dan Dare) and Mark Betts — another lost soul from Embleton High school — were attracted to the 'do it yourself' ethos. Ken and Neil fell into the Stooges' sound whole heartedly, and the Ramones laid a road map that the less accomplished players felt they could follow. Perth's inaugural punk band, the Cheap Nasties, were set in motion.

The band (Kim and Neil on guitars, Ken on bass and Mark on drums) hung out and dissected punk. They set to writing songs and honing their sound, with an early and short-lived incarnation featuring Dave Faulkner as singer. He co-wrote two songs with Kim, including the band's theme song *Cheap and Nasty*. 'Dave wrote the words that I put it to an AC/DC sounding riff. Dave hates the words, but I still play it to this day.' Gradually, a collection of granular, snotty and poppy songs emerged, complemented by songs from the New York Dolls, Stooges, Modern Lovers, Stones and the Kinks.

A minor scene was developing around this miscreant collective and their new sound. Blues or cover bands still dominated, but pockets of the new aesthetic were springing up elsewhere in Perth. Future Scientist Tony Thewlis recalls that around this time 'you had a few people dressed as punks who hung around the Hay Street Mall, trying to sound English and wearing leather jackets in the 40 degree heat.' In a bedroom over in East Perth, another group of would-be punks were forming under the moniker of The Geeks (or The Hitler Youth). Featuring Ross Buncle, Rudolph V (Dave Cardwell), 'Lloyd' and James Baker, the Geeks never made it out of the bedroom, but created their own brand of punk and would later contest the Cheap Nasties' title as Perth's first punk band. The Geeks incubated one of the towering figures of Perth music in James Baker, another lifelong Kim Salmon collaborator and friend.

The Rivervale Hotel, mid 1977 saw the Cheap Nasties, the world's most remote punk band, debut in public. They opened for the blues band The Beagle Boys who were, to the Nasties' surprise, very supportive of this abrasive new music. Suddenly a tiny, grubby piece of Perth culture exploded open to let the light in. The punk scene had operated covertly, with its various factions operating in total ignorance of each other, but with the Nasties' first gig the veil of secrecy was lifted. The band played in front of a huge portrait of Nana Mouskouri that Kim had painted for a 'Nana Night' party. As they whirled through their songs, Kim tore into the painting, slashing it with a knife and defacing it with tomato sauce before turning the sauce bottle on the punters gathered at the front of the stage. The punks in Perth were few, but most of them were there that night, and they liked what they saw.

Two such punks, Roddy Radalj and Boris Sujdovic, didn't take long to sense the change in atmosphere. Roddy and Boris were hung up on music. They had had their heads snapped round by the Stooges and were looking for more in the same vein. Both would feature in Kim Salmon bands, with Boris in particular standing beside Kim on stage for the next forty years.

> *Me and my mate Roddy were just bored teenagers in Fremantle. We started getting into jazz, we dabbled with that for about a month. There used to be this jazz venue and we could get port and lemonade for 30 cents, so we thought, fuck this is pretty good! Then all of a sudden we heard punk rock … there was a fledging Perth punk scene of two bands and fifteen to twenty fans. We went to a hotel in the city on a Tuesday night and saw the Cheap Nasties and that's when I first met Kim. And that's when it all started* (Boris Sujdovic).

They first encountered the Cheap Nasties at Steve's, a blues pub in Perth. Kim recalls stepping off the stage to see 'a pile of smashed glasses around the bottom of my mic stand having been chucked at me, some of them by Rod and his mates!' After picking his way through the shattered beer glasses, Kim was confronted by the imposing Boris Sujdovic demanding to know why the band wasn't playing the Stooges. *No Fun*, *Search and Destroy* and *I Wanna be your Dog* obviously weren't enough! He wanted us to do *more* Stooges songs!' Kim saw Boris and Rod around a lot after that, quickly becoming friends.

> *On that night the fifteen people in the audience were the fifteen punks and the fifteen people we stayed friends with. The Cheap Nasties sounded great! It was the usual story, everyone in the audience started playing. Out of the blue, Roddy got this saxophone and said* I'm auditioning for a band, *which turned out to be the Victims. He sounded like a demented Steve McKay 'cos he couldn't play a note and they didn't get him in. I started playing bass and Roddy soon realised guitar might be easier* (Boris Sujdovic).

James Baker was another punk that Kim had seen around but not yet met. 'I recalled seeing an ad with a photo round '74 stuck up in 78 Records. It had two very glammy looking dudes with fancy writing saying what looked to me like "Slink City Boys" and they were looking for members. That always struck me as unusual for Perth. Thinking back, I wondered if they were "punk"'.[3] James Baker, with an authentic Johnny Ramone hair-cut and signature striped tee, was also in attendance at the early shows. On meeting Kim, James recalls the affinity of a like-minded rock 'n' roll devotee.

James Baker is a revered figure in Perth (and Australian) music. He was an early pioneer having gone on a world sightseeing tour at age 16.

> *I lived in New York and London when all that music scene was happening, the Sex Pistols and all that … I met a lot of 'em, the Ramones, The Clash and the Damned, the Vibrators, Dictators, Blondie. My girlfriend at the time was the door girl at CBGBs and she introduced me to them all, Johnny Thunders and the Heartbreakers, and lots of people there. It was a very small scene then. I met DD, went to a party with Joey. So what I bought back was a few records yeah, but mainly the whole idea of 'fuck em let's make a rock 'n' roll band'* (James Baker).

James had already played in some bands in Perth in the early 70s including a Beatles cover band and the New York Dolls-ish Slink City

Boys, and had nearly auditioned for the drummer's job with The Clash after meeting Joe Strummer and Mick Jones on his rock 'n' roll world tour. He was, and remains, an affable and gregarious presence. He had the right look and his 'powerful, furious drumming was legendary around Perth'.[4] Add to this his firsthand, international experience with some of the legends of punk, he was someone to know. When James collided with Dave Faulkner at the Cheap Nasties gig, they immediately hit it off. In mid 1977, James left the Geeks (taking Randolph V with him) and formed a new band with Dave: The Victims. Armed with a bunch of songs James brought from The Geeks, the Victims set off at a fast pace, establishing themselves alongside the Cheap Nasties as the dominant forces in the Perth underground. But while the Cheap Nasties at that stage channelled the strong pop sensibility of British punk, the Victims produced to a barrage of atonal noise.

Kim, both friend and competitor of the band, watched them closely:

> *They all moved into a squalid fleapit of a house in East Perth. They cleaned out all the 'hippy dirt' from the previous residents and painted over all the bad art on the walls, dubbing the place 'Victim Manor'. It took about a month for them to let the 'Manor' slide back to such a filthy state that none of them except for Rudolph could live there. There, they threw a party where they performed their first show and instantly became the darlings of 'the scene'.*

Over the next year, The Victims acted out a drama parallel to that of the Sex Pistols, being banned from various venues and the bass player cultivating a drug habit. They also managed to have a truly original interpretation of the punk sound. They left a couple of recordings, including the classic *Television Addict*. In time, due to having no regular venues to book them, The Victims found a jazz club called Hernando's Hideaway and managed to secure a Wednesday night residency there. With a place to hang and for its new bands to play at (supporting The Victims), the 'scene soon sucked up all kinds of dubious trash from the suburbs and grew.'[5]

During 1977 the Victims and Cheap Nasties dominated the landscape with inspired shows at the Governor Broome Hotel or Hernando's, honing their unhinged craft, largely unaware of their place in the Australian music story. But elsewhere in Australia, the movement was unfolding rapidly.

In Sydney, Radio Birdman had released their 'Burn My Eye' EP and 'Radios Appear' album and, by April 1977, had largely departed the scene they'd spurned out of their Funhouse venue at the Oxford Tavern. By the end of the year, they had relocated, fatefully as it turned out, to the UK to record a follow up album and tour relentlessly. Numerous acts sprung up in their wake, including the Hellcats featuring Ron Peno, who would later have a unique and enduring role in Kim's musical journey.

In Melbourne, the Boys Next Door had put together the elements of their explosive live show by the end of 1977, and were just around the corner from the arrival of the transformative Rowland S Howard. Gary Gray, who would go on to form the Sacred Cowboys, was starting to stir up his dark, maniacal cowboy punk sounds. 1977 Melbourne's grim underground was supported by exceptional public radio 3RRR (soon to be joined by PBS) and developed by passionate entrepreneurs like Keith Glass and Bruce Milne, who would go on to run pivotal labels and record shops Missing Link and Au Go Go respectively. Bruce Milne and Au Go Go would soon collide with Kim Salmon, transforming both their destinies and catalysing the spread of Grunge's early tentacles.

In Brisbane, the Saints had released their *Stranded* album at the start of 1977 and had a large profile on the East Coast and overseas. The acclaim they attracted early in their career did nothing to prevent unwanted attention from the notoriously leathery Brisbane police. Locked out of established venues, the Saints turned their dwelling at Petrie Terrace into their own venue, the 76 Club, but by mid-year were en route to the UK to commence their own battle with record labels and internal division.

Despite this remarkable surge of activity, very little trickled all the way over to the Australian west coast. Ross Buncle recalls:

> *No one in Perth had heard of Radio Birdman at that time, and we didn't know of any other punk-style bands on the East Coast until way later. It seems incredible now, but without electronic communication networks shrinking the continent — or the world — to the easily manageable size it is today, we had no way of knowing what was going on over the Nullarbor until the first records were released, apart from actually going there. The first wave of the punk movement was over in Perth before anyone had heard of any Eastern States punk-style bands other than The Saints.*[6]

Kim bluntly agrees with this view:

> *We were on the other side of the country and didn't give a shit about Radio Birdman, the Saints, or the Boys Next Door. As far as we were concerned, we'd been doing punk as long on our own and didn't need their input.*[7]

Perth music was shaped by geographical and cultural forces that were quite distinct from the Eastern states, accentuated by its isolation. Thousands of kilometres and a two-hour time difference away, Perth music was largely insulated from the movement in the Eastern States and was taking its cues from sporadically available US or UK punk singles or magazine articles rather than from membership of a broader Australian punk scene. This isolation was an important factor in the evolution of Kim's sound — a factor which former Black Flag singer and longtime fan Henry Rollins recognised.

> *It was listening to the Scientists decades ago that made me wonder if the sheer geographic placement of Australia had anything to do with how Kim makes music. I always had this*

romantic notion that albums would wash up on the shores of Australia and people like Kim would find them, source the one record player for hundreds of miles, and dig the sounds at their most pure and potent form, free of commercial sensibility and corporate compromise (Henry Rollins).

The sunlit lifestyle and slow politics also left a mark. If the Saints were responding to political oppression and police brutality in Brisbane, the motivation for the Perth based Cheap Nasties came from a more straightforward source. 'There wasn't a political dimension, a social fabric that we were rebelling against. It was just that we were drawn to the music rather than rebelling against something' (Neil Fernandes). The Perth scene was musically active and socially comfortable, not hung up on politics or social conditions. Ross Buncle from The Geeks recalls, 'We had no such issues. Even if you were unemployed, life wasn't too bad in the dumb sun of the lucky country way out west. We loved to complain, of course, but our dissatisfaction didn't really amount to much. I think it is a fair call that we were generally pretty hedonistic, and self-focused.'[8]

The song writing in the Cheap Nasties and Victims reflected this. James Baker, the Victim's primary lyric writer, was concerned mainly with girls and TV, and even if their most effective song *Television Addict* held a dark message, it was still after all about spending time 'in front of the window of the world'. The Cheap Nasties too steered clear of disaffection and the simplicity of punk rock coalesced successfully into Kim and Neil Fernandes' early songs.

Neil's aspirations were never to have complexity in his music. I learned a bit from Neil and we quickly got into competition with each other. I learned to push his buttons and shit stir him until he was never calm around me! Our song writing process was one of us would bring an idea and the other would disparage it ... and then add bits to it. And they all benefited from that, they were water tight by the end. We wrote together,

> *and left no shit bits in. I thought he was a fantastic guy, a sweet even tempered laid-back guy, generous nice bloke to this day.*

Neil remembers the collaboration on one of his songs, *Hit and Run*, which was written in a warm major key but embellished with an edgy Kim Salmon lead break — played in a minor key! 'It was magical that he could have thought of that, distorting this song' (Neil Fernandes).

The first phase of the Cheap Nasties was, according to Neil, 'unquestionably Kim's band', with Kim as the driving force, singer and main song writer. To Neil, it was clear that Kim was absolutely single minded that music would be his life's calling. Gradually, Neil exerted more influence as his song writing developed. Kim and Neil shared vocal duties and the Nasties gigs were fast, fun and shambolic.

At Kim's urging, the band absorbed his friend from art school, singing aspirant, Robbie Porritt (aka Robbie Art), who through sheer will and bluff assumed vocal duties. 'He was fully formed, one of those cats who knew the score. He was so ahead of the curve he had his own jargon.' By July 1977, Robbie was in front singing Kim and Neil's songs, and the Cheap Nasties evolved further. Robbie was drenched in charisma and won over the small but animated audiences. The Cheap Nasties storm trooped their way through the disorganised haze of Perth's punk vista, leaving the old establishment in a pile of dust.

In what would be their last show, the band were hired by the police department for an end-of-year party to which an uninvited biker gang showed up and raised the stakes. During a break between sets, one of the bikers gave Kim a beer that he razed in one gulp. 'They were all round me. I think they didn't approve of a squirt like me trying to look tough in a leather jacket. Anyway, the guy then handed me a beer glass full of tequila which I downed. He was smirking at me and then handed me a jug of beer which I then attempted to down. I don't remember the rest …'[9]

'The rest' involved singer Robbie heading to the emergency department with a split lip and cut forehead following an errant punch from one of the bikers during the Salmon induced melee. A completely bombed Kim Salmon went to his singer's defence but dented the biker's brio not even a little given his state of drunkenness. The Cheap Nasties final gig ended, literally, with a bang.

Sometime in the year of 1977, the band bunkered down with a mixing desk in the dining room of 53 Third Avenue, Mount Lawley, Perth, where Ken, Mark and Neil lived. They recorded a live rehearsal, the resultant demo capturing the band's furious energy. The band didn't record again, and the demo remained dormant for over four decades before being released first as a digital recording and then as an LP released by Hozac Records in 2018. Hozac describes the recording as:

> *Ten songs of blistering teenage slime, screaming guitars screech in and out of the chorus, drums bash relentlessly, and that special Australian something you can't ever put your finger on. It's trashy, raw, and brutal punk slop at it's finest … such raw phenomenal stuff. But remember, this isn't for the weak or the elderly, and it's definitely not for audiophiles, but it will now sit alongside … The Saints* I'm Stranded, *and Radio Birdman's* Radios Appear *albums in OZ punk history.*[10]

•••

Kim was by now firmly down the path to his future self, and affecting the right rock 'n' roll regalia to invoke this was demanding serious attention, with mixed results. 'My experiments in style had gone awry. I had a Tony Barber hair do. I would go to op shops and buy leopard skin shirts and wear ladies' clothes and look stupid. I got my mum to make me some vinyl pants, but they were thick and sweaty, and my shoes filled with sweat and created their own ecosystem.' Sister Megan remembers Kim sporting a pink, yellow and red gaberdine suit with stove pipe trousers. 'No one could fathom standing next to him at the traffic lights!'

Kim's sartorial sensibility was emblematic of the cracks beginning to form in the Cheap Nasties, and he was dissatisfied with the band's direction. 'They weren't going to be punk enough for me, the idea of new wave came along and that's where Neil was very comfortable, the idea of a white shirt and tie and jacket … I railed against it and wanted to do my own thing.' The band's ideas compressed, consolidating the frenzied palette of Kim's early song writing and performance style into a more refined but milder proposition. Kim's internal edict of originality above all else grated against the new direction, and his natural tendency to stay on the outside built distance between him and the rest of the band.

The Cheap Nasties had emerged from a virtual void of home grown influence, succeeding in spite of the turgid local music scene and sparked by the sounds of overseas punk. They raced into the Australian punk future, playing live shows that were ragged, loud and alive. Propelled by the sometimes complementary, sometimes competing internal forces, the band were short lived but earned their place in punk history. 'The compromise of directions no doubt stifled the band's potential … As one might expect of a band that was pursuing something unknown, there was more than one idea of what that thing was.'[11]

In December 1977, the Cheap Nasties gathered for rehearsal in a studio set in the bushy hills outside Perth. Conditions were perfect, but the rehearsal broke down as the Nasties started arguing again, one fight too many. Realising they didn't *have* to do this anymore, they broke up. But it was really Kim that was cut adrift. 'Within a few weeks they reformed without me! They were looking for a name and their new identity, and I was a shag on a rock. There was a scene there that I probably brought to the town, and there I was … shut out of my own party.'

7

Pissed on Another Planet

In the wake of the Cheap Nasties gig months earlier, Roddy Radalj and Boris Sujdovic formed The Exterminators along with two other Perth musos, Johnno Rawlings and Mark Demetrius. 'I think we only did one show, and we just did basic punky stuff. Mark the singer was a kind of journalist guy and he'd write all these lyrics about how fucked Perth was,' Boris recalls. 'It was real basic stuff — we could hardly play a note.'

It was 1978, and with the Cheap Nasties in recess Kim was at a loose end. 'I don't know if he took pity on me but Rod Radalj decided he'd let me play in his band.' With Mark Demetrius excused from vocal duties Kim was invited in, under instructions to sing and *not* play guitar, and The Exterminators duly morphed into the Invaders. Kim was instantly enamoured of the Croatian guitar and bass player. 'Kim seemed to like Roddy and I, maybe some romantic notion that we were like Ron and Scott Ashton or something. We were maybe a bit tougher looking or stood out. I don't think it was because he was super impressed with the Exterminators first gig!' (Boris Sujdovic). A review at the time noted, 'It is hoped that the musically adept Salmon will be the cohesive factor the band appears to need. This band can only go up … They were a bunch of bumbling beginners and were very un-together. Kim joined … and they tightened up considerably … but were still a fair way from perfection.'[1] The band forged a Stooges and New York Dolls sound, operating in the general musical location that Kim was looking for but without the chops to pull it off. The highlight of their act was an ode to Perth called *Asshole of the Universe*. The band were starting to sound promising, but the drummer John was always at loggerheads with Roddy and Boris, and by May 1978, he was ditched from the group.

Meanwhile, the Victims had petered out through a combination of boredom and internal unease. 'In April 1978 they released a single, *Television Addict/I'm Flipped Out Over You*. This took most of Australia by surprise and generated some rave reviews. Even some of the British music papers were able to bring themselves to give it a favourable comment. 1000 copies were pressed, and it rapidly sold out. The group broke up the following month …'[2] With James Baker now available, Kim swooped and asked him to join the Invaders on drums. James accepted, but knowing Kim's guitar playing was going to waste, agreed to join on the condition that Kim play guitar. 'So, we went around to Victim Manor, a squalid hippy joint that was basically a drop-in place for all of the vagrants in that scene. It was a rehearsal place and we had all our gear there.'

With James at the drums, things coalesced immediately. He offered some rough lyrics about a girl and mumbled an even rougher tune to match the words. Bouncing back and forth with James, Kim spun a melody around the words and assembled a couple of chords. 'The combination of that and the punk racket of ragged two note bar chords and floor-tom-heavy drumbeats were like a collision between the Stooges and Herman's Hermits.'[3] With Kim back on guitar, the band now had a twin guitar attack. Whereas the Cheap Nasties had played with a counter point style — Neil Fernandes playing power chords and Kim stabbing noises over the top — Roddy and Kim played dual power chords, with Kim embellishing with arpeggios and creating a rich, jangly and distorted sound. 'It struck me as something new I hadn't heard, and we had a successful rehearsal. Straight away I heard a *sound*.'

Afterwards, with their instruments idle, the band hung out on the porch of Victim Manor, aware that something significant had occurred in the rehearsal room. This new sound seemed like a new band, not just a new version of the Invaders. As the Perth day dwindled, the four of them started throwing around potential band names. Kim was drawn towards a moniker that captured the sound he wanted: 'primitive and hardly any chords and so moronic that it's high art … so primitive that it turns into jazz, things getting thrashed into the ground.' Against that lofty mission statement, James said 'What about the Scientists? And that was *it*. It was never going to be anything else, and I was so happy that we'd found this name, we've got this new sound and the name just says it all, supremely ironic but sounds cool. That was it, the Scientists.'

•••

The Scientists set about forming their set list. James had a head full of songs that captured the freewheeling spirit of the Perth punk scene in contrast to the moodier atmosphere of Brisbane, Sydney and Melbourne. 'I don't know how I came up with the lyrics, they're supposed to be minimalist and rock and roll. And fun. They're tongue in cheek' (James Baker).

The song writing method of the new band was curious. James would invoke some lyrics and try to sing the tune to Kim, who then had to interpret the sound and create a fully realised song out of it. James is no singer, so Kim was really working off phrasing or collections of notes rather than a formed tune.

> *James would have these lyrics and he'd hand them to Kim and he'd say, 'it kind of goes like this'. But James just can't play an instrument so he'd kind of sing a drum beat in his head as the melody, it might have been an accident. He'd be humming a drum beat and Kim would think that was the melody. They kind of fumbled their way through it* (Boris Sujdovic).

Bantering back and forth with James, Kim would keep refining the chords or melody or sound until it clicked with some version of what James heard in his head. 'I couldn't read his mind, but he thought I could because he didn't know the difference! He knew it sounded good and then thought he must have written it! I always thought that was hilarious, because as soon as it was good he was like *oh yeah, that's it*.' James concurs, 'That's how we wrote songs, I'd give him the lyrics and a basic idea of how the song goes and he'd write the music. I'd give him my bastardised idea of a melody, and together we shaped it into a song.' The end results sounded like a mash up of the Sex Pistols and New York Dolls, filtered through the Troggs — power pop punk noise.

However, there were some constraints. James' lyrical themes had run their course, and by the time he arrived in the Scientists he'd moved from expressing social commentary to just expressing what he liked. Kim thought, 'Great! We're going to inherit this great font of lyrics, and this great cool guy with his stripy shirt and his Brian Jones haircut, he knows what he wants to do … brilliant, particularly the stuff in the Victims was great; comical kind of outrageous lyrics really. What I found was by the time he was in the Scientists it was a finite thing, it was sort of just the "girl" lyrics left, whereas before there was television *and* girls.' This was not lost on a gig reviewer who witnessed the band in Adelaide 1979: 'The lyrical content of some of the originals became somewhat monotonous after a while. The boy/girl line is fine, but the Scientists give it a hell of a beating.'[4]

However, Kim was impressed with his new band mate:

'I think about James Baker, as far as I can tell everything he did was a post-modern pastiche of the past done with strong minimalist and pop sensibility. But that's what I like and I'm projecting on to him. To him it's just good rock and roll and he'd hate that description. He's done it in a completely uncontrived way.' James' presence in the band was critical. He brought an unpretentious, simple style to the band that allowed Kim's vision to take seed.

And he was the first in a line of drummers with whom Kim would collaborate to capture his sound.

Boris and Roddy were like big, Croatian punk rock kids in a candy store. From a standing start they were in the centre of the scene and revelled in every moment. 'By this stage James was kind of a guru guy. He was a punk by 1972 and into the New York Dolls, driving around Perth all dressed up. Kim used to hang out, and he had his own thing going too … For Roddy and I it was great, all of a sudden we were with the rock stars. It was all excitement!' (Boris Sujdovic). The Scientists rehearsed in earnest and soon hit the Perth scene with a splash, horrifying and impressing audiences in equal measure.

While Neil and Robbie's new band the Manikins enjoyed a short while as the darlings of the scene, the Scientists were still *out*. Too loud, too arrogant, too British punk, too dandy. They just couldn't engender the easy embrace of the scant Perth music establishments, so the Scientists took a leaf out of the Victims book (and the Saints and Birdman) by building up their own scene at the Governor Broome Hotel. With James providing the entrepreneurial spirit, they talked the Gov Broome's owner into letting them play there for a small door charge. On the back of the Scientists blistering live shows, word got out and soon 'we were reining supreme in that particular scene'. As the most authentic punk band around, their popularity grew, catering for the true believers. 'If we played at a place that held 150 people, then 150 would be there … not super popular, but as popular as you could get in Perth' (Boris Sujdovic). Tony Thewlis recalls watching Kim at these shows, thrashing out *Teenage Dreamer* at some Perth pub and 'putting his entire body into the vibrato. It looked like a technique Bruce Lee might have used to kill people!' (Tony Thewlis)

Social etiquette at a Scientist gig was limited. Nobody clapped. Nobody showed enjoyment. If you danced, your head was down, staring at the floor. Pogoing was acceptable, but you would never use your arms. 'The scene wasn't super intense,' remembers Boris, 'even though the music was. It was less political. I guess no one had anything to be pissed off about.'

This circumstance triggered an artistic response in Kim, and before long, the contrary Salmon performance template took effect.

> *I remember right from the start Kim not wanting to do the popular songs. In the middle of 1977, right in the middle of the punk thing, you're in a punk band in a punk venue and Kim wants to do a John Cougar Mellencamp song,* I Need a Lover. *He goes 'yeah yeah, fuck 'em'. And a couple of punks stormed out! And maybe that planted the seed in Kim's head, 'This is great! I know how to piss people off!' And this was the formula for the Scientists. The attitude was 'let's not do what everyone else is doing'* (Boris Sujdovic).

As the band got more popular the shows got more crowded, and the audience more animated. The Scientists themselves channelled the UK oriented punk pop mood and thrashed about happily. Surely, thought Kim, they were building towards greatness.

•••

There was no shortage of evidence that a movement on the East Coast was building. In May 1978, up and coming music mogul Michael Gudinski released a compilation record of local bands called 'Lethal Weapons'.[5] While it missed the mark on presenting the true deplorables of Melbourne punk, it did feature the Boys Next Door and was early attempt by the music business to unearth the underground. Bruce Milne could be heard talking the new aesthetic during 1978 on his 3RRR Saturday morning radio show. Elsewhere, Dave Graney moved from Mount Gambia to Adelaide and teamed up with drummer Clare Moore to form first the Sputniks, and then a lifelong personal and creative partnership. Dave and Clare would soon come across the Scientists in full flight and recognised a similar impulse to their own creative output. Meanwhile in Brisbane, a young Gregory 'Tex' Perkins was looking forward to getting his first guitar for Christmas.

•••

The Scientists momentum was thwarted by some rapid and frequent personnel changes. The first of these was in August 1978 when Boris left the band. Fanzine DNA reported at the time that 'although Boris was a very competent bassist, the other group members felt that he wasn't sufficiently dedicated so he got the boot. Amongst other things, Kim was of the opinion that Boris was capable of performing back-up vocals, but Boris himself couldn't be bothered trying.'[6]

I'm in the Grace Darling Hotel, Collingwood with Boris and his partner Kat Amiss. Boris is thoughtful and gracious, super laid back but whip smart. As we talk, Kat seems as intrigued with his stories as I am, and prompts Boris' recollections with incisive questions. As we start on another round of cider and Coopers, Boris reflects on his exit from the *Mark 1* Scientists.

> *We were together for probably about a year, then I left. They kicked me out. I was getting bored. It was kind of like a surge from the middle of '76, but by the end of '79 it had started to peter out. Other things came in, but the actual punk thing seemed to get a bit tiresome. Maybe we all were getting a bit bored. But things happened at a super-fast pace back then, obviously now it would take years to get bored. Back then it only took six months, and everyone was like, what are we doing now! It was frenetic. We got along great you know, until they kicked me out! And then we still got along great!* (Boris Sujdovic).

Boris went from the Scientists to form the Rockets in April 1979, with Roddy Radalj who would also exit the Scientists original line up, uncomfortable remaining after Boris' demise.

With Boris gone, the Scientists laid low, scouring Perth for a new bass player until January 1979, when Dennis Byrne joined the band. 'When they returned to the gigging circuit they were by far the most powerful band around, not only good musically, but also confident enough in themselves not to kow tow to the promoters.'[7] It was this line up of Kim, Roddy, James and Dennis that entered the recording studio to record the band's first single. The result was the double A side *Frantic Romantic/Shake Together Tonight* released on DNA Records in June 1979. 'Legend has it that during the recording of this the band blew out the recording meters at the studio with the volume of their playing.'[8] Combining Kim's super catchy arpeggio guitar lines with James' unmistakable lyrics, *Frantic Romantic* is the quintessential example of the Baker/Salmon song writing approach. Kim sings this song forty years later and it doesn't sound dated or hackneyed, even with James' misty-eyed lyrics, just pure and poppy and great.

> *I love that single, how it came out. It's a real gem of a thing. Both sides of it, in fact. That was very important for me that experience of recording Frantic Romantic. I had gone in with a set thing to do and set about doing it. You don't have to have anarchy every time you go and try to do a piece of art. You try to execute something, an idea, to give it the form.*

In April 1979, after *Frantic Romantic* was recorded, Bryne and Roddy left to be replaced by Ian Sharples on bass and Ben Jupiter on guitar.

Ian turned out to be an effective songwriter and collaborated with Kim on several songs as James' well of lyrics started to run dry. This line up recorded the *Scientists* EP, which was released on White Rider Records on 28 February 1980. Featuring four songs, including the hit *Last Night* and *Pissed on Another Planet*, this record is considered by Australian musicologist Ian McFarlane as 'one of the most collectable artefacts of the Australian punk rock era.'[9]

•••

Desperate to get out of Perth, The Scientists literally begged their way into a tour of the Eastern States in December 1979. 'Their attempts to escape became increasingly desperate, to the extent that they began advertising this fact at gigs … The end result was a "tour" around Adelaide, Sydney and Melbourne'.[10]

Going East meant a three-day drive across the desert which the Scientists embarked on in convoy. Kim's first car was a Falcon station wagon, painted black and white with wood grain panels down the side. According to Megan Salmon, 'it really had this menacing feel to it'. The car seemed to glide or float rather than drive. Kim named it The Shark, and it was in this time bomb that Kim took his first trip East.

By this time, Kim was embroiled with girlfriend Rosemary Fearon, and she accompanied the Scientists on the tour. Rosemary was a wild child. She looked like Blondie and moved fast and hard. Kim had moved in with her and became enmeshed in her hoopla, even landing in the lock up for a night after their first date. Rosemary had a sister, Linda, who was studying to be a teacher, and together they made quite an impression. With Rosemary sharing the wheel, Kim set off East in his floating car.

With the gigs booked and the talent on the road, an agreement was reached that the band would take a percentage of the door, and hopefully make enough at each stop to propel them to the next gig. A review of Scientists gig in Adelaide, 1979 sheds light on their form …

> *The Scientists turned in two sets of powerhouse rock 'n' roll, the nature of which hasn't been seen here for a long time. They received rapturous applause throughout … the Scientists appeared to be a very confident band. The vocals were consistent and powerful, although Kim Salmon did admittedly have a few problems with some of the high notes. James baker did some interesting song introductions, and consistently came out with*

> *the relentless, powerhouse drumming. Kim has the occasional tuning problems with his guitar, but these were minor … Unlike many local bands, the Scientists see nothing wrong with the occasional bit of harmony singing, and this adds to the appeal of their material. Many of the cover versions sound better than when they were done originally. All in all, they came across very well, and were most enjoyable … Kim Salmon maintained a look of studied 'cool throughout …*[11]

The band blew back into Perth weary, but feeling like they'd accomplished something. But in spite of all the driving, loading gear and playing shows, they found themselves in an even worse position when they returned. Gigs in Perth were drying up, and the Scientists reputation as being 'too unprofessional' was not garnering them any favours with promoters. Unsurprisingly, the band jumped at the chance to get on the road, and in February 1980 they headed East again. But the second Eastern States tour was a washout.

> *We went on a national tour which was absolutely disastrous really, no good memories at all. Bad memories of being stuck with no money on the Gold Coast for seven days, supporting ridiculous bands like Mother Goose and Jimmy and the Boys, and Midnight Oil and all those bands we hated. Lots of driving and not good a good time at all. No good memories of the Scientists tour* (James Baker).

On the road for nearly two months from Perth to Brisbane and back, the band lost several grand and lots of weight. Booked into unsuitable suburban venues supporting incompatible headliners, the Scientists often played to crowds that were hostile or microscopic, which didn't bring the best out of the band. The Scientists just didn't make sense to followers of Rose Tattoo, Flowers, John Paul Young, Sherbert or Skyhooks, and they were routinely booed off stage or ignored. They were living off two dollars a day, and worse, many of the venues didn't even give them a beer rider!

There were triumphs though. They played a successful show with the Boys Next Door and headlined at St Kilda's famous Crystal Ballroom, pulling over three hundred people to a great gig. To their surprise, the band were invited to play *Last Night* on Australia's preeminent music show, *Countdown*. Molly Meldrum had heard a copy of the EP, liked it, and offered the band a spot. On a stage adorned with forty-four gallon drums and wooden crates, Kim looks like a mod, dressed all in black and buttoned up to his neck with white loafers on. Staring straight down the barrel of the camera, Kim is remarkably composed for a TV first timer. James valiantly plays drums at back of stage even though the set designers had decided the kick drum took up too much room and set up the kit without one! In Kim's view, the Countdown experience was a success. 'All the Aussie bands on there just looked crap. On our episode was Blondie and the Scientists, and I'm proud to say that the Scientists looked like we knew what we were doing. You can sort of see we had a plan and vision and sound'. The Countdown performance of *Last Night* can be found on the ABC music Classic Countdown compilation, listed appropriately between the Ramones and Ian Dury and the Blockheads. Now TV stars, the band returned to Perth with expectations of increased respect but 'no one gave a shit!' Well, at least one person, country boy and future Scientist Tony Thewlis, was impressed. 'I moved to Perth soon after the Scientists appeared on Countdown — in order to be available once they asked me to join them …!'

•••

Ben Juniper became the next Scientist to exit the band in May 1980, and the Scientists continued as a trio. Having pursued his favourite band, Tony Thewlis saw another opening: 'I tried to join the Scientists after Ben Juniper left … I met with James a few times until he gently broke it to me that they were going to continue on as a three piece. In that incarnation I think I saw every gig they played, and one day at the

Governor Broome Kim's girlfriend, Rosemary, noticed my homemade Scientists tee shirt and started talking to me. She introduced me to Kim (and to cider) …' Tony would remain loyal to Kim, and passionately committed to cider, for decades to come.

The three-piece Scientists scaled down the songs and rearranged the sound to fit the reduced line up. With more space, the songs took on a new life, and this version of the band momentarily put Perth on the canvas. But with the closure of key venues in Perth, the gigs dried up once again. 'The band started vegetating again. Song writing still went on happily, but they'd lost all enthusiasm for interstate touring and saw little future for themselves unless they left Perth.'[12] A lifeline came in the form of some committed fans and generous friends who pulled together enough money for the Scientists to capture these songs to tape. The three piece Scientists took over a studio for a weekend, recording their first full length LP, the self-titled album, known as the 'Pink Album', owing to its pink cover. The 'Pink Album' was released in August 1981 by EMI custom records. Ex-Scientist Boris sees it as an interesting, but not accurate artefact of the bands early sound.

> *They did the 'Pink Album', but it was not really representative of what the band was like, I don't think. It was too poppy. It sounded like the Scientists were a power pop band but I remember it live as more chaotic. Ugly pop, I used to call it … The songs were more Troggsy and primal than the 'Pink Album' suggests, but the engineer sort of cleaned it all up* (Boris Sujdovic).

Kim, too, was unhappy with the recorded depiction of the band. 'It was all done in a bit of a rush, and consequently, although the material was strong, the eventual recording wasn't as good as it might have been. We didn't know what we were doing, so the drums sounded like a bunch of cardboard boxes. The bass was wonky sounding as well. I didn't like the sound of my voice.' Kim described it as a 'dud' while

James Baker didn't even wait around to participate in the mixing. Sydney was calling and he bid Perth — and the Scientists — goodbye.

But the deficits that initially bothered Kim receded over the years, and he is now more charitable about his first full length record. 'I put it on now and l like my whiny voice. I like the primitive drums. It sounds like a post punk record out of England … I was kind of ashamed of the early band at one time, as the later stuff seemed like a much better representation of me. But I like it now'.

•••

In January 1981, the Scientists broke up 'in disgust at their unpopularity in Perth'. James recalls that they had 'had enough of Perth, and three years of the band was enough, no future for us …'

Their last gig at Hernando's Hideaway was supported by new band the Helicopters, featuring Tony Thewlis, who by now was friendly with Kim. Despite the clammy pall that Perth threw over the band, James looks back at this time fondly:

> *I didn't think I was going to change Perth, but we tried to give it a kick in the arse! We felt hated in our own city! We didn't have a lot of fans. But we have thousands now who say they used to come and watch us, but where were they when there was four people on a Sunday watching! We had fun doing it … We were just putting it up 'em in Perth really. And the friendship of all those people, Rod, Boris and Kim still remains strong today* (James Baker).

•••

The *Mark 1* Scientists came and went in a flash. They were really a transition band for Kim, between the hard and fast punk of the Cheap Nasties and the unique mess of the *Mark 2* Scientists to follow. They were a means to refine his song writing and performing, to learn who he wanted to play with, to consolidate his look, and to test his formula. The *Mark 1* Scientists drew Kim's identity into sharper focus, and he was clearly on the outside.

> *We were the next thing beyond punk (just plain contrary, in hindsight). We chose to take the next step that, to us, was to go through the rubble and pick up the things we liked and reassemble them ... We were perverse. We revered the stylish loser, the unsung hero, the uncompromising unconventional unseen dandy, and the misunderstood misanthrope ... Our heroes were incurable. They couldn't help it. They were rock 'n' roll to the core. And so it was for us. People had got The Victims. They didn't get us. We were loud, loose as buggery and yet had pop melodies and wore mop tops. And loud shirts. Were we punk? Old school rock? Or making some kind of art statement? Nobody could tell ... At first, we didn't care but soon it became apparent to us that we were becoming musical lepers around town. This only added to our righteousness ...*[13]

This enigmatic cauldron of noise, anti-style and fuck-off-attitude laid a large chunk of the conceptual template for the *Mark 2* Scientists. There would be seismic changes to the concept of the Scientists in its second coming, but this version of the band took Kim one step closer to the formula he was after. Kim was still on a messy transition from his invisible childhood in the swamps, but with the Scientists he caught sight of something he was chasing. He had found a gang of misfits to feel at ease with. The Scientists had delivered plenty of triumphs in spite of the general hatred in their home town, and although the immediate future was blank, Kim knew he stood at an open door.

> *I felt like I had an idea that was so strong that I believed in it, and it came from me and the guys. Finally, I was in a little scene, it was the club of four Scientists. And I belonged in that.*

And we defined the terms, we could go out there and people could interpret that how they wanted but we knew what it was, and people could say what they liked, take it as they would, but we knew it was strong enough as it was. And it was the first time where it was like we knew better than everybody else — you don't know shit! It was a great feeling. We were driven enough, me, James, Boris, we had enough drive. It's us against the world. It's good to be got. And the Scientists was a time where that happened.

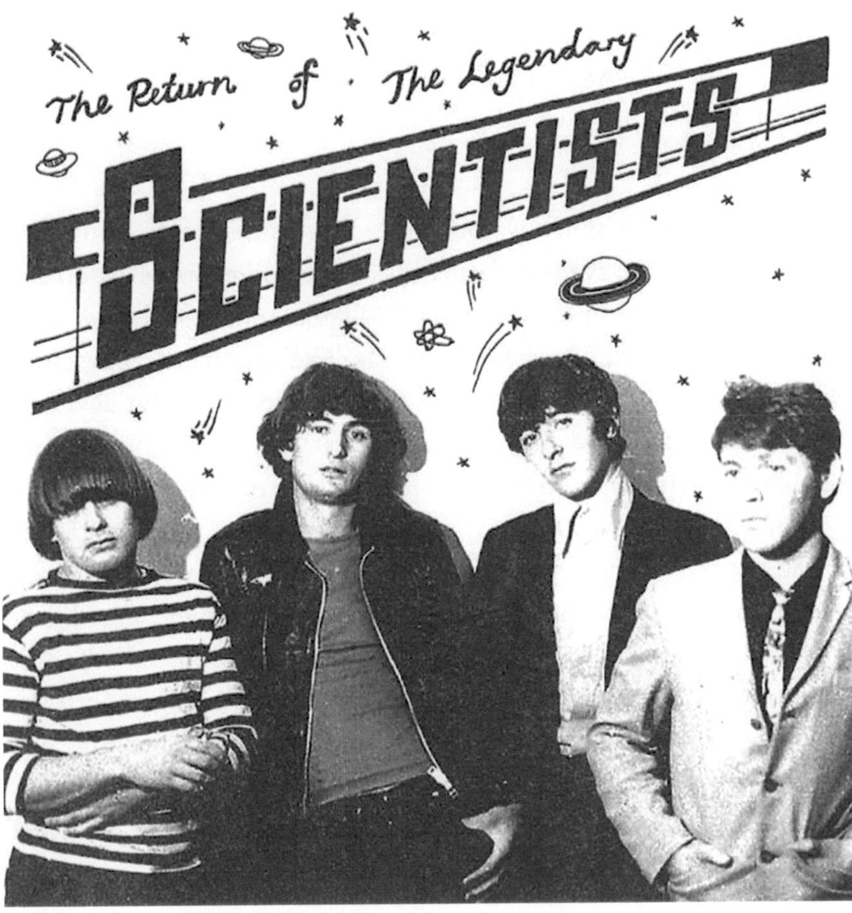

8

This is My Happy Hour

Now without both spiritual soul mates Boris and James, Kim hung around for a while, contemplating his exit from Perth. As a stop gap, he formed Louie Louie with Kim Williams and Brett Rixon. Kim (Salmon) described Kim (Williams) as 'like one of the guys from Hi Fidelity'. He had initially come into the Scientists orbit as a keen supporter of the band, having flown their flag in the Roadrunner fanzine and actually contributed to funding the recording of the 'Pink Album'. He enthusiastically signed on as bass player for Louie Louie, and would have a short, but substantial role in Kim's career. Replacing James would be hard, but Kim had spotted a drummer named Brett Rixon in a band the Screaming Fits who seemed to fit the bill. Brett was an immediately compelling proposition, surly and understated in disposition and stripped back but powerful in his playing. And so, Louie Louie was born, and was witness to a rapid Kim Salmon evolution. 'In Louie Louie, the Scientists sound was being formed already, with myself and Brett Rixon.'

Tony Thewlis now had his own band, the Helicopters, but he still had his sights set on playing guitar with Kim. Tony would manufacture reasons to run into him and got an early glimpse of where Kim's attentions were turning.

> *When the Helicopters were booked to support the Stray Cats at a large venue and I decided that my Musicman amp wouldn't be up to the job, which was basically an excuse for me to find Kim's parent's number in the phone book and ring to ask if I could borrow his quad box. He said yes, and actually drove it around to my place. He told me about his new group, Louie Louie, and enthused about the dBs and the Cramps* (Tony Thewlis).

Around about this time, Kim had been turned on to the idea of musical primitivism and was listening heavily to the Cramps.

> *After the initial punk rock thing, I heard the Cramps, and that reminded me what I loved about punk rock. It was primitive … it was raw and it was people going nuts! I heard a track and it was just feeding back and Lux Interior screaming, and I thought 'what the hell is this?!' It wasn't even like music … it was something much more primal. It was completely subversive.*

The primitivism of the Cramps was the skewed shape that Kim had been searching for when he sat outside Victim Manor with James, Roddy and Boris to name the Scientists. The first version of the Scientists had been captured by the momentum of Kim and James' earlier musical exploits and had retained that recognisable form. James' lyrics might have been postmodern and without affectation, but they did not lend themselves to the minimalist musical landscape that Kim was hearing in his alien brain. James' trip was punk pop, and with Kim at that time in the thrall of British style punk, the Scientists naturally developed that kind of sound. Kim's relationship with *Mark 1* Scientists was not straightforward. He was proud of their achievements, particularly getting up the nose of the Perth music establishment and ignoring the genre's favourite sons on the East Coast. He did, however, harbour frustration that the sound had never fully imploded into the sort of musical oblivion he imagined. The Cramps opened the door to that mayhem: 'There's always starting points in your life aren't there; these moments, like hearing the Cramps that time, it was a moment that really unlocked something. They were one thing that I really adored and took with me into the *Mark 2* Scientists'.

The Cramps producer, Alex Chilton, was another standard bearer.

> *He had an album called 'Flies on Sherbet' … It was so raw … the repertoire was really eclectic, there were false starts, it was like the band wasn't really acquainted with the songs, but it sounded incredible! It was the antithesis of pop production. I loved that. That really informed me, the whole way that the song was there and it was deconstructed.*

Kim quickly became obsessed with Alex Chilton, drawn in by his anarchistic terrain:

> *His version of* I Can't Seem To Make You Mine *where he breaks down sobbing in the middle of it, just like Lux Interior did in* Lonesome Town … *that was just such theatre to me. That was the world that drew me in and informed the Scientists.*

As Kim's musical reference points got more chaotic, so too did his personal life. After a fast paced but fun couple of months with girlfriend Rosemary Fearon, things started heading for a trauma.

> *It was pretty chaotic living with Rosemary. She was a total rock 'n' roll cliché, she was the wildest girl in town. She was blond and petite so you'd go anywhere, and you guarantee that any male in the room would make a bee line to her. I found it very boring in the end, it was always the same drama. By 5 o'clock she'd get this crazed look in her eyes and say 'I'm bored' which would mean we'd have to get trashed and wasted and go out on*

> *the town and have a big argument in front of everybody and then she'd come back at three in the morning and smash a glass down in the middle of the floor and wake me up ... She needed to have a drama around her.*

In fact, every day was drenched in drama. Kim sank into a dark period of 'getting wasted and taking serapax ... having big black outs and apparently doing bad things to myself'. While Kim was absorbing Rosemary's extremes, he would take refuge in Linda's more equanimous company. 'She had a kind of Monty Python-esque sense of humour, and Linda and I would share a joke, we had a shared a sense of humour, but nothing happened for quite some time after Rosemary and I split up. But we ended up together just before I was going off to Sydney'.

Meanwhile, Louie Louie had serious intentions, and Kim began writing songs for the project. 'I knew that I wanted to be primal, to get away from that poppy thing.' As was Kim's nature, he was looking to connect his songs with a concept or a totem. His radar picked up a vibration, and immediately something bubbled up. 'I read that the Cramps said in an interview "we want to be big, somewhere between the Beatles and Creedence Clearwater Revival. You got us wrong — we don't want to be underground!"' This resonated with Kim. His ambition to create discordant music did not exclude visions of great success, and by now Kim knew he wanted to in the best band in the world. If it's good enough for Lux Interior, it was good enough for him! And, they had referenced Creedence — one of his very first awakenings of rock 'n' roll and his first big concert. 'I just thought — Creedence, they were swampy! I liked that'. The home grown everglades of Perth were still fresh in his mind and seemed symbolic of the musical challenge he was setting. 'I just thought, swamps! ... so *Swampland* was like a mission statement for me'.

The song that would become the most enduring of his career didn't so much crawl out of some dark creative miasma, as it was constructed by the madly professorial Salmon. Although the song's simplicity and perpetual motion make it seem spontaneous, it actually had to be designed and manufactured. In fact, this particular swamp was a built environment. It started in fragments. 'I had a chorus — "in my heart, there's a place called swampland". Actually, I think it was "in my heart there's a *land* called swampland" and somebody corrected me and said maybe you should sing there's a *place*, so I got a little help. Too many "lands", which was a bad song writing technique.' The phrase in the chorus was the heart and soul of the song and laid out the manifesto on which the verses would have to deliver.

Every day at dusk when the sun fades
my mind returns to the everglades
A place of olive green mangroves and vine
shotguns and snakes, alligator wine

Music wise, Kim has constructed a chord sequence from G going down to relative minor E — honouring the initial Creedence inspiration. 'Very Creedency, Everly Brothers kind of thing. It's kind of an early rockabilly thing, in a poppy sort of way'. For the verses, Kim built a straight-ahead structure that pushed the song forward but, in a contradiction of design, built tension through tightly held restraint, as well. 'Kind of like a chugging swamp groove with rip offs of, I don't know if it's *Little Sister* or *Shakin' All Over*.' While the song looked back a little in its inspiration — early rock 'n' roll, swamp, pop, rockabilly — Kim wanted it to signal where his artistic impulse was pointing him. 'I wanted a bit more urban dissonance as well, 'cos we were post punk by this stage and I wanted that Television kind of jarring guitar.' *Swampland* had to wrap up all of these reference points and still travel forward in time.

Nobody knows so they never think to visit
Where the atmosphere's so thick that you could kiss it
I've never seen copper heads diving for their prey
or once mighty oak's with roots in decay

With all of this ringing in his ears, brain and guts, Kim presented the concoction to Kim Williams. He issued instructions for how the song should sound, what it should mean, how it would be sung — 'in kind of a bluesy sort of thing, and I had an idea of a Roy Orbison kind of falsetto inflection' — where the chorus and verses would be located and what the vibe was. And he handed his bass player the lyrics that were the song's motif …

In my heart, there's a place called Swampland.

'I just heard all these things that I wanted and put it together, constructed it. So it's got all these ingredients. And he came back to me with lyrics that actually had a formula it in …'

Nine parts water, one part sand.

Kim pauses as the story reaches its summit, and looks at me with a dry smile before delivering the punchline. 'It's the Formula for Grunge.'

•••

While the foundations for Grunge were being laid in Perth, in Seattle, a nineteen year old Mark Arm played his first rock show in his band Mr. Epp and the Calculations, adding guitarist Steve Turner to the line up a year later. In Olympia Washington, Bruce Pavitt — who, in 1988, would release the first single of Mark Arm's later band, Mudhoney, and coin the phrase 'Seattle Sound' — was starting a fanzine called Subterranean Pop and selling mix tapes of US underground bands. The tapes would eventually turn into a record label, and Subterranean Pop would be shortened to Sub Pop. Kurt Cobain, the singer in the label's most famous band, was sullenly contemplating dropping out of Aberdeen High School and discovering punk rock, unaware that he would be the figurehead of a global musical movement that was percolating 15,000 kilometres away in Kim Salmon's head.

•••

During the Louie Louie phase, Kim also wrote an early version of *We Had Love* and continued to experiment with a rougher, stripped back sound. Eventually, differences arose between the members. Kim Williams remained attracted to the Scientists power pop sound and was happy in Perth, while Kim and Brett were increasingly attracted to the swampier, dirtier sounds that were brewing elsewhere. They hated Perth and wanted out. After a few live shows playing to muted responses, Louie Louie broke up in June 1981. But before they did, Boris had planted a seed. 'One day when we were playing to ten people who didn't care, Boris came up to me and said, "Waddya doing this for? We could get the Scientists back together in the East and do a bomb! There are loads of bands over there copying it!"' Curiosity piqued, Kim contacted James Baker, who had already flown east to join Dave Faulkner and Roddy Radalj. James was by then embroiled in Le Hoodoo Gurus and declined Kim's overture to join the new look Scientists, but gave his blessing for the repurposed band.

> *Kim moved to Sydney about six months after I did. He followed me up and asked if I minded if he used the Scientist name. And I said no problem. I loved the* Mark 2 *Scientists. I saw most of their shows. It was different, a different band. Different people writing the lyrics. It wasn't really the same band, the name just remained* (James Baker).

The absence of James was offset by the stirring of something exceptional in Louie Louie's short lifespan. Brett Rixon had proved more than a competent drum player. He presented Kim a new tool kit to use in his song writing, a new means of expressing his musical designs: 'I think the sort of drummer that I require needs to be a very good musician — a better musician than I am.' In his quest for originality, Kim would tap out odd time signatures and drum patterns as the anchor point for new songs and transmit these to Brett. Brett was unorthodox enough to go with it, ignoring conventional drumming wisdom, and had the chops to pull it off. 'Brett … had an uncanny knack for interpreting Salmon's rudimentary instructions into the primal beats what would steer the bands sonic makeover. The two quickly became thick as thieves, developing their own language with one another, while getting into plenty of trouble along the way.'[1] Kim had found a new drumming accomplice to realise his revised vision for the band.

Not long before Kim was set to depart Perth, he bumped into the ever enthusiastic Tony Thewlis in the Hay Street Mall. Tony recalls, 'I asked him what was happening with Louie Louie and he said he was giving up on them and moving to Sydney to form a new Scientists with Boris and taking Brett with him, so he probably needed another guitar player. I immediately dragged him into an underground bar and bought him drinks all afternoon until he finally asked if I would be willing to move over to Sydney and join them'. Tony was stoked, but apprehensive, hoping that Kim wouldn't regret the offer made under influence of Perth lager. Kim reported at the time that he made the offer 'to be nice to the younger guitar player'[2], but it was a move that neither of them would regret.

In September 1981, Kim announced he was heading east and Linda, now his girlfriend, decided she'd follow as soon as she could. Without the means to wing it to Sydney, Kim purchased an old Leyland P26 — the world's worst car — from James Baker's girlfriend's brother. The Leyland's deficits were only overshadowed by the antics of Kim's travel mates, having somehow ended up in the car with two young Perth punks — Tony Pola and Brian Henry Hooper.

•••

When I moved to Melbourne in 1993, Brian Henry Hooper was the archetype of the perfect bass player and musical gang affiliate. He was male model material: good looking, with long, perfectly dishevelled black hair. He sported the ultra-cool uniform of sharp boots, narrow black trousers and wide-open shirts, and always had a cigarette hanging nonchalantly out the side of his mouth. This was all complemented by a natural rock 'n' roll swagger and general air of mischief, that, combined with his bass guitar chops, made him the full package. Brian Hooper was emblematic of the so-called Melbourne Mafia — a black clad troupe of bad ass musos who all played in each other's bands and seemed to be the custodians of Melbourne's underground musical atmosphere.

Brian's journey through music was punctuated by a terrible accident in 2004 when he fell off a balcony near Phillip Island. Out for brunch, he leaned against a balcony rail which gave way, causing Brian to fall and seriously damage his spinal cord. Paralysed from the waist down, Brian was told he wouldn't walk again, but somehow only a few months later he resumed duties with the Beasts of Bourbon at the Greyhound Hotel. The miracle recovery was supported by a walking stick that he would require from then on, and physically he was transformed from a lithe, whip sharp mafiaso character to a venerable journeyman of rock with a cane and distinguished limp.

The walking stick isn't in attendance as Brian opens the door to me at his lovely family home. His wife Ninevah patrols the lounge room floor, playing with their two-year-old twin daughters Ava and Charlize who, despite teaming up on their mum, don't manage to out-manoeuvrer her. Brian escorts me to the dining room and as I pull out the Zoom to record the interview, he gestures me outside and says, 'Let's have a chat and a smoke first'. Sitting outside with red wine, Brian talks off the record about his accident, health, tragedies, triumphs, and music. We revert to the dining table, refill our glasses, and by agreement, switch on the Zoom.

> *Having grown up in Perth and being part of the small scene that used to go to gigs like the Governor Broome, Hernando's Hideaway, places like that, I used to see the Scientists, the Mannikins, the Victims, the Rockets so that's where I first saw Kim … I was underage going to these gigs by the way, probably 16 or 17, and I'd wait for my dad to fall asleep, then I'd crawl into the bed room, sneak my hand into his the pocket of his pants that were slung over a chair at the end of his bed and get the car keys out, sneak out to the drive way and put the car in*

neutral and roll out the driveway in reverse, turn it into the street then turn the engine on where he couldn't hear it and drive in to the city. Get home at four in the morning before school started, slip the keys back and then go to bed for a couple of hours (Brian Hooper).

Given his regular attendance at punk shows, Brian had made an impression on Kim and the other Scientists. And so, when Kim needed company to share travel costs of the overland car trip to Sydney, it occurred that Brian might have the right amount of devil may care to take the ride. Sure enough, Brian and his friend Tony were up for it. They subsequently handed over petrol money, piled into the Leyland P76 and pointed it East.

I advertised in the paper 'drummer wanted for punk band, must be absolute moron' and Pola was the only one who answered it. He was a shepherd at that time, and he got me a job as a shepherd too. Looking after sheep and sheep shit. So we worked in the Midlands sale yards in the winter months. Farmers would bring truckloads of sheep in, and we'd haul sheep all day and get covered in shit and piss … and then you'd change your clothes and they had a bar set up there and you'd drink your wages after work and come home stinking of shit and piss and alcohol (Brian Hooper).

It wasn't all sheep though. Brian and Tony would play music in the tin shed at the back of Tony's Mum's place. 'I hadn't settled on whether to play guitar or bass, but 'cos I only had a drummer it made sense to get some rhythms going. So we played for quite a while together and formed a good friendship and worked out how to play together before we ever played with Kim' (Brian Hooper). Brian and Tony were seriously irreverent. They loved their music and had made some sort of mark on Kim Salmon, enough that he would willingly spend three days in a nightmare on wheels with them.

> *It was a horrible car! There was a swamp in the bottom of the car as the waterproofing was so poor. And Brian and Tony were a pair of hoons basically, they were younger than me, punk upstarts. Their idea of something fun to do was if someone was asleep in the back they'd slam the breaks on and you'd crash into the front seats and wake up terrified. They destroyed my car in the process. I got to Sydney and got as far away from them as possible! Trip from hell from west to east.*

Brian recalls colliding with a few kangaroos on the way and losing the muffler somewhere on the Nullarbor. 'When we arrived at Dave Faulkner's place in Sydney, the thing sounded like a tank and we got pulled over by the cops, and they put a blue sicker on the car just near his place. Dave didn't know me or Tony at all and he decided we weren't welcome there, but Kim stayed on. We did our thing and Kim did his thing. We stayed in Sydney for a year going to see Sydney punk bands, taking acid and getting drunk and all that shit, there was a lot going on' (Brian Hooper). It would be another few years until Kim would once again call on Tony and Brian.

•••

On the back of Kim's enthusiasm, Boris had already driven over to Sydney, joining James Baker and the other Perth musicians who had trickled over to the Eastern States. Dave Faulkner had arrived in late 1980 and immediately commenced looking to start a band. With Roddy Radalj and Kimble Rendall, he gave birth to Le Hoodoo Gurus on New Year's Eve of 1980. James would join a short time later.

Kim moved into Dave Faulkner's place in Darlinghurst, where Roddy was also in residence. James Baker was not far away, Boris was in Redfern and the Trade Union Club scene was on their doorstep. Tony Thewlis flew in next, taking a massive leap of faith to relocate across the continent to join a band he didn't know, hadn't played a note with, and that didn't really have any plans or prospects. 'Kim and

Boris collected me from the airport in Boris's panel van and drove me to their place in Redfern. For the first few weeks I slept on an air bed in Boris's room and in the days we learnt songs in the lounge room/ kitchen' (Tony Thewlis).

Sydney was a cornucopia of delights after the confines of Perth. In Tony's eyes, 'Sydney was another thing entirely. A proper city!' Boris's saw it as 'one of the music capitals of the world back then, every place you went into there were bands playing'. At the centre of this scene was the Southern Cross and Trade Union Club, where most bands hung out whether they were playing or not. Kim was in his element. 'Inner city Sydney was a tantalisingly wicked place for a bunch of Perth suburban boys who got taken in very quickly and nurtured down an inebriated path from their home in Nickson Street, Surry Hills to the Southern Cross Hotel, to the Sydney Trade Union Club and out into the oblivion of Sydney's pink bat-ridden night.'[3] Everyone was on the dole and poor as salt, so looking for corners to cut was always a priority. Dave and James pointed the newly arrived Scientists to the cheapest food joints in town, Skinny's and No Names, Italian 'restaurants' which were really just family homes serving cut price spaghetti and flagons of cheap wine.

When Linda arrived from Perth, she moved in with Kim and Dave before they all moved to Mount Street Redfern a year or so later. Amidst the rush of big city merriment, Kim and Linda's lives were about to undergo an unexpected but welcomed upheaval. At the end of 1982, Kim and Linda's first son Alex was born, and the young family gallantly negotiated their new circumstances. Being broke, playing rock 'n' roll and caring for a newborn wasn't straightforward. Alex was already sharp, but he wasn't an easy baby. 'He had too much going on to focus on some of the things he had to learn. He was already looking for information to compile.' Both sets of grandparents lived on the other side of the country, Linda had effectively frightened Kim's parents off, and Linda's parents were a difficult proposition. With no family support to help raise baby Alex, and Linda seeming to struggle with the parenting role, Kim was the primary carer. 'I was twenty-four when I first became a dad. And its stretched out. I've been a dad for a long time. It was unusual being a twenty-four-year-old rock and roll dad. I was often the odd one out.'

Kim tried his hand at working some night shifts at a nursing home to get extra money and spent most of his time during the day helping Alex interpret the world that he seemed so intent on absorbing. Linda required some looking after too, and combined with handling the song writing responsibilities, rehearsing and trying to get the Scientists happening, spare time was rare for Kim. While the other Scientists were hanging out together drinking, trawling op shops for clothes, or playing golf with James Baker, Kim had assumed more substantial responsibilities. He loved his new family but felt the pull of the carefree lifestyle of the others. He bemoaned missing out on what he referred to as their 'chummy lifestyle', and this set up a dynamic that would persist in the band where Kim was both central, but a little apart from the others.

Soon, Brett arrived in town, and he and Tony moved in around the corner. Boris was already entrenched in the Darlinghurst and Sydney scene. He seemed to know everyone who set foot in the Southern Cross hotel and had made some connections with other bands. By this stage, Le Hoodoo Gurus were making an impression. Their line-up was an oddity in the Australian landscape — three guitarists and no bass — 'they were like a poppy version of the Cramps'. Tony was keen to soak in as much as he could, and Boris who had been in Sydney the longest, was a willing tour guide.

> *Sydney bands really were completely under the thrall of the departed Radio Birdman and were all so similar to each other in sound and performance that it was difficult to remember which was which. Birdman's shadow covered the place — there were Radio Birdman symbols spray painted on every second wall and audiences seemed to measure every rock and roll band they saw against them. And most would fall short, obviously,*

by being so influenced and smothered by them that negative comparisons were inevitable (Tony Thewlis).

But the Scientists were outsiders to their core. The Birdman phenomenon had meant nothing to them over in Perth and meant even less now. They had a different perspective on the Sydney music scene, they looked at it with eyes unaffected by the *Yeah Hup* hype.

Boris recalls, 'It was a bit Detroit centric for us … We definitely set ourselves apart from all that, and it was good for us to come into that, if we'd moved to Melbourne the evolution wouldn't have been as quick, because we wouldn't have had to say, "nah were not going to be a part of that" … we could have just settled in, as there was more of an art scene in Melbourne. But in Sydney, we definitely had to go, "we are not going to play any form of melody, we're just going to go in there and make noise"'. Kim's reaction to this was typically stubborn — 'I was on a mission. I had the clearest idea of what the band should be. I didn't want to fit into the scene.'

•••

Think of it for a minute. Boris, Tony, Brett and Kim travelled 2000 kilometres across the Australian continent to form a band in a new city and they had never even played together before. It takes unique character to embark on such an adventure. So before going further, let's meet the band properly through the eyes of their leader, Kim Salmon.

It was Tony Thewlis who I spied one night playing some absolutely superb guitar with some absolutely god awful band at Hernando's Hideaway in East Perth. He thought the place I was offering him in the Scientists was the earlier brash 'pop' group he saw on [the] national pop TV show 'Countdown'. He moved to Sydney to join up, but when it dawned on him it was something else entirely, he began extracting all manner of dissonant, jarring, downright rude sounds from his guitar, probably to piss everyone off as much as anything else. He would refuse to play anything vaguely approaching a rock solo. He would be twice as inebriated as the rest of the band — he didn't drink beer so matched our beers glass for glass with cider or wine. He was quite a sight with his Johnny Thunders-style teased hair throwing his guitar at the floor, the ceiling, his amp or even audience members.

Drummer, Brett Rixon, brother of two years running Penthouse Pet of the Year, Cheryl, had on his wrist, a self-inflicted tattoo of a safety pin with two lines representing the bridge of skin the prong passed under. He was described by one Robin Gibson of Sounds magazine as having 'the demeanour of an assembly line misfit blankly contemplating murder'. He did have a dark sense of humour. For example, there is a tape in existence of him in a 'discussion' with Boris on the relative personality merits of two chaps they knew, one of whom had attempted suicide by hanging. Brett's argument against the other chap was that, 'If you were to find him dangling you'd give his leg a tug'. But Brett had an understanding of the brief.

Boris Sujdovic liked to act dumb to be left alone, but was actually a smooth talker when it suited him. Importantly, his laidback disposition made it very easy for him to adapt to the idea of two note bass lines. He was the tallest and meanest looking of us but was actually the one most likely to make a friend at the bar. He was also the member most likely to have a joke at the expense of the others.

I believed these guys were the perfect raw materials to work with (or just leave alone as the case may be). I thought I had it sussed. All they had to do was go on being themselves and let me point them in the right direction, that is, compose the right kind of material.[4]

•••

With all the key personnel in place, the band started rehearsing. Boris had access to a soundproofed rehearsal room in a huge loft in Campbell Street run by future Dubrovnik Peter Simpson. The *Mark 2* Scientists therefore, could make as much noise as they wanted. 'It was a massive warehouse in the middle of Taylor Square over three floors. Bands would rehearse there, fucking great, great times!' (Boris Sujdovic)

From the early rehearsals, it was clear that Kim had moved to an oblique place since the demise of the *Mark 1* Scientists. Gone was the punk pop; the music was now firmly anchored in the 'dirgey, swampy and doom-ish.'[5] They started by hammering out the old Scientist songs — *Teenage Dreamer*, *Shadows of the Night*, and *Dropout* — and some covers to test out the new line up. Immediately it was different — wild, heavy and noisy. Boris saw it coming. 'I knew Kim was evolving, even his playing in Louie Louie — he was evolving, and the sound was different right from the start, different drum beats. I knew it wasn't going to be the same as the *Mark 1* Scientists. But I didn't know what was going to happen!'

Tony took some adjusting. He had been accustomed to playing more breezy pop in the Helicopters, so he was pushed hard in this messy new direction. 'Tony was into the 60s pop thing — the Beatles, Who, Kinks and the Shadows. He was really into the Knack. You couldn't do a sound check without him doing *My Sharona*, or the Swingers *Counting the Beat* or the latest Cheap Trick number! Boris and I would want to jam on *Raw Power*, but he'd barge in with anglophile music and spoil our fun!' Boris recalls Tony's response to the challenge thrown down by Kim's new musical direction: 'when he got thrown into this rehearsal room, I don't think he knew what he was doing, so he thought "I'll just make as much 'fucken noise as I can and that will piss Kim off". And Kim goes, "yeah I love that!"' (Boris Sujdovic) To help things along, Kim gave Tony some clues to the formula: 'Tony was so loud, but it worked! I turned him onto Alex

Chilton, and that kind of enabled him to tune into what we were doing. Alex Chilton gave him a way into the murky world of *Swampland*.'

Boris seemed drawn towards a Spartan bass guitar sound, so he adapted to the new noise easily. 'Kim would just bring in a song and we'd start playing it, Tony would make this hideous din and Brett would play these kinds of rhythms that weren't strictly right, and Kim would do his stuff. I thought there's so much noise going on there's no point me trying to confuse it anymore, so I just evolved playing one note kind of stuff' (Boris Sujdovic).

Brett meanwhile, was a rhythmic anachronism, and really opened up the sound palette for Kim's vision. Not a conventional rock drummer, 'he had a full-on cymbal thing going on. It was jazzy. Well, I heard some jazz in it, and I suggested that we push that thing where the rhythm was on the cymbals a lot more, and big snare explosions. Brett and I were kind of doing rhythmically weird timing stuff, and Tony was doing sonically weird stuff. It was a really a matter of adopting what was happening naturally. Brett and I had worked on stuff together already, and Boris's inclination was to do the buzz saw thing anyway, so he just did that. So that was the combination we had to work with.'

And this combination covered a distinctly different topography to the *Mark 1* Scientists. After only a few rehearsals, they had already gone far beyond even Louie Louie's quick progression. They would soon be gig ready, and again Kim found himself searching for the right tag for the band. 'I remember we were trying to come up with a name, and we'd go through all these names and in the end we just thought "oh fuck it, can't think of another name, let's just be the Scientists again". Which we should have just seen straight away.'

•••

As their music corrupted further from the scene around them, so too did their appearance. Unimpressed by the attire of the other

Sydney bands they developed a distinct look in accomplice with their far-out sound.

> *I was getting ideas about interpretation and perceptions. Let's get some flashy shirts and stand out. So we fell into a kind of style with our clothes. It was kind of what you get from an op shop, what was readily available. So what you got was from the 70s, we adopted a look that was vaguely like yobbos. All the cool 60s op shop stuff had been taken. We did bad 70s stuff. We weren't looking to the 60s style at all, our hair was longer, we were more like the New York Dolls and the Cramps.*

For Kim the look has always been a significant consideration, but in the *Mark 2* Scientists it took on a greater imperative.

> *The look is important, you're presenting something, you can't ignore it. Appearances do say something, and you can use it in any way. You could tell we're in the same band, we all look the same and it was a strong image. Our band didn't look like other bands. We had genuine op shop stuff, rain coats on backwards, big zips. It was an important thing to us to look like we'd crawled out of something. It became something to be looked at and misinterpreted for the life of the band.*

Underpinning this was Kim's belief that it wasn't enough to just be the best band in town, you had to make people notice. Tony elaborates:

> *Kim had a theory that Australian bands like the Loved Ones and the Masters Apprentices were striking because of the time lag between hearing current English music on the radio and getting the English music papers … They'd hear 1967 Kinks doing* Waterloo Sunset, *but they'd see their pictures in the music papers from when they were doing Dead End Street in 1966, or whatever and base their look and sound on that. So Kim was very keen to get that discrepancy and make our sound and look jarringly incongruous* (Tony Thewlis).

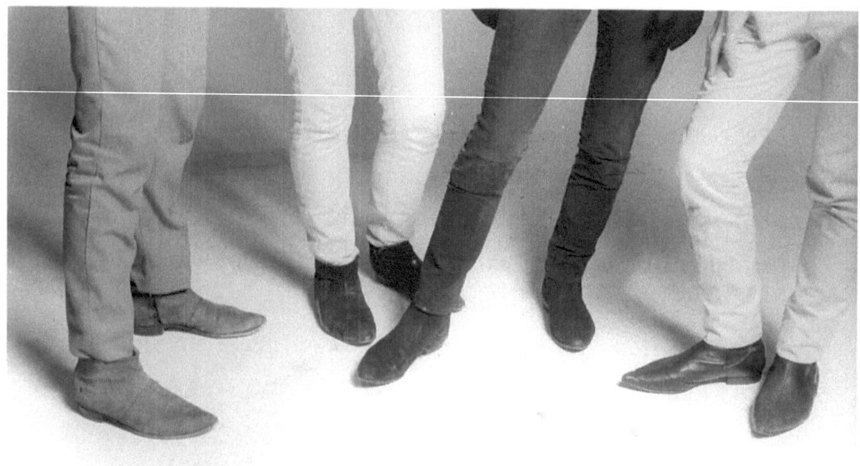

The other Scientists were on board with gusto. 'I got a bit obsessed with looking like Dolls-era Johnny Thunders, and Brett wanted to look like he was on the first Stooges album cover' (Tony Thewlis). Former Scientist and now Le Hoodoo Guru James Baker had a stall at Surrey Hills Market, selling his own off the wall shirts. In a nice slice of provenance Kim, Boris and the new breed of Scientists bought shirts from their former drummer to go with whatever garish things they could scavenge from Darlinghurst op shops. With money hard to come by, Kim's tailoring faced financial and intrapsychic constraints.

> *I was on the dole, Linda got a job, and I didn't feel good spending money on myself. I was in some funny psychological state where I felt I didn't deserve to have things. It was a bit about having the baby but just a hangover of things in general. The other guys were going down to Melbourne to buy pointy shoes and I was gaffer taping up points on my shoes and sewing hems onto my pants to make them longer 'cos I couldn't afford to buy new ones. Half my clothes were hand sewed together — I was a mess! If you look at the cover of the* We Had Love *single, I'm wearing a white business shirt with the collar turned up and I've drawn paisley all over it! But the Scientist version of paisley, 70s paisley not 60s paisley. It was more psychedelic.*

The other visual element that the Scientists would become known for along with flashy shirts and miscreant clothing was their hair. It became totemic and something for audiences to follow and critics to decry. 'I decided we had to grow our hair long. I was always cutting my own hair, so I had to stop that. The hair was definitely a big thing. Like the Ramones, you can tell these guys were in the same band. And we nurtured that idea. It was quite a strong image, people would remark on it too. Their sound is weird. Their look is weird. That was a really important thing for us.'

•••

With only a couple of months in the Taylor Square rehearsal room behind them, the *Mark 2* Scientists sound had now mutated severely from the earlier Perth incarnation. Kim was certain that there was nothing in Sydney that bore any resemblance, and that even at this early stage their music would make an impact. Through connections cultivated by the affable Boris, a gig opened up for the Scientists at the Entertainer's Club. It was New Years Eve of 1981, around three and a half years since the *Mark 1* Scientists had gathered at Victim Manor back in Perth. The set featured a mixture of the more raucous early Scientist songs like *Shadows of the Night* and *Teenage Dreamer*, the devolved songs from Louie Louie like *Swampland* and *Perpetual Motion*, and covers like the Troggs' *Gonna Make You*, and Leonard Cohen's *Suzanne* which had mostly been lifted from Louie Louie's live set. Tony remembers that they 'were very nervous and just trying to play everything right for the first few gigs, but then it got more relaxed as we rehearsed and played together a lot.'

Kim recalls the first gig as an unqualified success:

> *Everybody thought we were fantastic! We were the first rock 'n' roll band they'd seen that didn't sound like Radio Birdman. That was the closest I've ever been to being a hit! Tony had his hair and was chucking a wobbly every night. We really*

> *didn't have the direction we soon developed, we were playing a hotchpotch of stuff but I think we had already decided that whatever sound we had, that was going to be our sound for the night. So it didn't matter, that was it. It was like fuck you sound checks, fuck you good sound, whatever the sound is that night it will be a good sound. We'd already adopted that.*

The band combined rollicking good times and a little mayhem, with dedication in the rehearsal studio. They rehearsed a lot, growing in confidence and attitude, and Kim responded by bringing new songs that chartered the volatile progression of his sound, songs like *You'll Get Yours*, *Tiger Tiger* (written with Linda) and *Fire Escape*. The band initially approached the new tunes as structured songs, but increasingly they deteriorated to what Tony recalls as 'loud, violent and discordant' noise. Having seen the direction Kim was forging, Dave Faulkner donated a bass line that would mutate into the song *When Worlds Collide*. Repetitive and ominous, it provided another catalyst for the band to sink deeper into nothingness. Kim delivered a threatening lyric alternating between cool detachment and in-your-face caterwauling, interspersed with threads of polluted harmonica and jarring bursts of guitar. People were really starting to notice that something unusual was happening. Andy Griffiths is now a bestselling author and close friend of Kim's, but in the early 80s he had his place in Melbourne's dark musical underside with his prototypical grunge band Gothic Farmyard. With the Birthday Party and J.G Thirlwell as reference points, Gothic Farmyard supported the Scientists, and Andy was exposed to their toxic degeneration up close.

> *The Scientists stuck out for me. The more I heard the more I loved them. There was a song called* When Worlds Collide, *I used to listen to this song all the time and absolutely loved it. It had this incredible, slow menacing bass line and Kim growling and screaming over the top of it. It was amazing. So I always recognised there was a kind of purity and singularity, it boils it down to this primal gritty energy. It brings you back to ground zero - this is what it's about, purity* (Andy Griffiths).

Around this time Kim latched onto another couple of vital influences. First was Tav Falco's Panther Burns. Formed in Memphis in 1979, Panther Burns were the epitome of anarchy. Described as 'a Southern Gothic, psychedelic country band influenced by Memphis music styles,'[6] Panther Burns were off the wall; combining wild unstructured music with disorderly performances characterised as 'art damage'. Tav Falco confirmed Kim's prejudice towards the anarchic and his music followed.

The other breakthrough was Alan Vega.

> *A friend of mine from Perth, Nick Combes, played Suicide to me. This was electronic, minimalist, arty. It was the most punk rock thing I'd ever heard. One chord and just one little riff and he made it into a whole universe, it was like a pop art thing, it was just like a motif with no content, but it was so full of content because of the way he'd done it. It was a completely artistic way of coming at primitive rock. Everything had one motif, this was*

> *rock and roll planed down, flattened out and just one horizon. He (Alan Vega) had stripped it back to its raw essence, and done it electronically ... and I thought you can take it back to guitars and distil it even further, another stage of refinement. That was my turning point. The band quite easily knew my mind set and they got it. It was just a matter of waiting for the material to come to give the band some sound.*

Galvanised, Kim reduced some of the old songs to their barest components, and new songs degenerated even further to deep, throbbing noise over unrecognisable rhythms; fuzzed out slabs of guitar racket alongside sporadic commotions of snare and cymbal; howling wild cat vocalisation in place of melodic singing. There was no excess. Everything that wasn't absolutely elemental had been jettisoned, and only the raw products remained — the notion of a conventional song was abolished. It is said that Grunge, still a decade away, was a return to authenticity and simplicity in reaction to the excesses of the late 80s. In the rehearsal room at Taylor Square, Kim Salmon smashed out authenticity and simplicity naturally: not as a response to an overblown culture, but as a pure artistic instinct. He was not looking back in reaction but looking forward in creation. The road ahead was paved in the extreme expression of as little as possible.

> *We played* Rev Head *and there was no actual chord thing going on with the guitars, I told Tony and Brett just to do what they like, ignore the bass line and make it as much like a train wreck as we could. We grabbed the songs like* Burnout, *we took them and reduced them. Got rid of the chord changes and signature pop things.*

On stage, too, the band were transforming. They were establishing a presence, an authority. Seemingly indifferent to the audience, the band would glower under their hair and invoke a cauldron of noise both numbing but energising, both stupid in its simplicity and visionary in its conceptualism. 'People would say "what is that? There's no music in this song!" It was histrionic noise, but they'd want to hear it.' Tony recalls: 'The first time it all gelled perfectly and transcended the sum of all our parts, and we and the audience noticed, was doing *The Twang* at The Vulcan. It all came to fruition — a huge din played by four guys in colourful shirts with a "we know best and we really don't care if you like this or not" attitude.' They sounded wild and shitty, and the concept they were pursuing was really taking place. Boris got it, Kim and Brett had already worked on it, and although Tony didn't really get it his playing was so good it didn't matter. The *Mark 2* Scientists were something else.

•••

The Scientists had made an explosive entrance onto the Sydney live scene. 'We built up a good following in the Sydney Detroiters, the "Paisley Underground" of Sydney. Everyone would sing along to *Swampland* and *We Had Love* — it was going on at medium volume and then we'd kick it in at loud volume and everyone would pogo and leap in the air, it was crazy!'

Sydney was attracting an influx of other interstate musos. The Triffids had followed the Scientists over from Perth, and from Brisbane came Greg 'Tex' Perkins, who re-established his band Tex Deadly and the Dum Dums. Quickly orienting himself within the Trade Union Club scene, it wasn't long before Tex came across the Scientists.

> *The first thing I heard was the* Swampland/Happy Hour *single which I really loved, but it wasn't until I saw them live that I just went 'oh fucken hell' … It was like, there it is! It had every aspect that I hadn't even thought of, I was still formulating what I wanted to do with my music, but it had all the elements that I loved. That combination of the Cramps, the Stooges, Suicide, Creedence Clearwater — they were all my favourite things and they were all there together in one band! Song after song it wasn't just mere enjoyment, it was like being shown the way, the*

> *answer. They looked so fucken cool … an impression of a gang. They didn't look like they could win many fights but there was a unity, a brotherhood, and that was impressive* (Tex Perkins).

•••

In early in 1982, the Scientists scored a residency at the Vulcan Hotel. 'The Vulcan "Sats In May" gigs in Sydney were fairly memorable, although we were often absolutely plastered at the time' (Tony Thewlis). Kim was having a blast, both in the playing and hanging out with his fellow Scientists. They would sneak around late at night in Boris' van and stick up band posters all over Sydney. Boris would leave the engine rumbling in case of trouble, while the others brushed the back of the posters with the flour and glue mix before slapping the soggy posters on the wall or lamp post. Inside the hotel the shows were building force.

> *We were still working on our sound and image but Tony could always be relied upon to 'chuck a wobbly' and Brett and Boris were presenting a very granite-faced deadbeat hair in the eyes demeanour as we thrashed our way through a set that each week had fewer chords and more noise. Although we replaced the mandatory 'Detroit' buzzsaw guitar three chords with atonal guitar-scapes and two note bass lines our shtick was too 'dumb' to be art rock. Thanks to some wild shows it wasn't long before the Vulcan was packed with paisley-shirted and mini-skirted regulars singing along to* Swampland.[7]

There was a vibrant camaraderie around the Vulcan, Southern Cross and Trade Union Club that Kim loved. 'We all used to hang out at the Trade Union Club, that was the hangout for everybody — us, The Johnny's and the Hoodoo Gurus, John Foy and the Red Eye crew.' For Tex Perkins, Scientists gigs were events where important connections were made:

There was a very dedicated fan base, and I think everyone just wanted to keep their eyes on them. They played all round, but there was always mostly the same people that would go to the shows and I was proud to count myself amongst them. And actually, I met a lot of my long term friends and eventual collaborators at Scientist gigs. (Tex Perkins)

With all this intermingling of band types it was inevitable that Tex would meet up with Kim:

My band the Dum Dums supported the Scientist at a place called Stranded in Sydney. I was at the Trade Union club after that and Kim approached me and his question was, 'Are you serious?' which a fair enough question 'cause our band was just this side of the ledger of being a joke band. Musical proficiency and the great power of rock and roll wasn't part of our arsenal at the time, we were more into irreverence, stupidity and jokes. So even though we were an enjoyable act Kim genuinely couldn't figure out if we were taking the piss, which was sort of borderline. He wasn't trying to be rude, I think he saw the potential of what I could actually do and was curious why I was fucking around.

The Scientists were now a headlining band and had to select support acts fit for the occasion. Kim had heard of some band coming down from Brisbane called Tex Deadly and the Dum Dums, and booked them for the support on the strength of their reputation and name alone. Hearing what sounded like broken Johnny Cash vocals spilling out of the sound check, Kim walked up the stairs of the pub to find a ramshackle bunch of guys with a skinny Nick Cave look alike at the front …

… but a kind of bad version, like his hair had too much soap in it. He looked a little more like a hound than Nick Cave. There was something about him. They were almost like a cabaret act,

> *they were funny and I thought that's really cool, but I didn't know what to make of it really. I said to Tex, 'Come on what's your real name?' and he sheepishly replied, 'Greg'. He assures me that the suburb he comes from in Queensland is Aboriginal for* Swampland …

For Tex,

> *I just remember being delighted that the singer of my favourite band was talking to me. Slowly we became solid friends and I would actually travel with them just for the sake of it. Got in the band bus with them a few times just to go.*

There were perks being in a band too, other than meeting likeminded musical comrades. The Scientists were becoming a thirsty band, and the Sydney pubs were happy to oblige. Tony remembers:

> *Ron who ran the Southern Cross really liked us and the Gurus, mainly because our crowds bought the most beer. He'd moan that when he put the Triffids on their audience only wanted glasses of water. We used to get so many free drinks at the Southern Cross that there was one gig where Kim was practically unconscious before we played. I think he tried to stand up to do one song but then staggered and fell off the side of the stage. Luckily people like Dave Faulkner and Brad Shepherd were in the audience so Brett, Boris and I played a bunch of covers with them while Kim lay outside, for the whole gig, literally in the gutter, throwing up vivid green bile* (Tony Thewlis).

The Scientists had built such a loyal following in Sydney that they were emboldened to spread their wings. They travelled to Melbourne a few times in Boris' panel van, three of them in the front and taking it in turns for the fourth to lie on top of the amps in the back. Melbourne was receptive to the Scientists unconventional approach which included not sound checking. 'Dave Graney asked me the other day "So, are you going to do a sound check?", because we didn't sound check in those days. One time we came to Melbourne to play the Seaview Ballroom and we got straight out of the van and just started playing.'[8] The band were encouraged — it was time to take the new sound to the rest of Australia. In a rudimentary marketing exercise Kim produced a demo tape, handing out copies at gigs and sending them off to other markets to spread the word. The tape that we circulated was quite pivotal. Chris Logan, our sound engineer, was a bit of a slide-rule kind of guy, he was into the science of sound. So I thought let's do a cassette and sell it at our gigs'.

The cassette captured the interim period of the Scientists. Linda's song *Tiger Tiger* about vampires, a neo-Buzzcocks style song called *In Time*, *Perpetual Motion* which was going for the new urban sounds Kim was hearing, and one called *Monsters in the Back of My Mind* 'which sounds like a Queens of the Stone Age song.' Kim drew a wavy Scientists emblem for the cassette cover, which they sold at shows in Melbourne and Sydney, and a few copies trickled over to Adelaide and Perth. The cassette staked the Scientists claim as a truly original band. 'We were getting closer to the sound, but we didn't quite have it.' The next surge forward would need someone in their corner. 'Then I did an interview in Melbourne with Bruce Milne on his cassette magazine *Fast Forward*, and that was a pivotal step as well'.

•••

I park in an East Melbourne cul-de-sac of elegant, art deco apartments, make sure the Zoom has a live battery and attempt to locate Bruce Milne's place. The first record label I was ever aware of was Bruce Milne's Au Go Go Records. On weekend trips to Melbourne, a visit to Au Go Go, with its vinyl, CDs, posters and tee shirts crammed into the tiny Somerset Place store, was non-negotiable. Au Go Go was synonymous with Melbourne music of the early 1990s and it seemed like Bruce Milne had his finger of the pulse of all the great bands. Spiderbait, Magic Dirt, GOD, Meanies, Hoss; and international acts

Sonic Youth, Jon Spencer Blues Explosion, and prime exponents of the 'Seattle Sound', Mudhoney — they all had releases on Au Go Go. Bruce Milne is an icon of Melbourne music, in addition to Au Go Go, he was at the forefront of fanzines, community radio, band bookings and even owned one of the town's most venerable music pubs, the Tote.

I snake up the narrow stairs and ring the bell to Bruce's apartment. Bruce answers, and dodging his cat, I walk into a dimly lit room and come face to face with wall after wall of records. It's everything I hoped a Bruce Milne lounge room would be. 'Wow', I say to Bruce 'this is amazing'. Bruce, polite and erudite, efficient but friendly, is making a pot of tea for us. He calls out from the kitchen, explaining that the collection is now only a fraction of its former glory after he invested much of it in the record store and pub.

> *Au Go Go started in '79 because all my friends were playing in bands, and obviously no one was ever going to put out their records. So, I started in early '77 but I was just so young and naïve, because there weren't any independent labels so there wasn't someone I could ask 'how do you start an independent record label?' Luckily, what happened was, Keith Glass was running the Missing Link shop and he was starting Missing Link Records and he said why don't you come and work for Missing Link?* (Bruce Milne).

Bruce started distributing records for Missing Link, setting up Au Go Go as a hobby to help out young bands. Meanwhile his fanzine, *Pulp*, was selling a thousand copies an issue, and he was an active correspondent and sharer of cassette tapes with like-minded music lovers across the globe. Bruce became the Melbourne authority on independent releases and came across the Victims, and then the Scientists EP and *Frantic Romantic* recording. 'I liked the Scientists first single, the EP was a little too poppy. Then I started *Fast Forward* the cassette fanzine and Kim sent me some stuff, including *Swampland*, and I went "Woah! You've changed direction a bit! This is much more interesting"' (Bruce Milne).

Bruce had booked the *Mark 1* Scientists on their fabled Eastern States tour a year or two earlier but was blown away by the transformation of the *Mark 2* Scientists when they strode on stage in Melbourne. 'They looked like a surly mean gang; they *were* a surly mean gang. Kim and Tony used to fight on stage, and I mean swinging guitars at each other and walk off stage and not come back. It was like, the tension was part of the excitement of it' (Bruce Milne).

With *Swampland* ringing in his ears, Bruce reached out to Kim and suggested they catch up. Kim returned to Melbourne and recorded an interview with Bruce for *Fast Forward* cassette fanzine, and just hung out and chatted afterwards. Then Bruce said, 'Look I really want to work with you.' Kim recalls the meeting. 'It was at the Black Cat. There were no other shops on Brunswick Street in those days. So, he wanted to put out *Swampland* and he said he'd been thinking about it and all along there was a sound that he wants and when he heard the Scientists and *Swampland* that was it, that's what he was looking for for his label.'

Kim returned to Sydney with the good news: *Swampland* would be the first official recording for the *Mark 2* Scientists. They had another song for the single called *My Happy Hour*.

> *The writing of that was a funny thing. I was round at Tony and Brett's place with Boris, and Tony said 'I've got this song, it's kind of a Modern Lovers thing, all in a major key,' and I thought 'oh that's not bad'. And then Brett said 'I'm going to the happy hour. Who's coming?' And I thought, 'I can't afford to go, I'll just stay here'. So I took the riff and slowed it down, put it in a minor key and I thought, this is my happy hour! I was just feeling sorry for myself … It was very ironic and gloomy.*

Chris Logan — the slide rule guy — oversaw the recording of what would be the *Mark 2* Scientists first single. It was an easy process, the band went in with an idea, recorded it without any fuss and came out with a single. And it worked! Kim's favourite part is the slide guitar on *Happy Hour*, 'cos I told Tony to play slide guitar and he said "I'm not playing fucken slide guitar, I hate ZZ Top and Lynyrd Skynyrd … I'm not doing that!" So, I had to figure out how to play slide. And that was the beginnings of my actual slide style. It's a very beautiful piece of music.'

In December 1982, the resulting piece of vinyl, *Swampland/This is my Happy Hour* hit the streets. It was just a single, with neither the A or B side emphasised, so when it landed at national broadcaster, Triple J radio, it just sat on the *Happy Hour* side all summer. 'One day Bruce Milne said "Hey, somebody has flipped it over and discovered *Swampland* and now they're playing it non-stop!" Then they thrashed the pants off the song!' *Swampland/Happy Hour* ended up selling over 6000 copies at the time, vast quantities for an underground recording. It sold through at least six pressings, and every time it sold 1000 copies the cover was printed in a different colour. 'The Scientists did really well. We were actually a big selling band in terms of what an underground band could do, we were king-pins of the underground at that point.'

The pace of Kim's work rate — and evolution — continued to escalate. Rather than enjoy the success of *Swampland* and consolidate the song's popularity, he tore off towards the next artistic destination. Bruce Milne was planning out the next recording and listening with wonder at the Scientists output. 'I was just so lucky to be involved with them at that time because they were changing weekly. By the time the single came out Kim was over *Swampland* and *Happy Hour* and wouldn't even play them live! The band was moving forward so quickly, and the sound was really synthesising down to that primitive throb that they developed. It was getting to a point where the songs sounded like one note' (Bruce Milne).

•••

Boris' intuition that the Scientist's outsider status in Sydney sped up their evolution (whereas Melbourne might have given them less to rail against) seemed to be validated, as the Scientists received a warm welcome in the Victorian capital. 'Because of the hole left by the Birthday Party (who had left for the UK in 1980) we could come to Melbourne and be this band that people came to seek out. We were quite different from the Melbourne thing, we weren't trying to be tough cowboys, wearing shoelace ties. And up in Sydney we were filling the void left by the Radio Birdman. We filled both holes, but we weren't either of those bands.'

The Scientists felt an immediate affinity with the Moodists, who were also in Melbourne, and were Bruce Milne's other great love and recording project. The Moodists were the second major musical outing for Dave Graney and Clare Moore, who had left the Sputniks back in Adelaide and moved to Melbourne in late 1980. The band were underpinned by heavy bass guitar thuggery and Clare Moore's cooler-than-cool drumming, over which the seedy velvet nightclub majesty of Dave's vocalisations interplayed with jagged guitar lines. The Moodists released a number of records with Au Go Go, before heading to the UK in October 1983, now with future Dirty Three guitarist Mick Turner in the line-up. Dave Graney and Clare Moore have been consistently creative together for virtually their entire adult lives, and are great friends and collaborators with Kim today. It's been an extraordinary, long standing, intertwined musical comradeship between them for forty years. Dave remembers his first contact with Kim well, and paid close attention to the Scientist's exploits.

> *I ran into Kim at a Scientists gig in Adelaide in 1979. This was the very power pop version of the band … I never heard so many songs about girls from one band ever. The next year, 1980, we were in Melbourne and I saw the Scientists again. I think this was on their way back to Perth. Next time I saw him was in 1981 or '82 when we were both on Au Go Go. The Scientists were different. We could probably look at each other's bands then and see all the gears clunking, all the obvious things we were stealing from the same sources. Alan Vega, especially.*

> *Years later, Kim played with the Moodists at a reunion show in Sydney in 2005. He was hilarious at rehearsal, picking apart our precious songs and telling us what parts we'd stolen what from and how the Scientists had tried the same.*
>
> *He seemed to be a very skilled player even early on. Better than most of the people. Better than anybody I knew. I always found it easy to speak to Kim. He's a very straightforward fellow. I got into his music more and more over the years, always felt a kinship with him, perhaps more than any other musician of my peer group* (Dave Graney).

Kim recalls thinking that the Moodists were really sophisticated, but with the passage of time he realises that they were even more primitive than the Scientists. And much, much louder. 'Everything was louder than everything else in the Moodists! They didn't know how to not play on ten, they were deafening!'

•••

The next move for the Scientists and Au Go Go was to return to Richmond Studios to record again, with Bruce hoping to catch Kim's creative arc at a point in time before he disappeared into the horizon. Kim had plenty of songs emerging, but Au Go Go could only afford to do a mini LP of six songs that would become 'Blood Red River'. 'Blood Red River' was the Scientists substantial mark on the world, the artefact that would find its way across the ocean to spark a young Mark Arm in Seattle. It was already a big deviation from the single recorded only a short time earlier, showing the rapid change the band was capable of. Kim's view of the mini album? 'It's fantastic, it's one of the best albums made by anybody, in any universe, anywhere! No, its good, I love it. You know, it's got some shit lyrics and dodgy playing but I think somehow it's got its own rules and I can hear everything that went into making it'.

For Kim, it was his first collection of songs written entirely in

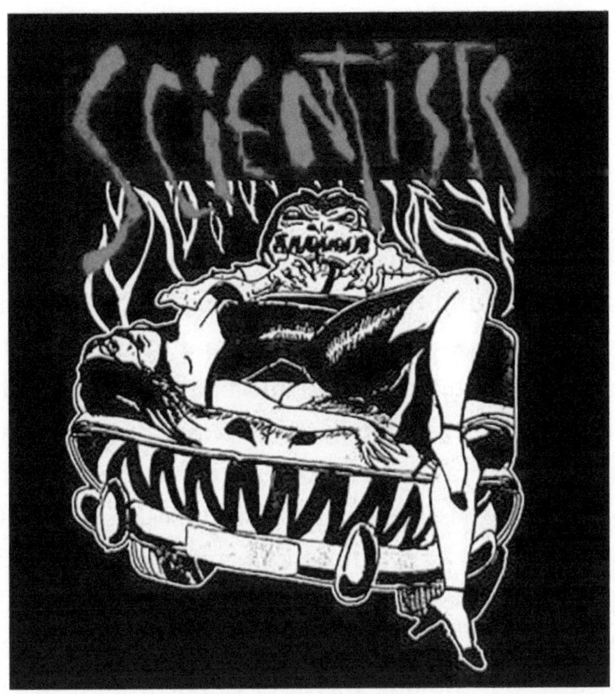

his own voice, and all vestiges of his past lyrical collaborations were gone. 'The recording of 'Blood Red River', what I've described about writing songs was really me deciding what it was meant to be as a work of art, using my vision, my way of looking at things.' Kim's ear for a neat turn of phrase was already in evidence, which laid out darkly comedic vignettes of inner city yobs getting up to mischief. 'Someone described it once as "a filthy sub-world of hate and lust". We were all from the suburbs of Perth, not from Caulfield Grammar.'[9] The intention of the lyrics might have been clear, but Kim's lyrical palette often told the story with amorphous images that could mean *anything* — or nothing. Some songs, like *Burnout*, however, were pretty clear …

Headed for my hour of glory my fate and I have met
There's magic in this bottle, gonna find it yet
Make a heap big heap splash, it's a wild bash
In the heart of this silent night
Oh woe is me, Calamity.

What'll become off, what'll become off, what'll happen to me.
Burn out all night
Sinkin son in the heart of suburban slime
A night of nights snowball in an all-time low
Going Hog wild, it's a low one on this silent night

With the songs ready, the band returned with Chris Logan to Richmond Recorders for some midnight to dawn sessions. It was a challenging experience. The band would get trashed and then go into the studio full of rock 'n' roll brio, being wild and bad and oppositional. There was always an element of friction in the band, and as they were tired and trashed it didn't take much to set it off in the studio. Kim and Tony would quickly dissolve into physical clashes and antagonism, and Boris was always happy to stir up trouble. Amidst the chaos, Chris Logan was the ideal engineer, and was meticulous about how the band was recorded. They had the mini LP in the bank, great songs, well recorded … but the mix was a mess. For Kim, it was a huge let down. His song writing was at its peak, the band was at full potency, and the sound that had been rendered so well in the recording had been badly diluted in the mixing.

> *It was a very underwhelming mix, I was really disappointed by it. And I sat on it for months, listened to it, and thought 'oh the snare needs to be more like the snare on Raw Power, that guitars got too much bottom end in it'. And I just thought about it and thought about it, and when we went back into the studio I had no idea about recording, but when it came to the mixing I was right over his shoulder the whole time!*

If Bruce was initially concerned about the setback, he soon realised Kim was on the right track: 'They went back and did it again and they were right, it was a whole new sound, a *reduction* of sound.' Having gone back to the studio and survived Brett's increasing frustration at being Kim's rhythmic mouthpiece, and in spite of the constant bickering between Boris and Tony, the Scientists found the sound they were after. It was worth it. 'I went back to Sydney and took it to a party and put it on and everyone was dancing and I thought oh this is really good now. So I realised that I'd got it where I wanted it.'

'Blood Red River' is an Australian classic and is widely recognised in the best of Australian albums lists. On the tail of *Swampland*, 'Blood Red River' captured something wild, a sound that 'forms the basis of the claim that the Scientists precursed, and influenced the development of that musical form identified with Seattle bands such as the Melvins, Mudhoney and Nirvana, that came to be categorised as grunge.'[10] Patrick Emery, who knows more than most about this area of music, writes:

> *'Blood Red River' withstands even the closest scrutiny. Rumbling beats, jagged guitars that hurl a spear through your musical senses, with Salmon's peculiar guttural vocal chants describing vivid tales of confusion and angst that could have been procured from an Edgar Allen Poe short story. 'Set It On Fire' — replete with Salmon's hair raising screeching chorus — remains a certifiable classic, while the fatalism of* When Fate Deals Its Mortal Blow *is as harsh as any convict novel.*[11]

On the back of 'Blood Red River', the Scientists were running hot. This review of the Scientists at Tivoli Hotel in August 1983 captures the mood:

> *The Scientists lurk about in the depths of a gloomy swamp pumping out a screeching wall of energetic dirge. The appearance all long haired, grungy old clothes with a lot of worn out paisley and battered beaten boots, very intense and to some extent aloof from the audience. I found it hard to recall any high points from their performance because all of it was a high point. Rev Head was probably my favourite song, this song hitting its peak with guitarist Tony thrashing odd ghastly tortured noise from his guitar, and mangling his hand in the process.*[12]

The Scientists travelled and played widely in 1983, performing well over a hundred shows, and all from outside the conventional structures of the music business. 'Basically, all the agencies told us to fuck off and we did it on our own'. Typically, they avoided suburban beer barns favoured by the likes of the Angels, Icehouse, INXS, and instead targeted inner-city rock 'n' roll pubs. They did however successfully team up with the Hoodoo Gurus, the Sunnyboys and the Church and razed the Sydney scene with these bands.

•••

In late 1983, on the back of triumphant shows, the super well selling *Swampland/Happy Hour* single, and the classic 'Blood Red River' album and video, Au Go Go commissioned another single. Kim was not resting on the laurels of success to date, and he continued to refine the band's vision, pushing the band to find something new to challenge the audience.

> *If ever there was a band that was going from strength to strength ... Every gig got bigger and better and more like what we were aiming for. We were evolving to the point where we just had two notes, weird drumming and a whole lot of guitar and the singing was just like a train wreck. The whole thing was just a twisted wreckage really, sort of like a car crash in motion.*

The recording process was challenging as Kim was chasing an elusive sound, something different but still true to the primitive mantra he had laid out for the Scientists. A reworked older song, *We Had Love,* was the perfect potion. For this recording, English BBC producer Peter Watts was behind the desk; a professional who diligently captured the band's sound. Everyone was pleased with the takes, but Kim was not satisfied. 'I said to Tony "come on let's turn the treble off", so he got this really thick fuzz, it was quite an exercise in pulling teeth to get him to do that 'cause we just played the way it was, but

I really wanted this muddy sound.' Tony was up to the challenge — 'Kim thought of making my guitar really bassy and with as much amp distortion as possible, which immediately worked' (Tony Thewlis). Kim was impressed — 'And then for the solo he must have seen what we were doing 'cos he was magnificent. It does not sound like a guitar at any point in the song. It goes from sounding like a weird synth to a vacuum cleaner!'

If any Kim Salmon song is aligned with Seattle Grunge, it's *We Had Love*. Built on the motif of a simple three note riff, *We Had Love* was operated by the loud/soft dynamics that would be used, with less discretion, by many of the Grunge bands of the early 1990s. 'That's one thing that has a bit to do with grunge, its only got dynamics to work with'. The dynamics were controlled by the archetypal Scientists two guitar sound.

> *Tony is a great guitar player and I saw myself as a songwriter, but in those days I wasn't a lead guitarist, I was just a guitarist. I didn't use effects I went straight in to an amp and Tony had all the fuzz. It was natural to have a two-guitar sound. It was a very three-dimensional sound scape. It didn't occur to us to have the guitars pressed together doing dual harmonies, it wasn't Blue Oyster Cult! I'm really proud of that and Sonic Youth ended up doing that and we were in that mind set at the time, the sonic experimentation of the guitars. And I'd try and hide the harmonic element and make it look like I just picked up a guitar and made some noise, but I thought long and hard about it, and all those really simple riffs took me forever to write.*

The sonic experimentation kept the Scientists sound plummeting towards the minimal. In November 1983, they returned to the studio and put down a further five tracks for another 12 inch EP. Titled 'This Heart Doesn't Run on Love', the new record mapped out where the band was heading. If anything, it's even more minimal than 'Blood

Red River', and there was some very off the wall timing going on. Kim explains, '*Nitro* was in 5/4, *Solid Gold Hell* is in 3/4, 5/4 and 6/8 or something and it just goes from section to section and maybe you don't even notice it. The lyrics were throwing in as much about snakes and swamp and fire as I could, just having something to hang the riffs off. But musically there is quite a bit going on'. In Bruce Milne the Scientists had a sympathetic ear and soul: 'They were moving and refining, making it hard to sell records obviously, I mean give me an album of *Swamplands* or *We Had Love*, but by the time we get to 'This Heart' it's like this is just a ferocious throbbing roar, but it's the reason I set up doing records, I want the thrill of working with this kind of thing' (Bruce Milne).

The new mini-LP was in the can and set to be released the following year. The Scientists were now hot and in demand. Their appeal was stretching beyond the inner-city pubs and out to new markets, and by late 1983, agents were bashing down Kim's door. Playing was still ferocious, and Sydney was still fun, but discontent was starting to surface at the back of the stage. 'We pretty much conquered the scene in the inner city. We were doing gigs on the northern beaches of Sydney, getting to be popular in different places. I know Brett didn't like it, having surfies coming to our gigs and saying "you guys are dead set. You guys are the shit". He really wasn't keen on that.'

In fact that wasn't all that was bugging Brett. He had been increasingly frustrated with his role in the band, which was at once aligned with Kim and critical to the Scientists sound, but did require some personal ego repression. Brett may or may not have been a budding artist with his own creative voice, time didn't give its fullness for that to be revealed, but in 1983 he was starting to feel like his avenues for expression were limited by just playing Kim's beats. 'And he was the one in the band who needed to be kept happy, he was going to be moody and stomp off. So keeping him in the band was key, I thought "oh god if we lose him that would be the end" … he was the lynchpin of the sound. He really did those things that were beyond the guitars.'

Brett was grumbling more and more and making noises about wanting a change of scenery overseas. Around this time, the Scientists got a good review in the British music magazine NME, who were not known for their charitable views of Australian bands. Forces were converging when Boris had dinner with his parents one night who said: "'We're going back to the old country, do you want to come?" and all of a sudden it dawned on me — "fuck, what are we doing here? Why don't we just go overseas?" And I bumped into Kim and said, "why don't we go overseas?" And he said, "yeah alright'" (Boris Sujdovic).

> *So there was a plan. London made the most sense to us, we didn't speak German! It seemed like London was the place to go. Linda was into that idea being English, and Tony was the same. They had hung onto their English-ment, so going back to England was quite significant for both of them.*

Preparations were made for the trip to England. A farewell tour in late 1983 was quickly thrown together to help fund the journey. The band did a series of shows across Australia to great response and general uproar. But one show in particular has gone down in Scientists folklore: The Paramatta Leagues Club.

•••

In October 1983, the Scientists were paired, somewhat oddly, with the Angels for a show at the Paramatta Leagues Club in Sydney. The Club was barely a band venue and was more accustomed to hosting jubilant rugby crowds celebrating a Paramatta victory. But not this night. The thousand strong crowd were not celebratory, they were pissed off. Their team had gone down earlier that day and now here they were, assembled *wholly* to see the Angels, the epitome of Aussie Pub Rock, and instead they were being subjected to four long haired, oddly attired, surly freaks who barely looked up and made noise, not music. The Scientists, it must be emphasised, were on a very different trip to the Angels. The Club was already soaked in beer and crackling with machismo and hostility when the Scientists took to the stage.

'It started when we introduced a Captain Beefheart song to the crowd, which was not really going to win them over when their footy team had just lost. "Who the fuck is this? Scientists? They haven't got a brain between them!"' The packed crowd booed and jeered, swarming and moving to let patrons loaded up with bottles from the bar back and forth through the throng. Scuffles broke out, but the antipathy was well and truly directed towards the stage. It was a scene that stuck with Tony. 'The Parramatta Leagues Club experience was, at the time, pretty terrifying — we really could have died for our "art"'.

As the Scientists moved into another song, a beer bottle, then another, flew from the angry horde at the stage. The first slid harmlessly across the stage, past Brett's drums and into the dark recesses of the Club. But the crowd were inspired by the wayward throw and started hurling their own bottled missiles.

> *More and more bottles were thrown. I was arcing it up, it was a bit of theatre. Dave Faulkner told me off saying 'you did that on purpose. You can't complain, playing Beefheart up there, what did you expect?' Whatever we did it wasn't going to work so I thought we might as well make it worse rather than just fizzle out. I started a riff in 5/4 time, and as we were busy being bottled off stage I said, 'hey guys, let's turn it up a notch, here's this riff!' It was this completely unstructured thing, so to turn it into a song I yelled some unintelligible lyrics and it had all these crazy guitar and drum bits in it.*

This was taking song writing to a new place entirely. 'Some of the songs evolved out of adversity. At Paramatta, he'd just make up a riff, and he'd say "just play this, guys", and infuriate the audience! And then a song would come out of it. The more antagonistic the audiences got the better it was for us' (Boris Sujdovic). That song would later morph into *Nitro* and be the anarchistic, thundering doomsday centrepiece of many Scientists shows thereafter. 'So we did *Nitro* and made it worse! A full bottle of wine nearly hit me in the face, and I thought "that would have hurt!"' Sensing that the mood had turned from dangerous to deadly, the band stuck their fingers up at the crowd, spat back some insults and skulked off stage, leaving a near riot of outraged Angels fans behind them. The band took this near-death experience not as a setback, but as validation. 'It proved my point that the establishment could not help us. That's a key moment for us, proving that we're going to do things on our own terms and that for the Scientists that was going to be the only way.' It showed the ferocious potency of the band, in attitude and form, they were un-paralleled in Australia. They had built up a fearsome live show, recording success, a loyal following and an expanding footprint. The doors to success were open.

> *It seemed to me at the time that suburban pub rock Australia was indeed promising itself to us. But before it could be had we were in London leaving the way open for The Celibate Rifles, Died Pretty, Painters and Dockers, and a plethora of post-punk rock bands to fill a new demand for 'underground' hard rock.*[13]

In March 1984, Boris, Tony and Brett departed for London, with Kim to follow soon after. For the music community left behind, the Scientists left an intense impression, their absence accentuating their unique proposition. There had been nothing like them and there would be nothing like them to follow. Tex Perkins, for one, was sorry to see them go. 'The Scientists were very clear about the way they were doing their thing. I won't say there were rules, but they did act like they were the best band in the country. And that was fair enough, because they were.'

9

Save Me a Place

> *Boris phoned me up and said, 'why don't you do this band? They won't give you any money, but you can drink beer all night and all you do is old Creedence covers. And I said 'okay, count me in on that one!'*

I'm talking to James Baker, former Victims and Scientists drummer, at his hotel in Fitzroy. It's early, and James is in bare feet, black jeans and a raggedy black stripy knitted jumper. He looks just like … James Baker! The night before the *Mark 1* Scientists played at the Corner Hotel in Richmond, with the original line up of Boris, Roddy, Kim and James. The set list was predominantly songs from the 'Pink Album' and self titled EP, and after hearing Kim play mostly *Mark 2* Scientist songs, the show was a revelation. This morning we're sitting in James' hotel room while his partner packs their bags for the trip back to Perth. Before we finish the interview James gives me a postcard from the Berlin Ramones Museum, a copy of his new 7 inch single, and a bottle of vodka. We're talking Beasts of Bourbon.

Where is the gig? At the Strawberry Hills Hotel in Southern Cross, which is walking distance to my house. Oh, this sound easy!

The catalyst for the band that would go on to take the mantle as '*the* best rock and roll band in the world'[1] was the untimely desertion of half of Tex Perkin's band.

I had the band the Dum Dums and we had a residency at the Southern Cross Hotel and two of the members disappeared, literally, we just never saw them again. So I had these gigs and I had a friend called Spencer Jones who was with me a lot of the time and Spencer was a very much 'up for it' sort of guy, especially in those days. It might have even been his suggestion; we'll do those gigs (Tex Perkins).

Spencer P Jones had come to Australia from New Zealand in 1976 and had been a working musician since his feet touched the Melbourne docks. He'd played in a series of bands: The Emotional Retards, Country Killed, Cuban Heels, Beats Working, and North 2 Alaskans. Mick Thomas, one of Australia's most celebrated singer/songwriters, moved into Melbourne from the country and met Spencer when he was playing in cabaret bands in the early 80's:

He was very helpful with me. He seemed so fair and reasonable. I came up from Geelong and never felt part of the scene here in Melbourne which was really high minded at the time. But Spencer never seemed to have any judgement about me personally being a kid on the outside, it was never a problem. Spencer was never one who would talk down to you or anything (Mick Thomas).

Mick quickly found that a charmingly wicked streak coexisted with Spencer's generosity:

He was outrageous. He'd take off his clothes and play. His band the Johnnys and my band the Weddos played a big gig

> *in Queensland and it was a circus, it was pretty wild after the show. I was standing next to him and a girl asked him to sign her hat and I didn't see him do it but he wrote 'fuck off' on it. The next day he said to me, 'I got in a bit of trouble last night'. Turns out it was her Dad's hat and they were really straight and the cops were called and everything. He was always in trouble, he was kind of mischievous, cheeky. He always had funny things to say.*

Spencer's band North to Alaskans ended up in Sydney to play with the Scientists one night, where Spencer hooked up with Kim and Boris for a post gig drink. Tex encountered Spencer in 1983 when he moved to Sydney to join The Johnnys. The Johnny's arose from the ashes of a badly executed audition by Graham Hood to play bass guitar for the Hoodoo Gurus, who had decided to leave their unconventional three guitars and no bass format behind, and were rapidly moving toward safer musical waters. Former Scientist Roddy Radalj, now going by the moniker Roddy Ray'da, took a shine to Hood, and they started the Johnnys with the mission of playing New York Dolls-esque rock 'n' roll under the guise of a country and western band. With Billy Pommer Jr on drums the trio dressed in cowboy hats and string ties and forged what one of Australia's most enduring careers in Cow Punk. Spencer joined on guitar, wrote their first original tune, and before too long had replaced Roddy as singer. Roddy left the band *and* left the Hoodoo Gurus, leaving him with the unique legacy of being a founding, but not long term, member of three of Australia's most distinguished bands.

The Sydney scene at this time was rife with bands springing up out of nowhere, new line ups and combinations forming. And centre of much of this activity was Tex, who had been adopted by the Scientists. 'My close dependable friends at that point were Spencer and Boris. Boris, I still see him like he's a big brother. It was me, Spencer and Boris and the Dum Dums drummer that filled the first gig spot. And then it just evolved' (Tex Perkins).

Kim was focusing hard on the Scientists world domination, but quickly heard about Tex's new outfit.

> *Tex had this band, 'I said oh yeah what's the name? Beasts of Bourbon ...' I just laughed, I thought it was funny, a bad pun. And what happened was, I remember being around Nixon Street and Boris had filled in with this band the Beasts of Bourbon at the Strawberry Hills and Tony and Brett were ribbing him about it. Boris said, 'you play a bunch of Alice Cooper songs, Stooges songs, Creedence songs, all our favourite songs really and get all the beer you can drink ...' So he didn't think it was so stupid!*

In his 2017 book, Tex describes that he originally conceived the Beasts as a 'throwaway band name for a bunch of guys who'd gotten together to play a couple of shows and we'd have it for maybe two or three nights and then move on with the rest of our lives'. The inspiration for the name was not directly related to booze at all, in fact it was taken from an article about the Gun Club — a band that Tex, Spencer, Boris and Kim all loved. Given the close consortia of Sydney's underground music types, it was maybe inevitable that Kim would join, too. A chance encounter with Spencer P Jones, who was double booked for an upcoming Beasts gig and looking for a way out, provided just that opportunity.

> *I was at Roger Grierson's place picking up some money or something and Spencer is there, and he says, 'Hey Kim, this might be a good one for you — I got this gig ...' and pretty much said the same line that Boris had about Alice Cooper songs and beer. So I said, 'okay, I'll do it'.*

Kim dropped round to Tex's place and they played some of the songs Tex was proposing for the band. They wrote a song that would make its way onto the Beasts first recording called *Save Me a Place*. When Dum Dum's drummer Fruitcake dropped out, Richard Ploog, the drummer for the Church, was called in. Although he was a very good drummer, his time in the embryonic Beasts of Bourbon was short lived. Kim explains:

> *We were doing* Bad Moon Rising *and he was putting a Ramones beat on it, it was way off and we had to explain to him the two four country beat that he didn't quite get. Very soon after that James Baker came in, and Richard had to go back to Church.*

For James, it just seemed like a fun couple of nights with minimum fuss. 'And there's a drum kit there!' He signed up enthusiastically. Kim, Tex, Boris and James got into the rehearsal room, and then suddenly Spencer's back and he can do the gig after all! Now, they were a twin guitar band, and, as Tex said, 'Pretty much from that point that was the line-up. And it worked out quite well for a while.'

Kim's first impression was that Spencer and Tex had 'got onto this whole kind of cornball shtick, and it sounded like a cabaret band. I thought "we're a rock 'n' roll band, I'm not doing cabaret". But maybe it was great, maybe I should have gone with it? I pulled a Rixon in other words — I'm not playing that shit!' In any event, the group developed a sound that was more tongue in cheek than cabaret. James was up for anything: '... so we learned a few Creedence songs that we knew, and then Tex introduced a couple of originals' and off they went. The first Beasts show featuring Kim was at the Strawberry Hills Hotel, and it quickly descended into chaos. 'It wasn't the tightest band in the world, it was a bunch of distorted Johnny Cash riffs and a few Alice Cooper covers; Tex with his shirt off and two microphones, screaming his lungs out. There was a lot of string breakage and anarchy, lots of drinking. Kind of like a Scientists gig, really, with Spencer Jones thrown in'. Mick Thomas had moved from Melbourne to Sydney to play music and hang around the Hopetown Hotel, and saw the emergence of the Beasts.

> *They were pretty wild. They made me very aware of my suburban upbringing! I heard them and realized 'fuck these*

> *guys are good'. It was the spectacle of the Beasts — they always seemed taller than other bands you know, they all seemed to grow when they got on stage* (Mick Thomas).

This early line up didn't do that many shows, but played enough to attract some attention. 'Roger Grierson saw us and said, "that's fantastic, you got to go into the studio and work with Tony Cohen"'. So the band had quickly progressed from throwaway fill ins to bone fide recording artists. 'They got a bit more serious and they threw us in the studio to make "Axeman's Jazz"' (James Baker).

Roger Grierson was on a seismic transition from punk rocker to record label owner, promoter and band manager. He was definitely someone to know, 'he had a vision that we'd just go in there and record it live 'cos it wouldn't cost as much, I guess.' The venue was Paradise Studios in Sydney. Build into the side of a rock cliff face, the recording rooms were basically made of stone and sounded great, the cool qualities of which come through on the album. It was October 1983 by Kim's estimation when 'Tony came in and it was one of those sessions. I don't remember it 'cos I was off my face. And it's become legendary.'

> *Recording 'Axeman's Jazz', Spencer arrived having not slept. It was his last night on tour filling in for the Gun Club, so he'd been up all night, accompanied them to the airport and arrived maybe an hour late for our session — I think our session was 12 midday to 6pm ... Spencer was incredibly drunk and high when he arrived ... we were all incredibly drunk by the time the session ended* (Tex Perkins).

The Beasts of Bourbon had only formed in August, played a handful of gigs and were already in the studio a couple of months later. It was either a lucky break or a visionary move, but either way, the band didn't approach the recording session with more than cursory preparation. 'It was hardly thought out in any way, it was just the repertoire we had. *Drop Out* was in because James and I had been mucking around on the old Scientist song, and Tex said "What's that? I love that,"' to which I said, '"Okay then, lets do it". There was *The Day Marty Robbins Died* which was a Tex and Spencer song. We had *Graveyard Train*, *Save me a Place* — just these different songs that we cobbled together. And it all sounds very cohesive.'

In fact, it is a miraculously cohesive (if not entirely coherent) record, full of great playing, free natural ebb and flow and little imperfections that make it just about perfect. 'Listen to the guitar playing on *Lonesome Bones*, the slide playing was Spencer … it was him saying "I want a go at playing the slide". It's hilarious! It's so off key, and it's great because of it, but it was so bad!'

If the Beasts were playing up a little, the man in charge of them — Tony Cohen — was not renowned for his temperance. 'Tony Cohen was hilarious. There'd be lines of coke in the studio and he'd say "oh, that's kiddies drugs". Tony was a very good engineer, one of the best. He worked with Molly Meldrum. He'd done the hard yards and made a name for himself with the Birthday Party and Models. This was the beginning of a nice, strange relationship I had with Tony Cohen'. Tony Cohen would appear in many more studios with Kim, producing Surrealists and Beasts records, along with Paul Kelly, Maurice Frawley, Tex, Sacred Cowboys, TISM and just about every other significant musician from the Australian underground. In August 2017, Tony passed away, aged just 60, having attained near legendary status. Recorded live to tape and not requiring any mixing, maybe Tony didn't have much to do that day in Paradise Studios, but maybe he was the perfect producer to stand back and let the Beasts of Bourbon go for it.

The record, sounding home spun but great, was released in July 1984 on Grierson's Green Records. With no apparent promotion or support, and without even the full band in the country to play it live (given the Scientists were overseas), the album gathered momentum. *Psycho*, a Leon Payne cover, was released as a single and became the highest selling alternative song in Australia for the year, a mark the album achieved not long after. 'Axeman's Jazz', in terms of an independent, underground release, was monolithic. There was a lag between its recording in October 1983 and release in July 1984 — an eternity for creatively restless punks in their early 20's. With the passage of time, they were 'not at all' aware that it was such a big record, 'because by the time it did come out I'd kind of moved on, kind of moving into the more *avant garde*, noisy weird stuff so by the time it came out it was kind of "oh yeah *that* stuff"' (Tex Perkins).

Kim and Boris had left for the UK before the album had even been released. At the time, the album's significance wasn't obvious to the departing Scientists. 'I liked Tex, he was my mate and it seemed like we had a good time recording it, but I thought the album was a kind of lame version of the other things we were doing, and that was it really'. When it was launched in July, Tex and Spencer gathered a make shift line up of to do a few promotional shows. In 1988, the original line up reconvened and did a European tour, when it dawned on them the magnitude of affection for 'Axeman's Jazz'. 'It wasn't until we went to Europe in '88 or something, a few years later, with the original proper line up that we realised how widespread the album was. It was just one of those records that people took a shine to' (Tex Perkins). Despite having very little record company backing, 'Axeman's Jazz' quickly sold over 30,000 records. But for not the first time in rock 'n' roll, the artists were the last in line for the spoils. 'Months after it came out, the record company distributor Big Time went belly up, owing everybody money and we never saw a cent or got any accounting from them' (Tex Perkins). None the less, 'Axeman's Jazz' has stood the test of time and it has earned the affection of the Beasts. 'Now it's probably my favourite Beasts of Bourbon record,' says Tex.

Kim's view is that the Beasts of Bourbon is a band that is hard to define. 'The first album kind of laughs at the idea of what a rock 'n' roll album is, but the *Low Road* kind of revels in the rock 'n' roll clichés. And the other two albums … no one could say *what* they were! The band doesn't really fall into a genre.'

When the songs were all safely locked up in Tony's recording desk, the Beasts of Bourbon picked each other up off the floor, gathered their assorted instruments, and stumbled out of Paradise Studios and onto the street. 'Apparently as we stumbled out of the studio and walked up to the main road, Kim just sort of wandered out into the traffic' (Tex Perkins). Luckily the band's singer was close enough to retrieve the seriously loose guitarist. 'I grabbed him by the collar and pulled him back from being hit by a car' (Tex Perkins). Neither Tex or Kim of course, really remember the event, both being too drunk to report the story first hand, but it was reliably witnessed by a studio staffer. Tex has the last word, 'It must be true. He's still alive …'

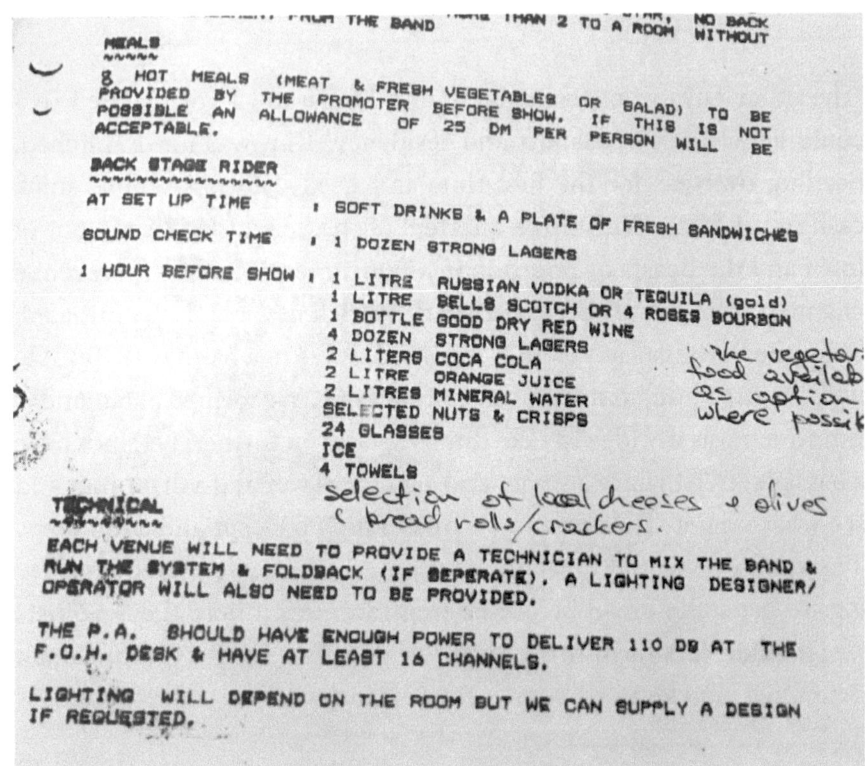

FROM THE BAND … THAN 2 TO A ROOM, NO BACK WITHOUT

MEALS

8 HOT MEALS (MEAT & FRESH VEGETABLES OR SALAD) TO BE PROVIDED BY THE PROMOTER BEFORE SHOW. IF THIS IS NOT POSSIBLE AN ALLOWANCE OF 25 DM PER PERSON WILL BE ACCEPTABLE.

BACK STAGE RIDER

AT SET UP TIME : SOFT DRINKS & A PLATE OF FRESH SANDWICHES

SOUND CHECK TIME : 1 DOZEN STRONG LAGERS

1 HOUR BEFORE SHOW : 1 LITRE RUSSIAN VODKA OR TEQUILA (gold)
1 LITRE BELLS SCOTCH OR 4 ROSES BOURBON
1 BOTTLE GOOD DRY RED WINE
4 DOZEN STRONG LAGERS
2 LITERS COCA COLA
2 LITRE ORANGE JUICE
2 LITRES MINERAL WATER
SELECTED NUTS & CRISPS
24 GLASSES
ICE
4 TOWELS
selection of local cheeses & olives
& bread rolls/crackers.

the vegetar
food availab
as option
where possib

TECHNICAL

EACH VENUE WILL NEED TO PROVIDE A TECHNICIAN TO MIX THE BAND & RUN THE SYSTEM & FOLDBACK (IF SEPERATE). A LIGHTING DESIGNER/OPERATOR WILL ALSO NEED TO BE PROVIDED.

THE P.A. SHOULD HAVE ENOUGH POWER TO DELIVER 110 DB AT THE F.O.H. DESK & HAVE AT LEAST 16 CHANNELS.

LIGHTING WILL DEPEND ON THE ROOM BUT WE CAN SUPPLY A DESIGN IF REQUESTED.

10

A Place Called Bad

'The other guys went to England, and Linda and I got married so I could get a British passport and residency.' Kim was newly hitched, heading overseas for the first time and needed to raise some quick cash for airfares. With three quarters of the Scientists already out of town and the Beasts of Bourbon in adjournment, Kim's main revenue channels were cut off. So in February 1984, a new band was initiated. 'After the Scientists left to go to England, I was in a band with Tex. He was the guy I hung out with most of the time. We formed Salamander Jim which was my idea to take things back even further. Let's not have a bass player, let's have a singer and a guitar player and a drummer and see what we got.' The band was a mix of high concept and commerce. Tex recalls, 'Essentially, Salamander Jim was Kim needing to do a few gigs to get some bread before he went overseas to join the Scientists … He said, "let's form this group, I've got some songs, you me and a drummer" and away we went' (Tex Perkins).

•••

Salamander Jim rustled up enough cash to land air fares for the Salmons, and in March 1984, Kim, Linda and baby Alex headed for London. Boris, Brett and Tony had already settled, crashing at Brett's sister's spare room. Initially things were pretty lean, as Tony recalls:

> *Life in London was fairly tough as we were strapped for cash most of the time, but that was pretty much considered normal and we were used to it and just got on with it. After another month, Brett's sister took it upon herself to find the other three of us a flat. One of the main things I remember about it was we didn't keep up the rental payments on the TV that was there when we moved in, and one night we were just sitting down to watch 'The Young Ones' when there was a knock at the door and men came in and repossessed it. We stared at the space where it had been for half an hour, then pooled all our money and realised we had just enough for a pint each in our local pub.*[1]

As Boris, Tony and Brett relocated to a place in Fulham, Kim, Linda and Alex moved into Brixton with Kim's old friend from Perth, Nick Combes. Nick played an important role in helping orient Kim into London life, and eventually, filling a place in the band. As a British citizen, Linda was able to get the dole which kept the wolf from the door until the band could get its foothold. Alex was about 15 months old by this stage, and Kim dove head first into negotiating the British early childhood health system. The share house was full, but fun. And it was here that Kim met Nick's house mate Leanne Chock.

Hailing from Newcastle on the NSW coast, Leanne was an avid primary school glockenspiel player and was used to hitting things. She was vaguely interested in working in the music business, but wasn't sure what or where. 'I had to get out of Newcastle, and London seemed like as good a place as any — and I was fascinated by the music scene there. I just packed a bag and got the hell out of Newcastle. I didn't know the Scientists at that time, it was just luck that Kim and Linda came and ended up living in a share house I was in. Even at that stage

I was blown away by Kim's talent, I guess. But he was a really nice guy' (Leanne Chock).

London was edgy, and nothing like Australia. There were lots of skin heads around slashing people with razor blades, and racial tension were palpable. It was a tough part of town being the scene of the Brixton riots years earlier, and Kim and Alex got held up at knifepoint. 'Obviously they chose the wrong people because Kim had nothing to give them' (Leanne Chock). The share house would eventually disband with Kim, Linda and Alex heading for Notting Hill Gate at the top of Portobello Road, surrounded by musicians, artists and food.

The Moodists were also in town. Dave and Clare were struggling to step out from the shadow of the Birthday Party that the British press had unfairly cast them in, but the Moodists remained a potent band. The complementary mindset of the two bands brought them together for performances, and consolidated the friendship between Dave, Clare and Kim. 'I knew Kim in London in the 80s as well. They made a much more vivid impact with people than we did. I always enjoyed playing with them. Kim was still the easiest to talk to' (Dave Graney). Kim remembers, 'I used to bump into Graney, we kept to ourselves but Dave would ring me up for a talk just to say hello and tell his stories. We'd bump into them quite a bit. It's great we are still friends. And making music together. A wonderful thing..'

Kim and Linda had built a friendship with Bruce Milne and his partner at Au Go Go, Greta Moone, and once the band were settled Bruce and Greta travelled to London to check on their prospects. Recognising Linda's 'take no prisoners attitude', they suggested she should manage the band and recommended a trip to booking agency All Trade. Linda took to managing the band with gusto, doggedly ringing around to arrange gigs, hassling the four Scientists into rehearsals, and appointing new friend Leanne Chock as tour manager. Leanne had developed a hunger for the rock 'n' roll lifestyle, and had virtually become the fifth Scientist, always hanging out with the band.

Leanne was one of the very few who could tune into the Scientists on the right wavelength. She exuded the right mix of acerbic wit, simmering hostility and gang mentality to fit right in, and she took to road managing with Novocastrian stoicism.

> *I had nothing to do so, I volunteered to be their tour manager. You just bluff your way though, sheer bloody balls. We just split any money that came in five ways, you'd get 10 quid each, and I was happy to do it because I was sitting around doing nothing, destroying myself with destructive practices. And basically, it was getting the equipment, carrying it in, helping with the driving. You'd sit in the back of the ford transit vans, and if you got out without gassing yourself that was a good night* (Leanne Chock).

The Scientists had left Australia on a high, lingering concerns about Brett's disposition towards the band notwithstanding. Kim knew that he had pushed the Scientists into the right shape for the next phase. 'In a way our sound was formed. All that time in Sydney was spent getting there and being belligerent about how it had to be. Our hair was preposterous, our clothes were gorgeous. And it was the same dynamic'. The Scientists were no more conventional in England than they'd been in Australia. They just didn't fit in.

> *By this stage, I was into Chelsea boots, pointy Rolling Stones shoes … anything that was hipster - tight, taken in pants. Brett showed up in really low black jeans, he'd cut the top off them and we all lowered our pants to see who could wear their pants the lowest. And shirts … funky black guy body shirts, shirts with frills, see through shirts, lace shirts, satin shirts, pimp shirts, big collars and lots of colour! Bad shirts, and lots of hair …*

Sections of the UK music press vociferously expressed misgivings about the Scientists. 'We were called the "lowest form of anti-social filth" in the press. After all that punk stuff, to be called that was really a feat! We were lower than any of the other anti-social filth …!" (Boris Sujdovic) This over the top description seemed to fit the model of appraising Australian bands. Radio Birdman had been greeted with muted enthusiasm in the UK, the Saints had been vilified, and the Moodists copped plenty of stick. It wouldn't always be that way for the Scientists. Kim was soon approached by increasingly enthusiastic media, but at the start, it was tough.

Appearances aside, the Scientists quickly made an impact. Back in Sydney, Kim had written a song *Backwards Man* while walking to Tex's place and had been concocting weird drumbeats. '*Backwards Man* is in 5/4 but it follows the singing and the timing jumps from phrase to phrase, and I just made up the singing! This was my most primitive song ever.' *Backwards Man* and another new song *Lead Foot,* were the first songs that Kim instructed the band to start playing in order to make their mark on the UK. Bruce's referral to All Trade paid off, and the Scientists set to work on freaking London out. They got a stack of shows at places like Dingwalls, The Electric Ballroom, The Clarendon Garage and The Lyceum.

> *One of the very earliest shows was supporting Nick Cave and the Bad Seeds at the Lyceum, a big theatre on the Strand. I'd been there a couple of weeks earlier to see The Heartbreakers so I guess I assumed it was normal to be able to basically come from nowhere and easily walk into such prestigious gigs and we started getting a following straight away* (Tony Thewlis).[2]

They gained further ground through Ken West, who knew the Scientists from booking them in Melbourne the year prior. 'We ran into Ken West who gave us some names including Rob Gretton who was the manager of New Order'. Kim took the recommendation and, with Leanne in tow, made the trip to Blackpool to meet Rob. Kim played 'Blood Red River' to him and he flipped: 'he loved it, and said "it's like the Birthday Party, only better! Peter Hook [Joy Division, New Order] would be in to this." He immediately gave us a gig at

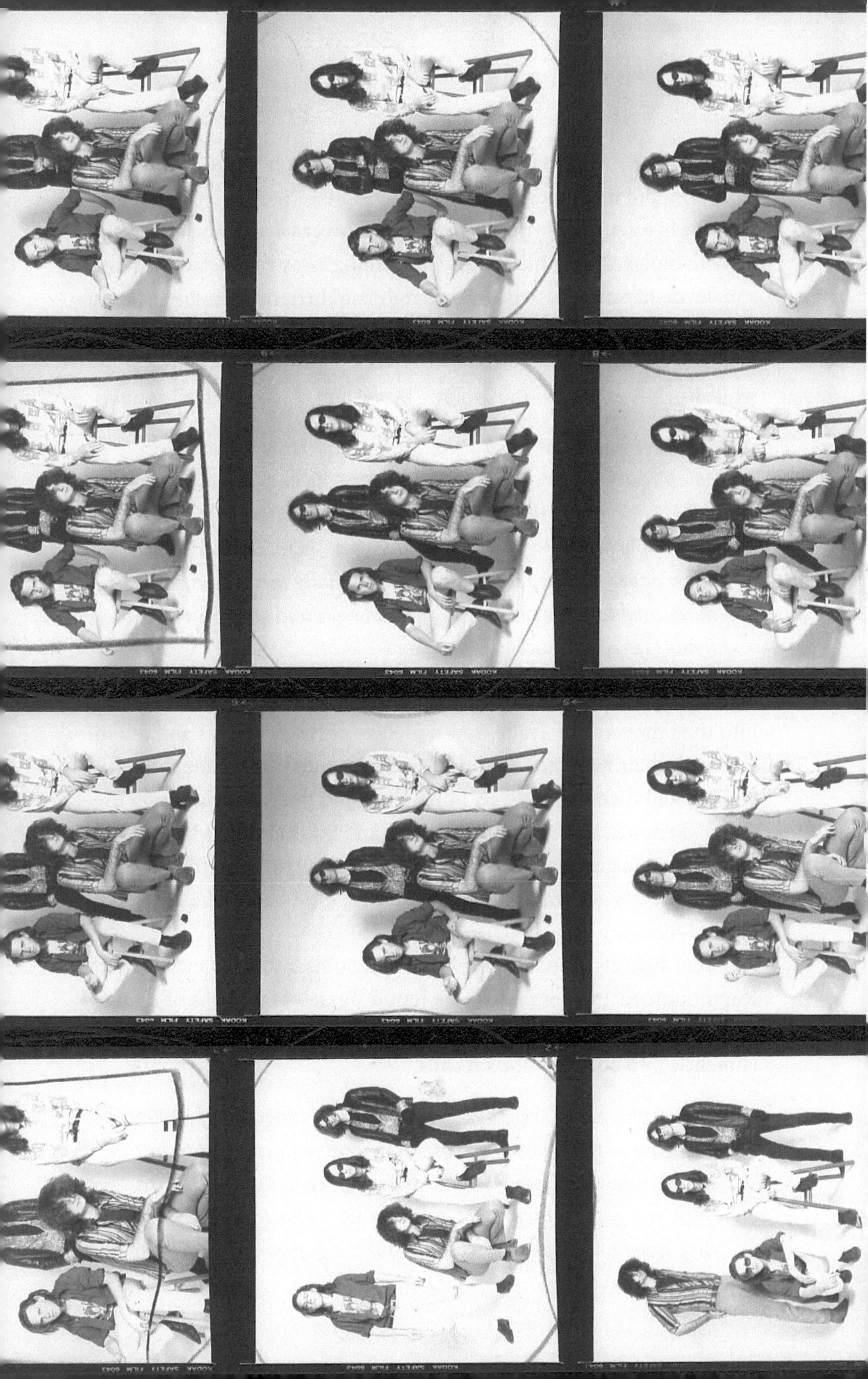

Southampton.' And to make matters better, Rough Trade, All Trade's label arm, put out a local release of 'Blood Red River'.

The live act, meanwhile, was going into overdrive. Tony would end up with blood all over his guitar from flailing away, while Kim was like a malevolent tornado, twisting left, right and bent over double, always with a sneer and contemptuous look at the audience — or his band mates. Brett lurked behind the drums, looking sinister and disdainful, while Boris lurched around looking bored and threatening all at once.

> *On stage it was all quite wild, and at that stage the audience would get wild as well, pogo and crowd surfing. It was pretty wild. They were still doing the punk thing, there were many gigs where people were throwing things at them, throwing beer cans, paper cups, one weird gig they actually threw coins. The band used to jump down into the audience and get involved in fights* (Leanne Chock).

Something was really going on. A band booker from Holland walked into the offices of All Trade, saw a picture of the Scientists and fell in love with their hair. He instantly declared his dedication for the band and booked them for festivals in Belgium and the Netherlands on the spot. 'There was a festival in Rotterdam and I don't know why we even got it — some guy saw a picture of us and thought "who the fuck are these guys, let's get 'em on!" I don't think he even knew who we were!' (Boris Sujdovic)

The festivals were *Futurama* in Belgium and *Pandora's Box* in Rotterdam. 'At Pandora's Box, we found ourselves in front of a huge jam-packed room which moved back a full metre the moment we launched into our set!' Boris recalls:

> *We got there and there was some kind of buzz going on. 3000 packed into the room to see us. They were really packed in but I don't think they knew who or what we were, they just heard 'fuck you gotta go see these guys'. So we walked on stage and they must have thought 'what the fuck is going on here' 'cause*

of the way we looked, and when we started playing they all took a step back! And I don't know how they did 'cause it was really packed in. I remember, physically they recoiled! (Boris Sujdovic)

The Scientists had effortlessly walked into these sought-after gigs, played killer shows and garnered great reviews.

After that we got our picture taken a lot and I ended up having to do loads of interviews for foreign mags that I would never be able to read unless they were in the three sentences of Deutsche that I know. As Boris pointed out to me, this gig set us up for Holland and Belgium over the next couple of years. It wasn't long after these festivals that we made it to Paris and then Hamburg.[3]

For some reason the Dutch were particularly enamoured of the Scientists, and the band returned there over again. They were hanging out to record, but conditions in London with Au Go Go weren't conducive, so a few months later, when they were approached out of the blue to record in Brussels, they jumped at the chance and were soon in the studio.

For about half an hour of that week, the band managed to be in the mood to play something and the tape happened to be running. It was rough as buggery but in my humble opinion there was enough power and feeling committed to tape in that time to make up for the rest of the dicking around. That session became the Demolition Derby *12 inch.*[4]

On another Dutch incussion the Scientists put on a huge show at the Melkweg (Milky Way) in Amsterdam, and then landed in the bar drinking hard. The Melkweg arose from the decay of an abandoned dairy, and a low haze hung over the dance floor and bar, as if in memory of the early morning mists in which the dairy had operated. Outside the air was static, frozen still by the penetrating winter snow and ice, but the post show Melkweg was hot, crowded and bristling with machismo. A couple of lippy Dutch locals circled the four Scientists, looked them up and down and sneered at their clothes, their hair and their accents. They were big oafish cats, their black tee shirts and tailored pants in stark contrast to the flouncy, frilly, satin shirted Scientists. As the Heineken kept flowing, the taunting escalated, and every disparaging Australian trope was wheeled out and spat at the band. Matching insult for insult, Boris fired back until a particularly sharp suggestion about where else the famous Dutch wooden clogs could be shoved raised the pressure to boiling point. Enough was enough. Boris put down his beer, left aside his smart ass comments and stomped directly to the opposing interlocutors, fists raised and ready for action. As Boris squared up the other Scientists fell in beside him, when suddenly — *sploooosh!* — they were knocked backwards by the high pressure stream of a fire hose. And that's when the realisation dawned — their combatants were the venue's bouncers! Before they could pick themselves up off the soaking wooden floor, the Scientists were violently bundled up and flung out into the wintery street, the fire house torrent following them out into the snow and propelling them scrambling across the canal bridge away from the Melkweg. 'I still have a satin shirt with a rip in it from being turfed out of the club. And the lesson was, you don't get in a fight with the bouncers!' Another Scientists show had come to its end.

The Scientists continued to build a solid audience in the UK, France, Belgium, Germany and the Netherlands, careering around the continent in an old black tour van. It was a precarious and not always reliable approach to touring. On one occasion, the van broke down and the band abandoned it somewhere in France. Later on, they somehow managed to cajole the locals (in broken French) to fund their train fares to Brussels, and Leanne gallantly tried to keep the band in line as they stepped off the train and wandered off in four different directions down the train platform.

Touring was done on a shoestring, but between the *per diems*, generous riders and judicious use of hotel breakfast bars, they made ends meet. As they kept touring, music press entities like NME, Sounds or Melody Maker continued to create interest in the band by demonising them with over the top antipathy. Kim lapped it up: 'I was quite happy at that stage of my life to be referred to as the "lowest form of anti-social filth" so long as they meant we were great. We got quite a bit of coverage and most of it was positive in that kind of way'.

Some nights though, the Scientists tumultuous stage show and unplanned hostilities didn't do them any favours. Kim had been courting French indie label New Rose for a deal after Alex Chilton had entered a lucrative arrangement with them. 'I really wanted the Scientists to be on New Rose, that was going to be a cool label. Once we hit London everybody said, "you should go on New Rose, they'd love you". And it was going to happen'. New Rose were coming to a show at the Lyceum in London to check out the Scientists with a view to taking them into their stable. But that night, the band had other ideas.

The New Rose executives took their place at the back of the Lyceum, but as show time ticked over they were still staring at a dimly lit, empty stage. Where was the band? The crowd was bristling, calling out for the show to start until there was a muted cheer as Kim stalked onto the stage, guitar slung on, shoulders hunched. He whirled around and barked something off stage, looking furious and ignoring the calls from the audience. One by one the other Scientists dribbled onto the stage. Tony stopped to remonstrate with Kim before the two of them shoved each other in the chest, reeling to opposing sides of the stage. Boris looked implacable but Brett seethed behind the drums underneath a wall of hair. Kim finally faced the assembled mob and started the set not with a song, but by pointing out and abusing a punter in the front row. The band then lurched into a cacophony of atonal mess that was supposed to be their opening number but turned out to be a platform for recriminations, the airing of personal grievances and the issuing of threats of violence. The longer the performance went on, the drunker and angrier the band became. It was a horror show. 'The Scientists did have a reputation for getting trashed, that's part of what we did. How could we be angry apes if we didn't get trashed, if we didn't reduce our mental faculties somewhat? We had to get primitive.' Before the Scientists had even evacuated the stage, the New Rose contingent had left the building. Their firm message back to the band was 'Its not going to happen. No, no way'. The Scientists would not be joining Alex Chiltern's label after all, the deal was off the table.

> *There are consequences for what you do. They would have been the one, they would have been the label and just 'cause of that one time you know ... The gig before we got this glowing review ... 'oh these guys are everything rock 'n' roll should be, these guys are magnificent'. But this one wasn't to be.*

Undeterred, Kim kept writing new songs and experimenting with lyrics. Keen to differentiate the Scientists from the Birthday Party, Kim steered the new songs away from angst and started injecting more levity. 'My solution to that was writing trashy things. *Murderess in a Purple Dress* was from that batch and I thought that was great, I lucked out on a bunch of good phrases there and I still haven't got a clue what the song was about.' Other songs like *The Last Thing That I Do* and *Shine* were the introduction of more narratives in Kim's stories, the former capturing the mood of Taxi Driver and *Shine* being Kim's ode to the Tarantella Tavern back in Fremantle. In most of these new songs, the drum beats remained central, he would start with a drum pattern made up in his head, and augment this with noise, fuzz and yelping or howling. The writing was aimed at collating a good and ever changing live set rather than designing an album. 'It was about defining the band, this is what we should be. By trying to change it all the time it made it good and kept me honest. It meant at least that every time I wrote a song and the band played it, it wasn't fixed. I didn't want us to be misrepresented, I wanted us to be true, even if it kept on shifting.' By trying to define the band, Kim was in fact out manoeuvring definition.

Looking for a boost, Kim had the idea of getting onto a quality tour as the support act. And his first thought was Brian Tristen, better known as Kid Congo Powers from the Gun Club. The Scientists had played with the Gun Club back in Sydney the year before and the fit was perfect, Kim was keen to recreate some of that magic. Cutting out the suits at the booking or management agency, Kim went straight to the source …

> *I got Kid Congo Powers' address, and Tony and I drafted a letter that would guarantee he'd tell us to get fucked. I said, 'I hear you're coming over, guess what? We're going to support you! Tell the blond one to lay off the drinks 'cause we're going to need those!' And he got back to us — and said yes! So we toured with the Gun Club. And I become good friends with Kid.*

Kid Congo Powers is a seriously credentialed artist, having done time in both the Cramps and The Bad Seeds as well as the Gun Club. To this day, he is still going strong with his band the Pink Monkey Birds. Kim and Kid remain good friends, with Kim joining Kid on stage whenever he tours Australia. After his UK tour with the Scientists in 1984, Kid returned to America and did an interview with *No Mag*, in which he was asked if 'there any bands from out of town that you think people in LA should hear.' He responded:

> *There's a really great band in Sydney, Australia. They're called The Scientists. They affected me deeply. They have an EP out but I've never seen it in a record store here. I have a copy of it. They're really wild like a good sound of hell.*

As well as giving the Scientists this glowing review, Kid also introduced Kim and the band to Sonic Youth, who were touring the UK at the time. Sonic Youth were blown away by the Scientists and helped spread their legend in the US. They would borrow from the Scientists sonic template too, building the momentum of the fledging grunge sound.

While the Scientists were garnering currency in the States, Kim's more immediate concern of conquering England was aided to no end by the Gun Club tour, which raised the band's profile considerably. The tour was in October 1984 and was the zenith of the Scientists' time in Europe. The band were running red hot, mastering the combination of tested material and increasingly off the wall new songs, and building a reputation as a fearsome live act. For the Scientists, the Gun Club tour arrived at the perfect time.

'That seemed to clinch it,' Kim reflected, 'taking care of exposure over the rest of England for us'. For Boris, those days on the Gun Club tour were the Scientists at their apex. The ferocity, the singularity, the down-right unique presence they imposed.

> *We were in a battle, but in a bigger battle now on a world stage. We were getting noticed, fighting big battles. We knew that if we were upsetting people, upsetting the masses and still exciting people at the same time, that we had kind of reached our pinnacle* (Boris Sujdovic).

Kim felt like it was all coming together. The UK was won over, Europe had got the picture and the States were beckoning. They were getting offers from labels and had arrived as a sought-after band. They were pumped and canvassing their options. There was just the matter of Au Go Go back in Melbourne, who had put out their records to date, but they were sure that wouldn't be a snag. 'It was all ready to happen for the Scientists. 1984 was amazing, it was a really landmark year for the Scientists. We thought it was our birthright. And then it all went bad.'

•••

For Bruce Milne, what happened next was painful. 'I'd gone to England and set up a deal with Rough Trade so that we could release Au Go Go records in Australia but press them through Rough Trade in London. That was the plan … I'd set up this thing for the Scientists, it was fairly informal, but we signed an agreement before they moved to London. Then things went to shit'.

Kim agrees:

> *It all turned to shit overnight. We'd signed this deal with Au Go Go and we thought if it was agreeable we would be able to recontract, that it was a handshake deal. It turned out that they weren't going to let go of us. There was a big squabble over ownership and they kind of got into cahoots with Rough Trade and over the next couple of years every record we'd do there'd be another release in tandem from Rough Trade. We'd begun recording, the last thing with Brett, at a place called Berry Street with Peter Watts, the guy from BBC. We were recording 'You Get What You Deserve' and it also came out as* Atom Bomb Baby *minus a couple of tracks. So everything we'd do the sales would be affected, we were still charting in the alternative charts but we just couldn't really get there because of that.*

For Tony, being a little removed from the brunt of Kim and Bruce's negotiations, this was a nightmare that he could see impacting on the band. 'Brett was frustrated that nothing was happening and was threatening to leave, and Au Go Go were constantly telling us they didn't have any money for us to record'. Tony was also convinced that the impasse with Au Go Go was preventing the Scientists from landing with a label that would launch the band into the States.

If the Scientists were frustrated, Bruce was equally mystified: 'We thought we could resolve it. Tearing up the contract is one thing, it was terrible and devastating and I'd put all my heart and soul into the band and was very out of pocket having done that, and you're the guys that I had really wanted to make my mark with, and now you're not talking to me.'

The long term ramifications of the dispute would damage both the band and the label, but in the short term a solution was concocted. 'Eventually our manager, the uniquely un-shady Nick Jones, sold some of his precious record collection in order to fund the recording of what became 'You Get What You Deserve' and keep us going and together. Brett was still unhappy, but willing to stay if we were recording and something seemed to be happening. We told Bruce he could have the rights to release the record in Australia but that we would be releasing it on Nick Jones' new label, Karbon, in the UK' (Tony Thewlis).

The contract situation did seem to contribute to one of the hallmarks of the Scientists — their confounding back catalogue. Much of the Scientists recorded output has been released on multiple records or compilations, and its initially hard to piece together a coherent recorded narrative of the band. Irrespective of any impact the situation with Au Go Go had on the Scientists, their releases seemed naturally inclined towards shorter play releases. 'We're a singles and EPs kind of band. We kept on just doing things in other words, gathering songs to define the band and play live'.

These days both Kim and Bruce are reflective and, having reached a settlement over the matter, bear plenty of regrets, but no grudges.

> *Things went really badly, and I wish we could have found a compromise which meant everything could have moved forward. One of the frustrating things is it stymied Au Go Go,made us look bad and made us broke when we had very little money, and it stymied the band's career at a time when they should have taken over. They should have been one of the big bands, one of the notable bands, they should have had records coming out, carefully planned, so it hurt both of us and no one benefited from it. Just a mess. It was a band I was passionate about and loved and was willing to put my hard-earned money into* (Bruce Milne).

Kim's career to that point had been largely self-managed. For a band with the Scientists' potential and activity, the infrastructure supporting them had always been inadequate. Things were done on the fly, and planning stretched only as far as making the next recording, not mapping a long-term career over multiple albums. A band is ephemeral, and the impulse to sign first and get advice later can be irresistible. Essentially, Bruce was passionate about the Scientists and wanted to put out their music, and the band connected with Bruce and were grateful for his early support. That things went so badly off track is a story as old as rock 'n' roll itself, as both parties rushed headlong into arrangements they never imagined the consequences of.

> *I put it down to inexperience and none of us really knowing. Bruce was a pivotal part in the Scientists history a couple of times, he even booked our Melbourne gigs on the first time to the eastern states. What happened, it's just the whole dark side of the business.*

In spite of these complications, Kim and Bruce are friends again now.

> *In the end, we're both part of the Melbourne music community. We've both done the hard yards. I'm still going to see his music because I love it and he's still going to bump into me 'cause I'm there, so we just slowly worked it out* (Bruce Milne).

•••

The band did make it into the studio to record their next record, 'You Get What You Deserve'. 'We managed to get through it, but all hell had broken loose at that time. And we'd really been kicking goals. From that gig in 1981 to sometime in 1985, it was just a steady arc, it was just brilliant'. But the curve was now heading south.

Nick Jones, who managed the Sisters of Mercy loved the Scientists and took over management duties from Linda, who, by this point, needed a break from haranguing Boris and Tony and worrying about Brett. 'Linda handed management over 'cos she was over the whole thing, but she did a lot of good work and was a pivotal part of the band'. Following Linda's departure, Nick Jones booked the Scientists as support for the Sisters of Mercy UK tour in March 1985. After the rigours of facing off against their record label, recording at Berry Street and trying to humour the increasingly down beat Brett Rixon, the tour was welcome news.

But then 'Brett decided he wanted to leave. It just wasn't happening for him ... it might have been because he wasn't writing songs. He wasn't satisfied. And it was really devastating for the band'. Brett always carried a dark underside, which for the purposes of looking surly and badass on stage was perfect. But this disposition, which aided his filtering of Kim's rhythmic idiosyncrasies, constrained his ability to move towards his own creative output *or* be satisfied with his lot in the Scientists. It was a self-defeating mindset that had come close to sinking the band already. And now, in the heat of battle for world domination, Brett folded. Kim was angry, knowing how hard it would be for someone else to not only come in, but to *get* the Scientists, to understand all the nuances. The band had come through the stoush with Au Go Go and were still on the verge of great opportunity, but Brett couldn't wait for it. Brett Rixon, who had been a pivotal interpreter of the Kim Salmon vision, simply sold his drums and walked away from Boris, Tony, Kim, and the Scientists.

•••

As Brett slunk back to Australia, the Scientists were faced with the pressing task of finding a drummer for their Sisters of Mercy tour. It would not be a straightforward process.

> *It was suggested we get the drummer from Public Image Limited (PIL). He had short hair and wore a suit so he didn't look the part ... after a day rehearsing with the PIL drummer, Boris says, 'I can't play with this wanker!' And I'm like, 'Come on man, we got this tour ...', and Boris is saying 'I can't do it, he's got my spark. He's taken my spark. He can't take my spark!'*

At a loss, Kim turned to manager Nick Jones who suggested his mate Lucas Fox, who had recently played with Motörhead. 'He seemed like a good bloke, he didn't look like one of us, but that didn't matter'.

Having learned the Scientist songs, Lucas proved himself a serviceable drummer, and the Sisters of Mercy tour went ahead without a hitch. However, it was clear to Kim that 'it wasn't quite the Scientists. We could sell it as that, but you were being conned'[5].

Emblematic of this was Fox's overblown drumming approach in contrast to the super minimal Rixon.

> We Had Love *starts with drumsticks being tapped together — click, click, click — at the start of each bar. When Brett did that, nothing of him moved except his two wrists, which moved maybe a centimetre each. No effort was expended at all. Lucas had every drum and cymbal mic'ed up — he had about 20 microphones around him. He'd do the click, click, click on a different microphone for every bar, stretching and contorting himself to reach them* (Boris Sujdovic).[6]

Tony and Boris, gifted shit hangers, found this hilarious and wasted no time taking the micky out of their new drummer, and he didn't last long. In fact, the Scientists unit had invested so much into being a gang, a bunch of outcasts, that it was a hard cell to break into. The fashion sense was paramount, the reference points critical, and the ability to move from brooding angry ape to erudite piss taker was essential. Added to this was their righteous self-belief, and singular commitment to their own sound and feel. It was simply too far removed from the regular world for most people to bridge. Kim was finding that for it to sound like the Scientists, it had to be played *by* Scientists. And Lucas was not a Scientist. Necessity dictated that the empty seat had to be filled, so they trialled some more drummers.

> *1985 was a search for a drummer. It was a massive distraction. We got an American guy Phil on board who did some touring with us. He was a bit bemused by me, Tony and Boris bickering all the time, but for us it was a way to keep ourselves amused. Constant bickering, we got it to an art form, arguing for the*

> *sake of arguing. About anything. Boris and Tony particularly. Boris enjoys a stoush, and Tony gets really wound up — but he's a really funny, witty character as well. So it was quite an amusing sport.*

The trouble was, the new drummers were able to play the songs, but something was missing. Or, more accurately, too much had been added. Kim's vision for the band had been finely honed minimalism. The heavy-handed percussion was a distraction to the fine balance of Boris's fuzzed out, two note throbbing pulse bass and the freaked out maniacal guitars. The drums had to sit *behind* all this. To Kim, they had to support the oddball rhythms rather than drive it with a loud, hard beat, which really was more the role that Boris played. The songs happened, but the spirit was missing. 'We were finding that the spark was gone, it wasn't really happening for us anymore. Again, the drummer was too heavy handed. It wasn't anything to do with him, it's just because he wasn't in on the ground floor of that evolution'.

In effect, the Scientists had evolved to such a unique place that no one else could play their music. For the formula to work, it needed the right mix of surly energy and broken chemistry. It turned out however, that someone close to the band had already cracked the code.

When Brett had quit, Leanne had purchased his drums leaving him unencumbered to return to Australia and Leanne with a new instrument to learn. As tour manager, she had watched Brett from the side of stage over and over again, and she knew the songs well: 'I just sat there night after night and studiously watched Brett play the drums, I was quite mesmerised by it, actually' (Leanne Chock). Leanne noticed some of the intricacies about Brett's playing, his soft touch, his use of cymbals in preference to the hi hats, the nuanced placement of his drum sound in the overall ecosystem. More importantly, she *felt* the atmosphere Brett created, and understood what the Scientists were about. All the while, Brett's drum kit sat in her Fulham apartment, quietly waiting for her. Initially, Leanne sat cautiously behind the kit, viewing the drums with apprehension. She aimed at the snare and took a few tentative hits, the sticks bouncing just a little on impact, creating a satisfying reverberated crack. She splashed the cymbal, watching the brass disc vibrate and shimmer as the sound resonated: a lot of noise for very little effort. She activated the kick drum and then found her soft spot, the floor tom, and using it like a hi hat she carved out a rudimentary beat. Leanne practiced, day after day, recalling Brett's moves and repurposing them as her own. Eventually, she built up sufficient chops to take Kim and Linda into her confidence that she was now not just a tour manager, but a drummer too.

As the band churned through a succession of drummers, it became apparent that Leanne had eyes on the Scientists drum stool. 'All the while Leanne is scowling more and more because she's got Brett's drum kit and thinking "why aren't we calling on her?" Linda would say we were "utter bastards because she'd do anything for you guys"'. Leanne continued to practice, aspiring towards more than just managing the touring schedule.

> *One day at Kim's place he showed me a couple of Scientist songs and beats, and then one day we went into these jam sessions in a rehearsal studio in West Kensington, and we were going to start our own band and call it the Shags or something silly. I can't remember why, but Tony was there one day and we played some Scientists songs and they sounded okay. They must have discussed it and then asked me if I wanted to join. I would have been off my face, and I said 'sure'* (Leanne Chock).

Kim was cautiously elated. Maybe their drumming dramas were over.

> *Leanne, because she taught herself, all she knew was from watching us play. So she was sort of tainted, cloned in a petri dish. It was done scientifically in a way, and lo and behold she does kind of sound interesting. So we gave it a go and played with the band. And she was kind of crap. But it sounded like the Scientists again!*

With Leanne performing a resurrection of the Scientists sound, Phil was told it wasn't working and was asked to leave. He took it hard, and didn't understand the reasoning, but the band needed it to happen. 'We could have … adapted, changed. But we were a bit inflexible. This band doesn't rely on musicianship at all, it's about nuance and alchemy. And the chemistry was so powerful, our chemical thing felt so scientific, you can't turn your back on that kind of thing'.

•••

Leanne officially took up drum duties just in time to embark on a massive tour with Souixsie and the Banshees. They'd hardly had any time to rehearse before the first show, which was an enormous affair at the Glasgow Barrowlands. It was a disaster: 'We had the unenviable task of distracting the disgruntled Banshees fans who had come to see the Banshees not some antipodean yobbos with a bad drummer.' These were the kind of conditions the Scientists thrived on. They got angrier and meaner, louder and more dissonant. 'Having to distract them from our new drummer, we kind of amped up our punk shenanigans and carried on and the fans threatened us. Luckily, there was a crash barrier between the band and the increasingly angry mob. They were even trying to bribe the bouncers to let them on stage to bash us up! I yelled at the crowd, "Lucky for you lot there's this barrier"'.

Tony was loud, but scared:

> *Siouxsie was livid as well, but out of jealousy because her fans always loved her and she couldn't get such a hateful reaction out of them no matter what obnoxious thing she did. We made her fans want to kill us without even trying. I tried to go out into the audience to watch the Banshees after we'd played and the bouncers refused to let me leave the backstage area. They honestly said they couldn't let me go out there into the still baying mob as they'd be held responsible for my death* (Tony Thewlis).

They recovered from the first show and ploughed on. One of the highlights was the chance, on a day off from the tour, to support Alex Chilton play at the Mean Fiddler. They drove from somewhere in the Scottish wildlands back to London, supported Alex Chilton and then drove back up to the next Banshees gig. Soon after a support slot for Alan Vega at the Clarendon materialised, and Kim was well on his way to supporting all his musical heroes.

Leanne joining had salvaged the true Scientists.

> *We were ramshackle, deconstructed as all fuck and that's saying something for us. It was a baptism of fire, but however bad it might have been, it was actually the Scientists again. And the tour got better and Leanne got better. She had a rudimentary way of playing but it was the way Brett played, the lightness of touch he had, it glided into the sound rather than thumped behind it. But the thing she had that Brett didn't have was a metronomic quality; she could play in time. Brett went in and out of time but Leanne was solid in her beat.*[7]

Leanne had another thing going for her … exactly the right look and attitude to fit the Scientists.

> *Being a good musician has nothing to do with good music, it all has to do with chemistry. Leanne wasn't a musician but taught herself how to play. … She's dark and angry, silent and foreboding, but she has a heart of gold once you get to know her.*[8]

•••

The Scientists had been tested by the UK, but they prevailed in a blaze of hair, touring, drinking and menace. They were mean, hateful and triumphant, and international acclaim followed. However, the Scientists were always close to combustion, and London eroded and finally ended the band 'there was a protracted period in 1986 where the band kind of disintegrated'. Brett had left, Tony and Boris were tired out, the rigors of living poor in London and constant touring had taken it out of them. Even for Kim, the Scientists had become difficult. 'I think by that stage we were on our descent. Having Leanne gave us more mileage out of the band, but when it came time to create, we didn't really have the spark to take it anywhere'. In an effort to release some recordings that weren't attached to Au Go Go, the band went into the studio in 1986 and recorded 'Weird Love', which was essentially a compilation album.

> *Nick Jones had just got us a deal with Big Time records, for over half a million dollars all up over a period of time. But first thing on the agenda was to record our back catalogue, because that's what they were really interested in of course, our back catalogue. That's what 'Weird Love' was, it was a rerecording of everything to date that mattered.*

'Weird Love' was a miracle. It captured the best songs the band had done, and no matter what the state of things internally, it documented excellent and in some cases enhanced versions of the material. The producer had made hits, with the Fall, the Birthday Party, Wall of Voodoo and many others, and knew how to present the band's songs at their best.

'Weird Love' was recorded at a time when things for the Scientists were about to fall apart, but the band was a tough enough machine to make work even though the chemistry was dwindling. 'Weird Love' stands as a document of the best of the Scientists. But the recording experience was marred by an escalation of bickering between Boris and Tony, and more terminally for the band, significant conflict between Linda and Boris about his attitude towards resolving his British work visa issues. Boris had effectively been directed to return to Australia, but rather than challenge the ruling he was avoiding it, and Linda was livid.

> *Boris is a very affable, lovely guy, but he loves to bait people. He is a bit playful, he can't help himself. He's a very smart guy, he plays dumb but he's very smart. Linda was being critical, tearing strips off Boris for not sorting out his visa. I was conveying Linda's message to Boris and eventually he just said 'I've had enough', and off he went.*

Boris couldn't avoid the visa issue any longer, and it was to him, in the end, a relief to leave London and the Scientists behind. 'Weird Love' was still being assembled, but Boris had already laid his bass tracks before he departed. With a tour in the planning to support the album, a friend of the band, Joe Pesido, was drafted in to play bass on the road.

> *He did a creditable job, but the Scientists thing was from an outsiders point of view … it sounds very simple, but there's a whole world of nuance. He kind of got it but there were things like Leadfoot which he kind of never got this head around. To an outsider it probably sounded good but inside it never really felt right. And if it doesn't feel right it's hard to put it across. We did a bit of a tour around UK, Europe, that kind of went for a bit then fizzled out. It was good, but more the internal thing, the chemistry wasn't going to be sustainable.*

The revolving door of Scientists members claimed another casualty as Joe was exited from the band when they got back to London. They were tired, depleted in numbers, but Kim Salmon had yet another radical tangent for the Scientists. Enter the 'Human Jukebox'.

•••

They were now down to three — Kim, Tony and Leanne — and had established that replacing Brett had been a miracle that would not be repeated twice by finding a replacement for Boris. So the Scientists made their final stand in the UK as a three piece, with Kim taking up the bass.

> *I was playing a bass guitar made of balsa wood and an amp, which I had overdriven to the shit house, from a hock shop in Notting Hill. I didn't really want to be a power trio, I wanted to have something else there. So I was experimenting with dissonance and distortion and some of the things I still do came from that period. I started experimenting with little cassette players and drones and I had a tape player on a stool with a microphone like it was its own performer. I could hear things kind of working. We were in new territory.*

Leanne had learned the Scientists sound, style and rhythm from the ground up which made her authentic. But, not for the first time, Kim had taken the band careering down a new creative path. The songs he was writing now were verging from the minimal into the surreal. It felt a little as though Leanne was perfectly calibrated for the *Mark 2* Scientists, but the sound was in effect moving towards a third phase, and Leanne was having trouble keeping up. Kim coached and coaxed and challenged Leanne to free her playing, to open up to the new and spontaneous Scientific combustions. And she tried, listening to the new songs and practicing, practicing, practicing. But Leanne had been cast immovably in the sound and style of Brett Rixon's *Mark 2* Scientists, and the feel just wasn't there for the new songs.

> *Leanne never had any idea she'd be in a band or play music, she just got it in her head that she could play drums for us. And it's to her credit she was that diligent and single minded that she taught herself and went on the road, toured with the band and did all that stuff. She put herself through what must have been incredibly nerve wracking stuff, it shows incredible strength of*

character. She bought continuity and dedication and tenacity, but she wasn't really a musician.

Leanne didn't really have confidence in her improvisational skills, and you need someone to interact with to really make creating new material work. I realised that Leanne was going to have to step aside for it to happen. She had learned from the old Scientist sound, and that's what she could do at the time. There wouldn't have been another record if we'd continued that way. It was awful - I just said we need this to happen and you're great at what you do but you can't do this new stuff. It was a really hard thing to do.

Leanne, whose personal life was pretty torn and frayed by this time, was a little relieved to have some of the pressure off and departed with no umbrage.

Once Boris left, it was clear things were starting to fall apart. I didn't leave the UK, I didn't come back to Australia til 1996. It wasn't weird for me. I didn't keep in regular contact with them once I left the band. I was more self-absorbed in London at that time. I stopped playing music. It wasn't really until I got a job as a teacher in the UK and became really good friends with the music teacher there and she got me to join a wind band with her, the Portobello Symphony Orchestra, so I joined that and played timpani which was pretty funny. I was the percussionist in operas and stuff. It was fun (Leanne Chock).

The replacement for Leanne presented itself in the form of Kim's old friend Nick Combes. Nick had been part of the punk scene back in Perth, even playing in a band with one time Scientist Ian Sharples, and retained pretty rigid views on what was acceptable. As he spent more time in the Scientists inner circle, he increasingly became a sounding board for Kim, a firm opinion at which to throw ideas. 'He'd say "oh that's dreadful, that's shit" … he'd be honest about stuff and I gravitated towards him'. Now two members short of the original Scientists, Kim put it to Tony that Nick join the band, and even though the pair were geometrically opposed in nature, style and taste, Tony agreed. And it worked. They undertook what would be the final Scientists European tour for more than twenty years as a three piece, and landed some punches. 'We did a few shows at a club in Hamburg which I remember very fondly. We called ourselves (only jokingly and to ourselves) The Hamburg Power Trio and they were the best gigs that we did as that line-up' (Tony Thewlis).

•••

In the end it took Royal Decree for Kim to leave the UK, with an emissary of the Princess of Wales paying Kim handsomely to leave his flat, which was apparently required by the Windsors. 'We lived in a placed called Chepstow Villas, a block of flats in Notting Hill Gate, in the street where Prince Harry and William went to crèche'. The rental laws at that time in London stipulated that six months demonstrated rental afforded additional residential security rights. Kim had duly documented over six months of rent payments when there was a knock on the door.

> *I was on the phone to my manager and somebody came to the door. Linda was talking to them for ages, and I got off the phone and they said 'Mr Salmon, we represent people who have just bought the property you live in and we've been going around making offers to people about relocating and providing the expenses. Your wife has said she wouldn't think of moving for less than 30,000 pounds'. I thought Linda was mad but good on her for having the hutzpa to put it on them. So they gave us 30,0000 pounds to leave!*

With the pay out in her pocket, Linda took Alex back to Australia to find a house to buy. Kim remained in London for a few weeks, walking the streets and hatching plans. One of these idea generating strolls resulting in Kim coaxing Nick and Tony to a low rent, eight track recording studio underneath the railway arches called Reel to Reel under the pretence of doing some demos.

> *My agenda was always to record an album. We started jamming, and Tony said he had this dream and there was a song in it, and it was going 'I am a human jukebox'. And I had this distorted Eddie Cochran riff, I discovered the nuance that hadn't been done before. So I started playing it and Nick said 'that's great' and jumped on it. And we started recording it. I had the whining tape dictaphone going and we just jammed it, and Tony did the most crazy, fuzzed up dissonant things you can. So that was that.*

Kim added some wild dog, super distorted vocals bringing the character of the human jukebox to life. Nick chipped in with a crazy piano pattern over Tony's guitar, creating a weird melange of lo-fi, garagey sounds. Next was a version of *Shine*, Kim's ode to the Tarantella Tavern back in Fremantle which the trio had been playing around town. With haphazard, echoey drums puncturing Tony's broken, wayward guitar the Tavern is brought graphically to life. You can smell the cigarette smoke and stale beer in every second of the recorded document. Kim had also constructed some dissonant, industrial numbers: *Distortion*, *A Place Called Bad* and one called *Hungry Eyes*. 'A lot of it was really just jammed, an atonal jazz post punk work out. I'd just discovered you could put two-time signatures together so on *A Place Called Bad* and *Hungry Eyes* Nick is playing in one time signature and I'm playing bass in another. Put them together and it come out almost sounding Latino. So the poly-rhythms were going down. It was quite a joyous process, really.'

But then it was time for Kim to follow Brett and Boris back to Australia. He left Tony and Nick finishing off the *Human Jukebox* film clip, and Leanne wondering what to do with her drum kit in Fulham.

•••

The time in London had stretched from early 1984 to mid-1987. It had been hard and delivered brutal disappointments along with tremendous success. It had resulted in a churn of band membership and, in the end, an almost entirely new version of the band. It had seen Kim once again completely revise the sound of his music, responding in part to the new personnel and circumstances at his disposal, but a function of his restless need to push forward creatively. For all the growth and movement in the UK however, none of them could escape the feeling that they'd somehow missed an opportunity, that they'd dodged a bullet of success and fallen into the path of something more peculiar. Losing Brett had wounded the band, and the Au Go Go battle and subsequent constraints and confusion over their recordings had compromised their commercial advancement. It was hard to know if this was the fault of London, or just the hand fate dealt them.

> *Our biggest mistake was actually going to England. We should have gone to America. We didn't realise it, it was kind of that Rodriguez thing, we didn't realise there was this massive ground*

> *swell of stuff happening in America for us. We would have been much better off going to Seattle, maybe not artistically, but commercially we would have been better off* (Boris Sujdovic).

England had not delivered the band the riches it deserved. But when things worked on stage, it was undeniable that the Scientists had grown as a live performing unit in the UK.

> *All through England was a battle, constantly fighting with audiences and confronting them. The more antagonistic the audiences got the better it was for us. It was a battle, but that fed us. Most bands feed off cheers, we seemed to feed off jeers. Adversity — that was good for us. And Kim is an antagonist, he just has a contrary spirit, he's not a confrontational person but artistically he is* (Boris Sujdovic).

11

If it's the Last Thing I do

Back in Perth, Linda had bought a house with the proceeds from Notting Hill Gate, and Kim eased uncomfortably into suburban life.

In Sydney, Boris resumed duties as King of Strawberry Hills. Tony remained in England, but in late 1987, he dropped into Sydney on holiday and caught up with his old bass playing band mate.

> *I was playing snooker with Boris at the Trade Union when Denis (who ran the place) wandered through and saw us. He did a double-take and spluttered, 'What are the pair of you doing here? Where are Kim and Brett? You've got to get them over and do some shows!'* (Tony Thewlis)

Kim describes Denis Stoneman as 'the living personification of Lance Boyle, the Barry Humphries character — he was scary! He knew we were in the country and said, "let's do a couple of nights at the Sydney Trades Union club and a couple in Perth"'. Denis scheduled the Scientists nights at lightning speed, moving other shows around and generally terrorising people to make it happen.

> *He treated us like returning Kings, giving us the whole second floor of the Trade Union as our dressing room, complete with access behind the bar … It was the first time Kim, Boris, Brett and I had played together for several years, but the old power of us all hitting F sharp and E together magically appeared again* (Tony Thewlis).

Kim and Brett converged on the Trade Union Club, ready to play. It was Kim's first contact with his ex-drummer since Brett walked out on the Scientists.

> *I met the new Brett Rixon who had started reading books and had suddenly turned into Max Cady from Cape Fear. He was like a prison guy reading up on Nietzsche. He'd become an intellectual. It was quite bizarre because he was a smart-alec yobbo before. He'd always been frustrated I guess feeling like he had to help me realise my vision and I think he was frustrated he hadn't been able to express himself, so I think books were his road to self-improvement. So over the years I got to know him again. He was a different Brett but a great friend.*

The Trade Union Club shows were a huge success. 'Apparently we had the record for booze drunk backstage at the club, an enviable but dubious reputation. We hated the idea of playing to an audience that was more inebriated than us'. The shows were a lot of fun, the classic line up was back together and, free of the complications in the UK, they blasted and contorted their way through the set. Denis was ecstatic and suggested the band do a national tour, which he promptly set about organising. But 'little did he know that that it wasn't going to be the classic line up'. In fact, for this tour they would be promoting 'Human Jukebox' which was the artefact of a substantially different band. Nick Combes came out from the UK to resume drum duties, and while he was serviceable, he was not the sophisticated drummer that Brett Rixon was. 'He had a couple of beats and he could improvise, but basically you had to get his attention to stop him trampling the song into the ground after ten minutes'. Meanwhile Brett, who was

Kim's drumming muse, came back on board but inexplicably was assigned duties alternating between guitar and bass. Brett's history playing guitar hardly credentialed him to match it with Tony Thewliss or replace Boris. His limitations added an erratic element to the Scientists show and defused the cohesion of their pummelling sound. Kim was combining bass or guitar with commandeering his whining cassette tape sound, while Tony belligerently stuck to his turn it up to ten guitar assault.

This version of the Scientists was, according to Kim, 'doomed'. 'It was a head scratching line up for many people. We started in Sydney and people were walking out furiously'. The Scientists had often fuelled their shows with a strong dose of on-stage animosity, but there were moments on this last tour where the dynamics *really* sizzled and some of the historical frustrations bubbled to the surface. Staring into the bewildered crowd Kim launched into another song but was swamped by a swirling blast of Tony Thewlis guitar dissonance. 'Tony just did his thing of being uncompromising, he had his guitar up full and I couldn't hear a fucking thing, all I could hear was him'. Kim's blood boiled, as if things weren't already hard enough. 'I couldn't play in time, I couldn't get *anything*. I got so angry I remember grabbing him by the ruffles of his frilly shirt and shaking him'.

Accentuating the odd line up and ungodly noise was the song choice. There was no *Swampland*, no *We Had Lo*ve, it was mostly 'Human Jukebox' numbers which were challenging even for rusted on Scientists fans. The material was new and unfamiliar, and the band played up to the hostility their hideous din activated. 'I have got reports of being so drunk I'm wandering around the stage on all fours with a bucket on my mouth going arrrrhgggh …'

The shambolic tour lurched north to the Gold Coast. By this stage the crowd response was so negative that the band conceded it should probably give *Swampland* a go, which they hadn't played in years. 'It was a millstone around our neck and we tried to let it go. So we played it, we made the concession but it was too late. People already decided they were going to hate us'.

The band made it back to Melbourne and Sydney and by this stage the act was showing signs that it might come together. The audience were pre-warned, and those that wanted to see the angry apes turned up and got a great show in line with their expectations. The audiences were smaller but discerning. 'It seemed like we were redefining our audience for that tour. People appreciated it, they could see what was going on, it was the extremity of it was what people were understanding'.

Kim's impulse was to keep redefining the band, to move beyond external ideas and precepts. *Swampland* and *We Had Love* would always be great songs for Kim, but he refused to let them define or limit what the Scientists were about. And on this tour he pushed that notion hard, landing it at the Shenton Park Hotel in Perth, November 1987; the Scientists last gig. It was not a glorious send off. 'It was a shambles of a thing. Although *I* thought it was good because it lived up to our ideals of deconstruction and driving everybody to the door.' After the gig, Tony and Nick returned to London, and really, that was it for the Scientists.

•••

I ask Kim about this decision to deviate from the warm reception at the first post UK show with the classic line up, to embarking on a challenging, nerve wrecking, confounding third generation Jukebox tour.

> *It was never a choice for me, it really never occurred to me. I was so driven by coming up with new ideas and exploring new things, it was never an option. It never occurred to me to keep doing the same thing. I don't think I was shooting myself in the foot at all. I wasn't courting failure. I just had a particular path.*

The Scientists would be put on the back burner for more than 15 years, and Kim would keep going on his peculiar path, taking him to

many new outfits, sounds and experiences. But the Scientists, even as they went their different ways, was always special for Kim Salmon. In summing up the band, Kim penned this manifesto, which is where we leave the Scientists for now.

> *We loved rock 'n' roll's tradition but despised traditionalism, hated artiness but naïvely believed what we were doing was art (when it worked). We believed we were on a mission to take rock back to its most basic primal essence. Only then could we add our own flavours which would be spontaneously concocted out of companion fuzz boxes, beer, various chemicals, anarchy and whatever else was handy at the time. At times it would be beautifully simple, at others quite tricky getting it right. Real rock 'n' roll was dumb, and sophisticated, serious and funny. A paradox. You couldn't hide behind a joke. You had to be prepared to go out and be a joke. The path of riotousness was the path of righteousness and only we were on it. We didn't just believe, we knew that we would be misunderstood first, worshipped and adored later. We did not want to change the*

world. It could sod itself. We wanted only to be left alone … and admired from a distance. And we believed, with absolute conviction and no irony, that we were the greatest rock and roll band in the world.[1]

12

The Surreal Feel

The London air was chilly and the sun was tepid, filtering through the small trees along the sidewalk and casting the Notting Hill terraces in soft, thin light. It was 1987, in the last weeks of the Scientist's life in London. Kim Salmon walked along the quiet streets, past the bookstores and the Coffee Cup's red awning. With his hands shoved into his coat pockets, bracing himself against the cold, Kim meandered past the market stalls, only half looking at the mess of goods on sale, not hearing the bustle of the commerce. His mind was slowly turning over the end of the Scientists, and even in their death knell, he was thinking of his next move. Walking through London, the prospective sounds were forming, the concepts distilling. It wasn't the Scientists and it wasn't punk. It was *surreal.* And it would set a sonic template for what was to come.

> 'I just had this idea for a song you know, this song just came to me and it was *intense.*

The world when seen
Looking through her eyes
Was not the world
Of you or I

I can't take that much credit for it, I actually wrote it without even holding a guitar, you just kind of imagine what it needs to be.

That's not to say
That I thought she was bad
Or even just
A little bit mad

It was a fairly atonal kind of a song. I knew if we had any tonality it would be kind of dissonant, I knew what I wanted it to sound like, the words would be very simple,

You have to live with this sad fact
The things that repel sometimes attract
The things that attract, sometimes repel
You could find yourself living in your private little hell
And loving it ...

but the idea of the song was a bit more complex and maybe ironic and a whole lot of other things. It wasn't quite what it seemed.

and its intense
intense
intense
INTENSE

So, that's when I had this idea of the Surrealists'.

The Scientists had built a fearsome reputation. They had a name, a strong identity and international prestige. The band, however, had focused so strongly on building their coherent image; they prioritised emphasising their look, their idiosyncratic sound and their angry antagonistic performances, that the identities of the people within the band were overlooked. Players had come and gone but they were subsumed by the power of the group.

> *I could see the band wasn't going to last. It was starting to implode in London. And in those last crumbling days of the Scientists, I had come to the realisation that when the Scientists are gone, my name wouldn't really mean anything, despite the reputation of the band people didn't know any of our names. So I thought, for the next thing, I'm going to have my name at the start. If I had my name at least the work I put into something can be carried over into the next thing. I don't have to start from the beginning each time I get an idea. I can build on something.*

Far out experimentalist content stuck in Kim's head. Around this time he had been turned onto Kenneth Anger's film *Scorpio Rising*, and films like *Eraserhead* or David Lynch's *Blue Velvet*, the song of which he had been playing before it graced Lynch's movie. Artists like Dali and Breton were intriguing to Kim; presenting wild illogical scenes with total sincerity but leaving perception and interpretation wide open. Surrealism's motivation was to turn the everyday into the unfathomable, to place the real and the imagined side by side, to surprise and bewilder. Above all, surrealism sought out the unexpected, and at its best this was delivered with authenticity, as an impulse not a contrivance. This was an impulse that was true to Kim, a vibration to which he was attuned. 'The idea that was going on around in my head was everything seemed to be *surreal*. I'd heard that joke, "How many surrealists does it take to change a light bulb? A fish …" And I thought, I think I'll call my next band Kim Salmon and the Surrealists.'

Along with this mindset, a set list was growing out of some experimental solo shows and in Kim's imagination.

> *I had this repertoire of songs in my head. Blue Velvet. Old Elvis songs. When I saw that Kenneth Anger film I thought that's going to be in my set, and it was. Things I grew up with like J'taime, they used to have it blaring around the speakers in my high school. Things like that seeped through into my consciousness and stayed there, they weren't things I'd really thought about they were just there … and I guess I wanted to put them out there.*

If the Scientists mantra had been minimalism and primitivism, the new band would start from a surrealist base and add a nasty dose of deconstruction. Crudely defined, deconstruction seeks to show the impossibility of using a form as a means of expression by breaking down the whole to its constituent parts. Deconstructionism suggests that clarity is fallacy, and that even in a reduced state, ambiguity thrives. 'That kind of approach was informing what I was going to do. I had ideas where we'll have a record where the band doesn't even know how to play it, we just do it. It was kind of an anarchist idea. So that's really the genesis of the Surrealists'.

Now back in Perth, Kim met up with Brian Hooper, his travelling companion across the desert from Perth to Sydney years earlier. Brian had ended up in London too, and had followed the chaotic arc of the Scientists up close.

> *I lived in London and saw the Scientists over there a few times, that's where I got to know Kim better. I'd go to far out places to see them play. I saw them play to empty rooms, I saw them play to full rooms. But what I noticed was that by the end of the gig, after people had been blasted from the front of the room to the back, generally at least half of them moved to the front again and started to understand what was going on. It was a bit weird, but they were a weird band. And I loved them!* (Brian Hooper)

Brian had been playing bass in a band called Modern Wimps, and also guitar in a group called Funken De Klumpen. And of course, where

Brian was, Tony Pola wasn't far away. DNA fanzine described Tony's drumming contribution to Modern Wimps as a 'sonic whirlwind' and he had gone on to play in another forgotten Perth punk band, Dismembered. Kim saw Modern Wimps and Brian stuck in his head. 'He said he liked my contempt for my instrument. I think I had a barb wire wrist band with blood coming out and I was trashing and bashing the bass a bit' (Brian Hooper).

> *I found that, as much as I couldn't wait to get away from the pair of them after that drive from Perth to Sydney, they were likeable rogues, immensely likeable. So I saw Tony around, but I formed the Surrealists with Brian. I told Linda I was going to form a band and she said, 'you got to get someone good looking in the band, you got to get Brian'. And I thought 'yeah he'd be good'. He was a bit of a star the way he played, he played with that forceful rock 'n' roll way of playing, and you noticed him, and that's what I wanted, I wanted everyone to matter in the band. I didn't want a band full of the guys in Oasis who aren't Gallagher's.*

Kim started indoctrinating Brian into the conceptual landscape of the new band. 'Over the course of a few weeks I explained to him what were these things that I had in mind. Then Tony Pola who was Brian's best mate, he couldn't *not* be in the thing once he found out about it, and it gelled. He was a really good drummer'. The three of them, despite — or maybe because of — the harrowing road trip in the Leyland P76, quickly struck up a strong understanding and friendship. 'We *got* each other because sometimes you know someone you've driven for four days straight with better than people you've known for ten years' (Brian Hooper).

With their disorderly collection of songs, the new band started doing a few gigs around Perth. It was low key and shambolic, but it held the promise of something more, and the trio were switched on. 'Our gigs were pretty amateurish from Tony and my point of view, we played in bands but had never done serious gigs like Kim was used to doing. Having seen what I'd seen in London, I was pretty excited' (Brian Hooper). This growing energy was to be complicated by geography, but the soon to be disparate living arrangements of the band were perfectly in keeping with the surreal and deconstructed template from which it was created.

> *Both of the guys decided they were through with Perth and Tony went to Sydney and Brian went to Melbourne. So, before they left I grabbed my friend's four track reel to reel and whizzed them into the studio with a couple of microphones, not knowing what to do. I taped us playing live on three tracks, leaving one free just for anything that I might want to do afterwards, as long as I got the band down there. And that was 'Hit Me with the Surreal Feel'.*

To call it a studio recording was an overstatement.

> *We did our first recording session in basically a tin shed, hired out as a rehearsal room. We hung one microphone from the ceiling in front of the drums and hung another from the ceiling in front of the amps and bashed out a rehearsal and called it a record* (Brian Hooper).

To concoct the right amount of deconstruction, Kim only introduced many of the songs to Brian and Tony right before the recording was made. *Blue Velvet* had hardly been played by the trio, and songs like *Bad Birth* or 'Hit Me with the Surreal Feel' were only just taught to them by Kim before the rehearsal. Kim had honed his concept, and now he wanted to hand the songs over fresh to his two new band mates to see what sort of filtration process they would go through to come out as recorded artefacts. 'I didn't let them get to know the songs too well. Back then I had this really strong idea that the way you heard a song, the way you heard any idea was never going to be pure, you're never going to have an idea that comes out into the world without being filtered in some way.'

For Kim, it was a test of artistic endeavour to cement the concept and leave the performance to the chaos of interpretation. For an artist so strongly driven by the conceptual, in just about all his musical outings, Kim has been very receptive to the expression and interpretation of his collaborators, and open to the impact of the artistic process on his creations. It would not be until SALMON, the double-drum-six-guitar-riff-heavy machine he invented years later, that Kim would be an authoritative conductor of his band. In the Scientists, he had worked with the quirks and permutations of his band mates to fashion his vision into something that worked. In the Surrealists, it was an even more open approach, taking a concept or idea and letting its performance create multiple impressions or meanings.

> *Because the song exists without its performance, in a way. If it's an idea, it only exists as an idea. But I've got this idea that a performance is like a salvage job. Any performance you do, you never get it the same way … it's always going to be different. You're always grabbing what you can get hold of and fashioning it into something.*

While the recording circumstances of 'Hit Me With the Surreal Feel' were opportunistic, there was also an element of contrary design to the production, and it enshrined the Surrealist's anarchistic, primitive and curious sound. Imagine listening to the record in 1987 when it was recorded, at the height of 80's production that emphasised crispness, definition and compression. The Scientists had resisted 1980's production through dogged commitment to their aesthetic: a singular and primitive focus on the baser elements of their craft, and haranguing any producer or mixer who tried to get in their way. The Scientists avoided the curse of 80s production that still haunt the recordings of many of their contemporaries — too much chorus, too much reverb and overly affected. With the Surrealists, it was Kim's impulse to strip the production of all fashion trends to leave the songs and their subsequent performance laid bare, but at the same time, cloaked in a mysterious fog of interference. It was a high concept approach that actually sought to protect the purity of the performance and the purity of the song.

> *Any performance that anybody does is purely subjective, so things like production, you know they're just these ideas that are subject to fashion. Even if you're doing Mozart and you're a virtuoso violinist you've still got to interpret those dots on the page and even as close to precision as you can get with those it's still completely subjective. There's always going to be a conductor who interprets the tempo and the dynamics.*

In his very threadbare approach to production, Kim was trying to take the conductor out of the orchestra. And the result was, not surprisingly, something that didn't fit the usual expectations.

> *At that point having distorted vocals was really bad, and that sort of low fidelity recording was not acceptable. Now, there's Jon Spencer, and everybody does it these days. It's quite expected to have microphones that don't put every frequency in, that don't record everything, that thin down the sound of the voice and make it sound like something out of the past.*

'Hit Me with the Surreal Feel' was released in August 1988. The whole project was executed on the run and for a budget of only \$60 (equivalent to \$130 in 2019 terms) at a time when recording budgets were generally bloated. But although the album sounds thrown together and an accident of time and resources, it endures today as an art record, where the songs stand on their own, the performances are authentically rendered and the audience can make any number of guesses at what the band were even intending to do. For Kim, it was a new frontier, and he was satisfied with the outcome. 'You go and try to do a piece of art, you try to execute something, an idea, to give it the form. And "Hit Me with the Surreal Feel" did that, it actually did do that.'

The album was from another planet, and it landed on earth with a bang. Gareth Liddiard, mainstay of the Drones and Tropical Fuck Storm, was floored. 'The main thing is that his music is weird. Like, the recording of the album "Hit Me with the Surreal Feel". What *is* that? It sounds like someone remembering a record that was actually a lot more melodic and lush and high fidelity' (Gareth Liddiard). The album would go on to garner international praise. Larry Hardy, who runs In the Red Records, and would later release the album in the States describes it as 'probably the most crude record Kim ever did. I mean, Scientists got weirder and weirder as they went along. And "Hit Me with the Surreal Feel" was going into an even darker, stranger place.' Former Black Flag singer Henry Rollins was also a convert.

> *I first heard Kim Salmon when someone gave me the Scientists 'Blood Red River' record in 1984. It was a lucky break for me as I didn't have money to buy records and could have very well not heard the band for a long time if at all. I liked it as soon as I heard it. That was the only record I had of Kim's until I went to Australia for the first time, at the beginning of 1989 I think it was. The first night I was there, only hours off the plane, I was taken to a Beasts Of Bourbon show. They were great. The next day, my agent from then to now, Tim Pittman, played me the 'Hit Me With The Surreal Feel' album and it was one of those experiences where you hear a record you've been going through miles of crates looking for but never really thought anyone would actually make. That's when it hit me that Kim was responsible for a lot of music and I had a lot of catching up to do* (Henry Rollins).

Brian Henry Hooper sums it up simply.

> *It was always going to be lo-fi. It was never going to be anything other than that. Kim did take it into someone's house with a mixing desk, but it was still very low-fi. We got a review of that album which said 'it sounded like a drunk being dragged off in a wheelchair through a public toilet screaming his head off' … I just remember thinking, 'this is great! This is what I want to do!' (Brian Hooper)*

The Surrealists had only been a working proposition for a few months, but had already recorded an album, forged an electric live show, and outgrown Perth. Tony and Brian once again headed east: 'I had a 1962 Chrysler. I shoved an arm chair in the boot, a couple of suitcases and a guitar. A pot dealer I knew was smuggling a few ounces, so we put that in the door panel …' (Brian Hooper) Kim, meanwhile, was making plans. Brian hung onto a comprehensive collection of memorabilia from his life in music, and when I spoke to him, he fished out a letter from Kim, who was at the time still in Perth, writing to Brian who had already moved to Melbourne. It was the end of July 1988.

> *Dear Brian,*
>
> *How's this for a possible plan? I'll use the money from the Beasts of Bourbon gigs to fly to Melbourne, stay with you or Tony, and we'll rehearse. I'll try to organise a demo tape to send to you to learn before I come, for a week or so, so it's as low cost as possible, and then we'll drive to Sydney. During the week days I could be rehearsing with the Beasts and I could maybe do a gig or two at nights. We can do the Beasts supports and even though it's a lot of work for me it tends to make the whole gig an event rather than just a band and support, and it would benefit us. After the Sydney gig we could drive back to Melbourne and support the Beasts and then do a gig or two around town … The only problems I see are is we'll need a car going by then. Say hello to Tony for me and if you get any ideas or if you can see any flaws in my plan let me know. By the way, when I say my plan it seems obvious that you have probably thought of something similar.*
>
> *Kim*

And so, that was the formation of Kim Salmon and the Surrealists in Melbourne. 'The plan came off', says Brian, 'of course it did.'

13

Non Stop Action Groove

The Beasts of Bourbon's re-emergence began as the Scientists total implosion was nearing its magnificent crescendo. In the aftermath, the development and activities of Kim Salmon and the Surrealists and post-'Axemen's Jazz' Beasts of Bourbon were closely linked. In time, Kim would become frustrated with the shadow that the Beasts of Bourbon would cast over the Surrealists, but from 1988 to 1992, the two bands were intertwined in what would be, for Kim, an incredibly satisfying creative period of nonstop action which would see four of his favourite albums created.

> *The albums 'Essence', 'Just Because You Can't See It' … 'Sour Mash' and 'Black Milk' are really linked for me. Brian, Tony and I would have these great times over these few years, where we'd only reconvene because I'd been able to get across the country to do a Beasts tour and we'd do a bunch of songs at Bakehouse, and we'd exist with these cobbled together ideas that I would have and was throwing left right and centre between the two bands and seeing what took root.*

The Beasts of Bourbon were in recess, other than some sporadic shows with different personnel, while Boris and Kim were in the UK with the Scientists. But when Kim and Tex reconnected in Sydney, things changed quickly. After one of the Scientists' goodbye concerts at the Trade Union Club in 1987, Kim was doing an interview on JJ Radio. 'I came out of the building and there's this lanky figure striding up and I realised it was Greg Perkins. He'd heard me on the radio and invited me to his place for dinner'. Tex was living at a place called The Gunnery in a disused navy building with an anarchist art community squatting beneath a big planetarium dome. 'He was putting it to me that we do the Beasts again to cash in on the "Axemen's Jazz" album. He wanted to get that line up back together. I said "sure". They were fun times. So that was the beginning of it'.

From this reconnection, the Beasts of Bourbon re-emerged in March 1988. Instantly, the chemistry of the band returned, as did the camaraderie. But it was clear from the outset that this iteration of the Beasts was not going to be an 'Axemen's Jazz' repeat. This time, the band would cast its net wider.

> *The '88 version of the Beasts was initiated by me and Kim. Spencer was a bit slow, he needed convincing, but not much! The last time we'd left the Beasts of Bourbon it was basically a piss up cover band so I guess he was right to be suspicious but no, this time me and Kim had more ambitious plans* (Tex Perkins).

Tex was, by now, hanging with an eccentric bunch of creatives and had teamed up with John Foy from Red Eye Records to create an offshoot, Black Eye Records, for the more obscure works that Tex was generating.

> *Kim went overseas, and I did the Black Eye stuff, and I went overseas too. And then in '88 we found each other again. I'd been making humour-based noise music for a long time, or noise-based humour music, so I was ready to make music with some kind of predictable structure. But not just straight-ahead rock and roll* (Tex Perkins).

There was little risk of Kim being involved in any straight ahead rock and roll. Tex heard the Surrealists first record and saw that it would be a good fit for the Black Eye stable.

> *Because my ideas about production were pretty unorthodox, and if I went where I wanted to go with the Surrealists, I didn't think it would get picked up in Australia. But this Black Eye thing sounded hopeful. I had recorded some things on a four track, and there were some pretty crazy things on it and sent it off and both Greg and John Foy loved it. As soon as I found Black Eye were kind of interested in it and I had a place to be I worked really hard at it. I set about writing a lot of material. And I found just from hanging out with Greg that you could be a lot more open about writing than I had thought.*

•••

Kim and Tex swapped cassettes of material, while in the background a run of Beasts of Bourbon shows was put together. Kim was as taken with Tex's new songs as Tex had been with the four tracked 'Surreal Feel'.

> *I knew the next Beasts record would be a different thing to the 'Axemen's Jazz', it was more bluesy, more avant-garde, more industrial. I was into it, I was inspired and I had a few ideas. The ideas I sent back were stuff that was pretty out there.* Playground, Elvis Impersonator Blues, Door to Your Soul, *it was a mixture of stuff that I sent over to fling at the wall and see what stuck.*

Playground in particular was a standout: a grating, industrial horror show. The centre piece is a harsh, repetitive, reverbed snare drum, offset by a splinters of abrasive guitar noise. It was a jumble of random half notes falling between the cracks of the overbearing guitar and drums, bristling with tension and foreboding. The solo stumbles in like a creepy drunk neighbour in a slasher movie, making you recoil but curious about the damage it will unleash. This oppressive aural landscape is the perfect bedrock for the lyrics, which suggest a suburban scene drenched in misery made more painful for its stifling boredom.

I live out in Yobsville ten miles out of town
Sitting on a bench in a deserted playground

Asbestos houses all around
Clicking insects the only sound
Nowhere could be as normal as this place pretends to be

The drunken manslaughtering and panel beater removes a dint from his car
The last 3 decades went by the family next door
There's incest in the kitchen in the house down the road
And a gang of cockroaches have moved in on me
The neighbours all look down their collective nose
If you look real hard you can see buggery abounds
Doesn't take much to hear the sound when you're lying face down on the ground

With Brian in Melbourne and Tony in Sydney, Kim remained in Perth madly writing songs for the two hungry musical outfits that were about to hit their prime. And the songs piled up, Kim looked back on the process fondly. 'I had an amazing time of song writing in that period. It was nothing like writing for the Scientists, which is the hardest thing in the world. I really wanted something original, that was my main concern, to be really original. I could write all this crazy shit for the Surrealists and the Beasts got what didn't fit the Surrealists'. As well as songs for what would become 'Sour Mash', the Beasts second album, Kim wrote the majority of material for the next two Surrealists records during this time.

Meanwhile, the Beasts were ramping up their live performances, which funded the blitzkrieg touring approach of the Surrealists. The disparately located Surrealists would convene on the East coast every time the Beasts of Bourbon would emerge. 'They'd do a bunch of shows and fly me out east and the Surrealists would do a run of shows at a much more grass roots level'. And the Surrealists had an appetite for playing:

> *Kim initially said take a week off work, but I never went back to work!* (Brian Hooper)

The Beasts, too, were motivated. In late 1988, they went into the studio and in another booze fuelled session smashed out fifteen new tracks. Kim loved it. 'On "Sour Mash" there was some covers, a Max Roach song, *Driver Man*, I thought it was fantastic, it was right up my alley. Absolutely what I wanted to do. "Sour Mash" was really like what the Scientists could have done'. Reviews were equally positive, with Ian McFarlane stating that it 'virtually redefined the parameters of guitar-based rock 'n' roll. The Cram ps-influenced swamp-rock of old had been discarded for a more adventurous slab of gutbucket blues and avant-garde weirdness.'[1]

They came out of the studio snarling. 'We just got on a roll. We made "Sour Mash", people liked it and we toured Europe' (Tex Perkins). The tour took them all through Europe, but it was in Germany that the Beasts seemed to really land a punch, serving it up rough and hard. 'That's what the Germans like and that's why they signed us up. *Hard Drivin' Man* which was full on distorted, that's how we started our set — I'm a mean mother fucker! Pay attention and get into this. Or else! That was it, take no prisoners from the word go!'

'Sour Mash' extended the Beasts of Bourbon reputation. They had transitioned from the image of a bunch of bent cowpunks having a drunken jam to a serious force of original and very confronting music. 'There was a lot of talk about 'oh the Beasts are the high priests of dirty gutter rock 'n' roll'. Pre-grunge kind of talk. Dirty blues, Muddy Waters on crack' (Tex Perkins).

•••

The Beasts of Bourbon returned to Australia triumphant after the Europe tour, with Tony and Brian waiting to crack on with the Surrealists' assault. In addition to Kim's songs, the Surrealists were developing a new avenue to expand their repertoire. 'Brian and Tony were jamming on this semi-funk groove, and I jumped on it and that became *Melt*. It was great fun jamming. The Scientists never jammed, we wrote songs and thrashed 'em about. But it wasn't like "here's an idea!" Whereas the Surrealists would naturally jam'.

Brian and Tony were eager contributors. 'Tony and I didn't do much song writing in the first one, in the second we were invited to. I came up with the bass riff for *Melt*, parts one, two and three. I wouldn't say that I was always given dues by Kim, but I was happy enough just doing it' (Brian Hooper). The second Surrealists album was recorded basically in between 'Sour Mash' sessions, and in an actual recording studio — not a shed with microphones hung from the ceiling. The collection of songs ranged from the fast out of the blocks groove of *Melt* (it was recorded as one long song but had to be split into three parts on the record because the band sped up so much during the take), to the tongue in cheek sleaze of *Je'taime* through to the curious discordance of *An Articulation of the Thoughts of Society's Bastards*. 'It was creepy where it needed to be, ugly where it needed to be' (Brian Hooper). Kim was relishing in being so productive with his song writing. 'I just wanted an outlet for my songs, it was a matter of trying it on and seeing what stuck. All four of those albums — "Just Because You Cant See it", "Sour Mash", "Essence" and "Black Milk" — were done really quickly, all with about as much material, and I venture to say none of them sound like each other!' Suddenly song writing was flowing and fun.

> *I'd left behind that thing I had created with the Scientists, and that had become difficult. I love it, and it was fun, but I am really the only person who can write songs for the Scientists, and the band are the only ones who can play it. I'm the person*

> *that's got the formula — and I don't even know what it is! I've got to get it in visions and I don't understand what it is. But there's not really much mystery with the Beasts, just get a bunch of songs together and it was easy and fun. I had a couple of new bands and neither of them as bizarre or difficult as the Scientists, so naturally I felt freed up.*

The camaraderie with his fellow Surrealists was also peaking. Kim would blow into Melbourne or Sydney from Perth for a few weeks and they would play hard, touring with big names like Tav Falco or the Cramps, and generally have a good time. They were on the same page musically too.

> *It was a few years of really fantastic times with Brian and Tony. Absolutely gold. We were all conscious of the same material too. I was at my friend Zelda's place and the other guys were going to come over later. And on the radio I heard Peggy Lee singing 'Is That All There Is?' and with this new freeing up sense of what you could have as a song, I thought that it would be a cool song to do a version of. Then Tony shows up and says, 'I heard this great song on the radio by Peggy Lee called 'Is That All There Is?' We ought to do it.' Then about an hour later, Brian shows up and says exactly the same thing! And so from then on, we would break out into at every opportunity! We never recorded it at the time, but eventually Spencer and I did on the 'Runaways' album.*

•••

The Beasts enjoyed the high praise for 'Sour Mash', but started to rankle at the industry's perceptions of them as just industrial, hard, dirty and bluesy.

> *And being contrary we thought it was time to show them we have other sides to us, I thought 'Sour Mash' was pretty varied but the perception was it was dirty blues, so 'Black Milk' was intentionally eclectic, to the point it was multiple personality disorders going on! Songs that just don't belong together. It was our 'fuck you don't call us dirty, we'll call us dirty!' album. Kim helped provide that change* (Tex Perkins).

'Black Milk' was largely conceived on the road. In Germany, Spencer Jones saw a place that had a sign that said 'Bad', meaning spa or bath. And he said 'Hey you got a song called *A Place Called Bad*! He'd heard "Human Jukebox" and he said, "Man that's one sloppy record … crazy!"' So the Beasts cut Spencer's song referencing the Scientists song that came before it. Meanwhile Kim was extending his song writing vista to examine nuanced lyrical ideas and more graceful tunes, after his punishing contributions to 'Sour Mash'.

> *When Kim started to bring songs to the Beasts of Bourbon they were kind of deliberately a lot more highbrow than what we'd become known for. Things like* Words from a Woman to her Man, Cool Fire, *softer, jazzier ideas. We wouldn't have done those sorts of things without Kim, we might have had a stab at it, but Kim was the man for the job, a little bit more intellectual. There are interesting periods with Kim's work, I think there's good stuff to be found all over it. I think some of them he specifically wrote with the idea of me singing them, some of the more low brow stuff, the more animalistic stuff* (Tex Perkins).

Words from a Woman to Her Man in particular introduced a distinctly different narrator to the Beasts, different really to most Australian music. Kim takes the woman's perspective in an introspective enquiry about a relationship running into fatigue and despair. While the song was actually about a couple who lived nearby in Perth, there were more than a few elements of the song that resembled conversations in the Salmon household as the years caught up with Linda and Kim. Whoever the subjects, the song remains a standout of Kim's contribution to the Beasts.

Well if 'I'm sorry' comes along and says its all okay
For you to walk out whenever it suits
And not spare a thought for me stuck here
And don't come back with nothing to show
When together we could be building something
That could take us out of this
Well you can take him with you
'Cos its obvious he's your friend.
You can keep I'm sorry, 'cos he ain't no friend of mine

'Black Milk' was released on Black Eye in July 1990. It was not reviewed as favourably as 'Sour Mash', but still made a splash. In his autobiography, Tex ponders — just like Ringo did about the 'White Album' — that maybe there were too many songs on the album. Kim however, was in his element.

> *We recorded this album with all these crazy new dynamics and there's too many ideas on it really, I love it! The band really believed we could do anything. In fact, people had told Tex he can do anything. I was willing to use that idea to get my songs on, like* Cool Fire *would never dare be presented to the Scientists — it's an old 40s sounding song. We're trying to be like Dr John, every song is different.*

If the album was a kooky mess of grime, glamour and finery, a harder, straighter edge was developing in the live show. The crowds were baying for rock 'n' roll, and as the band became more serious they started playing up to their growing reputation as the meanest, dirtiest blues rock band around. The more esoteric songs that made the albums so varied and compelling didn't come across quite so forcefully in this live environment.

> *The live show is probably an indication of where we should have gone in Tex's mind, but our mind set was we can do anything. The first three albums — everything is thrown in the mix, we can do anything, we can do what we like and we can throw it all in there. Tex's idea about where we should go next is very much evident on the next album — 'The Low Road'.*

•••

As the Beasts juggernaut gathered momentum, the Surrealists were having a blast. They had by now undertaken some significant supports and were absolutely razor sharp as a band. And Kim was about to deliver them an album full of some of his best ever songs — *Essence* — recorded in 1990 at Poons Head Studio in East Fremantle.

> *'Essence' was probably one of my favourite records. There are some ideas there. The crazy shit that goes on in life it comes back to you and you try to work it out. It's all therapy really. So the first two albums are the opening to that, and then this is what can happen because you've done that, and then here's the results.*

Probably the most varied and fully realised album that Kim would make until 'My Script' in 2016, 'Essence' starts with the wryly bombastic, epic rock number *Keeping You Alive* that Kim would hurl out into the Melbourne Cricket Ground full of U2 fans a few years later. There are moments of transgressive weirdness like *The Cockroach* and *The Butterfly Effect* that, even nearly thirty years later, sound like nothing else happening ever. Brian Hooper's bass leads some deep rock grooves like *28 Good Words* and *Self Absorption*, but it is the songs *Essence of You* — '*take your essentials, cook them in a stew. Reduce them down, to an essence of you. Take all your good things, and bad things too. Mix them together, to an essence of you*' — and *Sea Anemone* — '*deadly as you are, you cling to whatever touches you. I don't see an enemy. Just Sea Anemone. Nature with its rules and an irony that is cruel*' — that really stand out on this record. Fragile, curious, hypnotic: these songs are Kim Salmon at his most compelling. The album was an artistic triumph.

As they clocked up their third album in short space, Kim remained fond of his band mates.

> *You couldn't help falling for Brian. Very earnest and sweet and would do anything for you. And Tony was the same. He was sort of totally in the gutter but totally charming, a really fun, really funny guy. And basically, a decent guy, drugs just sent him down the wrong path. He was possibly able to intellectually rationalise some things, because he was a very intelligent guy, more easily than some of us others. So I was hanging out with Tony and then hanging out with Brian wherever he was, then*

jamming, it was a grand time. My trips to the Eastern states were these explosive creative great times.

These great times were however, contrasted with life back in Perth. Alex was now seven, and Kim was enjoying their relationship. But Perth itself didn't offer much for Kim, and with all his musical action on the other side of the country it was hard to focus on the west. He was bored, but didn't do a lot to push out of it. With money left over from their UK great escape, neither Kim or Linda had to work, and the down time bred melancholy.

Linda and I, our life was turning into a country and western song. I felt imprisoned in that situation. She had some very black and white views on the world, and it was her way or the highway, pretty much. She didn't have the capacity to see another idea to the one she had. She thought everybody was privy to her nuances. She'd crack these most absurd jokes, and no one would get them, except maybe me, because we were on the same page, but most people weren't. My expectations for partners and things were probably pretty low when you got down to it and I used to wish I wasn't in this. I think it all comes from being the invisible teenager, so I probably hadn't lived enough before I got into some pretty heavy-duty relationships. And with Linda, I felt trapped all the time.

As the Beasts of Bourbon geared up for another European tour to support 'Black Milk', the strain was really showing between Kim and Linda. What they really didn't need was for Kim to head overseas with a bunch of bad ass Beasts.

Touring with the Beasts of course, things happen. That tour was a bit of a rock 'n' roll tour. I'm a pretty good guy, but some things happened. It should be said that before the tour Linda said, 'If you want to go with other people that's alright'. It was basically a hippy idea. And suddenly I'd gone from a one person man to some sort of ridiculous Mick Jagger figure. I wasn't trying to get into groupies but being in a band like the Beasts of Bourbon eventually these things sort of happen. I was trying to work my way out of things with Linda I think. I let her know, I told her. I couldn't contain it. And that had an impact for Linda and me. It kind of upped the ante really. We nearly broke up and then didn't break up. These things have an effect on you and have an effect on your life, and this was quite momentous.

•••

The atmosphere in the Salmon house was doomed following the 'Black Milk' tour, despite the best endeavours of both Kim and Linda to make things work. Linda remained seething and suspicious of Kim following his groupie revelations, while Kim battled through competing bouts of guilt and suffocation. Increasingly, he spent time at Tex's place in Darlinghurst, 'and they were good times'. By this stage, Tex was performing with the Cruel Sea, and seemed to be the epicentre of a number of music scenes. Kim enjoyed his place in the artistic fold, but he was noticing that while everyone raved about the Surrealists, when push came to shove, the attention really gravitated to the Beasts. And, in particular, their singer. 'Tex is like a cult leader, he drew people to him and still does. I was living in his pad for weeks on end and having a great time, but I started to get a bit envious of his standing in the community. The cracks were probably beginning to show'.

Perhaps one band was not enough space for two front men to co-exist in harmony for too long. Kim and Tex had a great friendship and on stage were the generals in charge of the Beasts show. But both were front men really, Kim having led the Scientists and Surrealists, and it didn't always sit easily that Tex, by virtue of being the singer and front man and larger than life character, seemed to capture the lime light.

One time he was in Geelong and finishing Save Me a Place, *and with Greg his job is to front the band and he has a big say in*

> *the way the song is put across. But ultimately the counting and nuts and bolts are down to the band, and he'd just expect the band to fall in with in with where he was going. And sometimes it works and sometimes it doesn't. And this one time I got the ending wrong, we were riffing it and I didn't get it right and he kind of slapped me round the face. I didn't take it very well, I punched him in front of everybody, on stage.*

After another gig there was a scene in the band room, where Roddy Ray'da was holding court, shooting his mouth off. Booze and drugs were everywhere and Roddy strayed too far out of his lane, and was promptly correctly by Tex. 'I turned around for a minute and there a fight going on between Tex and Roddy, and the whole thing is mayhem. Tex wasn't in a thinking mood, and he said he saw a right that needed to be wronged. That was a bit of a turning point.' James and Boris objected, and threatened not to play the next show in protest. Kim persuaded everyone back on stage for the next show, but there was a lingering impression that something had changed.

•••

It was not long after, in February 1991, that James and Boris left the Beasts of Bourbon to focus on their other band, the Dubrovniks, who were taking off. They eventually achieved massive fame in unlikely places like the Greek Islands.

> *James and Boris were in the Dubrovniks and sold tens of thousands of CDs in Europe, so they quit the Beasts to concentrate on that. The Beasts had always been a fluid line up at that point, it was just another one of these things, lost a couple and get a couple more. Because we played with Kim, he recommended us* (Brian Hooper).

Tex knew Brian and it was quickly assumed that he would take up bass duties. 'Tex liked to have a couple of guys in lace shirts from

WA over there in that corner of the stage'. Kim was keen to include Tony at the outset but the other Beasts wanted to test the field. 'Then we played with Tony and it was like — oh yeah!' (Tex Perkins). Brian knew already that Tony's belligerent personality and way of pummelling the drums would fit the Beasts' music, and he locked in straight away. 'Tony already knew how to play with Kim and Brian, and it was just adding me and Spencer in. It served the Surrealists quite well for a while' (Tex Perkins).

So now the arch of the Surrealists and the Beasts, that had been running in a twisted sort of rock 'n' roll parallel for the last few years, joined. Tony and Brian had gone from being slightly resentful of the Beasts taking their band mate away, and slightly jealous of the bigger crowds that Kim played to as part of the Beasts, to now being in the Beasts' fold. And they adapted with vigour. Their inclusion in the Beasts of Bourbon had immediate implications for both bands. For Kim it was, in a way, the start of the clock ticking for his exit from the Beasts and the overhaul of the Surrealists.

•••

As their legend grew, the Beasts were invited back to Europe for another 'Black Milk' tour. The shows were successful, but Kim noticed the atmosphere was darker.

> *All in this time we did shows together through Europe and I found that very quickly, with those two in the band, the criminal element that was around the band was really gravitating, there was serious drug interest, and I was finding that people that I was vaguely scared of were around all of the time. It was getting a lot more bad ass.*

The internal dynamic was shifting too.

> *I noticed that my position in the band wasn't what it was, there were new guys there, Greg was enchanted with these new*

people. Tex found that Tony was actually this charming funny fellow, and Brian was this guy who would do anything for a dare. He was up for whatever! There were lots of good times on that tour, but the ante had been upped and the irony had gone out the window.

Brian and Tony committed to the Beasts of Bourbon hard, just as the band was really starting to elevate. The adventurous follow ups to the happy accident of 'Axeman's Jazz', along with a lot of hard touring, had hit a groundswell for the Beasts. They were a band to watch out for, their live shows taking on mythical rock status. They were getting a reputation for living as hard as they played, and it was starting to take a toll. 'I've saved Spencer's life, Tony's saved my life, we've all been in death defying situations — died and come back. We were the nastiest sounding underground band' (Brian Hooper).

Kim watched this warily. 'I never knew whether to get in the game and compete with them or just distance myself'. But more than anything it was his drive to create good art and perform that was the overriding impulse. Kim upped his solo performances, supporting Ed Kuepper all around the country and doing other high profile shows, including supporting Henry Rollins. The Surrealists were still going from strength to strength and picking up just about every major tour that came to Australia. The band went to Europe on an exhausting thirty date tour, only to back it up straight after with another thirty dates at the request of Nick Cave and the Bad Seeds: sixty shows in just about as many days. Notwithstanding the growing temperature in the Beasts, the Surrealists remained tight — the three musketeers — and their tours were fun.

I remember some great times, touring with the Surrealists trudging through the Black Forest not knowing where we are, tripping off our dials and finding some club in the middle of the forest and they're playing Hot Chocolate! Doing other stupid shit, me and Brian jumping trains, doing runners, getting lost … they were good times.

•••

The far out, 'anything goes' creativity of 'Sour Mash' and 'Black Milk' was starting to get boiled down to something more streamlined. 'We worked our way towards the "Low Road", which was destined to be played in rock 'n' roll clubs that we were playing all over Europe. Tony and Brian arrived so things got harder and funkier and louder, and we needed material to fit that new band' (Tex Perkins). One of the first signs of this was *Chase the Dragon*, a song that Brian introduced. It was a complicated bass line that Kim pared down, inserted a classic guitar lick, added some chord changes while Spencer went the full Jimmy Page trip. 'Suddenly, Tex has the lyrics for it and you could see that a new, different era was ushered in, and it was completely different, you could tell that the rules were not the same'.

At another rehearsal, Tony offered up some lyrics to Kim before the others arrived.

> *I said give them to me, I didn't even look at them. I could tell, just by sniffing that there was gold in there. And you could tell he was thinking about things. I thought Low Road was a gem. The Low Road, along with Drop Out [written with James Baker] remains one of the theme songs of the Beasts. So I am proud of that. I have had some good runs with lyric writing drummers!*

Another song, *Just Right,* introduced Kim as a virtuoso guitarist, a role he had previously deferred in preference to his song writing. He had been playing Hendrix style riffs which perked up Tex's ears and he jumped on it. 'So that album was sort of like being in this new band. I remember putting down *Chase the Dragon* and we needed a lead break — "Can you play something blistering?" — and there was applause and that was nice'.

Tony Cohen returned for the 'Low Road', and the album hit a vein. It was a great album, and Kim loved it. But his view of the Beasts of Bourbon and their mission statement was shifting.

> *It started out as this fairly sophisticated ironic punk rock band and it was very eclectic. For me it embodied the anarchy of punk rock in that way, there weren't any limitations to what it could do and the first three albums are like that — everything's chucked in there like a cauldron without really giving a shit about the consequence. And it kind of honed down into the pub rock, AC/DC thing.*

•••

Soon after the 'Low Road', the Surrealists re-entered the studio, again with Tony Cohen, to record 'Sin Factory'. The Surrealists were building powerful performance muscle, having been on the road, playing constantly and consolidating their strengths. The progress of the band had been building to this moment, the look and feel growing more distinct, and 'Sin Factory' would capture the final identity of this version of the band. The 'Sin Factory' era Surrealists were all about wide-open silk shirts, dark shades, big rock moves and good-natured sleaze, and all of this made its way onto the disc. It was distinct from their previous recordings.

> *Before that we'd reconvene in whatever city we were in, and the albums were done on the fly, in stolen moments every one of them. We weren't always playing consistently, it was just 'here's the ideas I've got, here's what this song is, we're just going to jam it out' and bang — there it is. Whereas 'Sin Factory', you hear the band playing, the band doing something that is well worn and specific.*

Kim was realising that he had surrendered some control over the concept and output of the Surrealists. While previous Surrealists song constructions had been about anarchy and ideas, there now seemed to be a template that the band had adopted. Previously they were open to nuance and tangents, but now the image of the three piece rock band seemed to be prevailing.

> *When you're with groups of people, everybody takes ownership of things. And that line up have got a certain amount of right to do that because certain things that they added to the performance. It's what my band had become, by that stage I guess I was the band leader letting it do its own thing.*

This had an immediate practical implication. 'Coming up with the material for 'Sin Factory' wasn't easy, it was getting to be like writing a Scientists album'. Difficult maybe, but the songs from 'Sin Factory' were more cohesive than previous Surrealists albums — *I Fell, Non Stop Action Groove, Rose Coloured Windscreen, Gravity* and *Desensitised* were pivotal songs and dominated this period.

'Sin Factory' was met with very positive response, and the Surrealists were as big as they ever were, generating a real buzz. Kim appraises it as a good record, but the Surrealists album to which he has the least personal connection. 'It's much more what the band became. We'd sort of reached our zenith when we recorded "Sin Factory", it's our best produced one and as a pop rock statement its better than the others. But I don't find it any more interesting than "Essence" or "Just Because You Can't See It". I think it's less interesting. But it shows the band firing on all cylinders'.

What it *did* do, was cap off a very productive period which manager Tim Pittman was able to capitalise on. Kim's publishing deal was structured so that whenever he recouped half his album advance, he was forwarded another advance. Combined with some lump sum APRA payments and good earning from live performances, Tim was able to put the band on a weekly wage — a major accomplishment for an 'underground' act. 'We were really building towards something' (Tim Pittman).

•••

In 1994 Kim called time on the Beasts of Bourbon. When I first got to know Kim I was wary of the Beasts. It seemed like complicated territory. Kim was always respectful but a little guarded when talking about his ex-band mates. Over time, I came to understand the set of interpersonal, artistic and commercial elements that made Kim walk away from the Beasts. Along with the highs of making great records and playing powerful shows and the life long bonds with his band mates, there were also brutal lows. Times when the relationships turned sour or were treated harshly, times when his artist standing was overlooked in preference for the cult of personality of the Beasts, times when the Surrealists in which he believed so strongly were left holding the bouquet while the Beasts did the main dance. By the time of the 'Low Road' tour, the Beasts of Bourbon held plenty of pain for Kim Salmon. As we talked, it was clear that any misgivings he had about the band after the 'Low Road' era were offset by great affection for his fellow Beasts and their creative output. But by 1994 the band had run its course for Kim. 'By that stage, I was a bit of an outcast. I was straight and you know, you had to be a rock 'n' roll bad ass and everyone was doing rock 'n' roll bad ass things. I was maybe an experimenter, but it wasn't my life choice'.

It's Brian who I talk the most to about this phase of the Beasts of Bourbon, and he is very straightforward about where the band was at that time.

> *It got to a point where, because we all had drug habits, he didn't feel like part of the gang anymore. It was nothing we did purposefully, we were just being stupid. He felt he was outside the rest of us. I didn't feel he was, but he felt he was. But it just so happened that he wasn't a heroin addict and most of the rest of us were* (Brian Hooper).

Kim Salmon today still knows how to have a good time, but a health scare in 1998 when he was diagnosed with (and later successfully treated for) hepatitis encouraged him to slow down. Over the journey he has soaked up his fair share of illicit substances; heroin however, just wasn't his bag. Nor was joining the club.

> *Something about my genetics was not to be a joiner. If it's something that everyone else is doing, bugger that! And it did get to be a bit of a bad boys club there, the rule of the club is you've got to be a bad ass, you gotta take drugs, do heroin … [but] if everyone's doing heroin I'm not going to. If nobody did, I probably would have! It's a perverse streak in me that I've always had.*

The band were aware that Kim was enjoying being in the Beasts less and less. He was candid that the Surrealists were more important to him, and chafed at the emphasis given to the Beasts. This dynamic played out on stage at times, with Kim not inclined to consolidate the perception of him as a sideman when in fact, he was a front man of his own band.

> *I enjoyed both the Beasts and the Surrealists, but I didn't want to be the singer so it didn't worry me, I was just the bass player. Kim wanted to be the singer, and the songwriter. He was the singer and songwriter for the Surrealists but he was just the guitar player and songwriter for the Beasts. And it got to him eventually, he thought 'right, I've got to make my own mark'. He was sick of being Tex Perkins' lacky, it was like that for Kim, that was his truth. He thought this was just hack rock 'n' roll stuff, what I'm doing with Brian and Tony is more interesting* (Brian Hooper).

Perhaps more pressing than egos at play, although no doubt they were, was the critical and commercial impact that Kim believed the Beasts had on the Surrealists. While it definitely served the latter band well and raised their profile, Kim was in no doubt that when it came to industry support, focus and resources, preference was given to the Beasts. Budgets for film clips weren't forthcoming, media focus was directed away, and the general impetus of the machinery around the two groups all seemed designed to benefit the Beasts. Tex appraises this pragmatically.

> *We never really looked at it as an overview of how it looks to other people or what it means to the big picture of our careers, we come together we create something, it worked, if someone gave a shit we'd release it and go and do some shows. For a little while between '88 and '92 the Beasts were pretty much what was working the most out of all the projects we were doing, it was the one that was selling records and getting us touring Europe* (Tex Perkins).

But Kim felt something more was at stake, and he was getting jack of playing second fiddle.

> *I was finding these double standards going on, 'Kim you'll get your time, Kim be sensible'. I was being patronised by the industry, and sort of steered in a particular direction, and unequivocally it starved the Surrealists.*
>
> *To this day I wonder how come the Surrealists weren't where the Beasts were, because the band was incredibly good. It was amazingly good. People who encountered us wanted us to support them. U2, Bad Seeds, Rollins — the band really had some currency there. But as a support band you know. Fuckin' hell, why weren't we headlining?! The Beasts weren't a support band, they were headlining. Is there any reason on earth why the Surrealists shouldn't have taken on the mantle of the Scientists? It's every bit as good a band. And why did that not happen? Because the Beasts of Bourbon were going on and I was being encouraged to steer that way all the time.*

When all is said and done, Kim concludes that 'it was a really bad idea for me to have the Surrealists on the same label. I was stupid letting that happen and getting Brian and Tony to play in the Beasts of Bourbon. I mean I facilitated that thinking it would work, and it just didn't work at all.' Kim eventually found himself in an awkward and high pressure dynamic of discontent with his Beast bandmates, which inconveniently as it turned out, also included his Surrealist bandmates. Tex described that Kim leaving the band gave everyone licence to behave as badly as they wanted, which by implication paints Kim as an unwelcome reminder of the valour of temperance, something the Beasts did not want to know at that juncture. And so, tired of the whole thing, Kim left the Beasts.

> *When Kim announced he was leaving it was like phew! Not that we didn't love him but it was 'okay, let's end this torture'. But then after that we didn't play for five years, we didn't have any intention of playing. He announced it, we knew it was coming for months, we planned some activities and he said at the end of that it will be it for me. But we didn't play for years so it was a moot point* (Tex Perkins).

Kim played his final show with the Beasts of Bourbon in Fremantle, with support from You Am I. It was a high octane show, played to a revved-up audience surrounding the stage like crowd baying for blood at a boxing match. Kim played like his life depended on it, Tex turned himself inside out and at the end of the gig the stage was littered with smashed up drums and other musical shrapnel. Afterwards Kim was looking to get undone. Leaving the Beasts was a relief, but a loss none the less. Wasted and coked off his face, Kim turned it on but wanted to shift festivities up a gear. Where could he find some high quality rock 'n' roll debauchery? Of course — You Am I's after party! Through the wasted haze he located the support band's hotel room and knocked loudly on the door, ready for action. Greeted with silence he knocked again, but still nothing. Kim was sure there was fun to be had, and all that was stopping him was this damn hotel door. 'I was in that much of a drunken state I thought "I'm going to kick this door down". That's what you do isn't it? So that's just what I did. I kicked it down. I literally kicked it down!' As the door slung off its hinges Kim was confronted with the bewildered Tim Rogers, Russell Hopkinson and Andy Kent quietly sipping tea and eating cakes. Slowly placing his tea cup back on its saucer, Rogers appraised the silhouette of Kim Salmon standing in the open doorway and said, 'you're a wild man Kim'. 'I guess the party is somewhere else then,' returned Kim, and skulked off down the hall. Sometimes the big moves just don't come off.

Many connections have come Kim's way through music. Brian Henry Hooper became one of the Kim's longest friendships, and its Brian who has the last word on Kim's exit from the Beasts of Bourbon.

> *I was enjoying it just fine up until the point he left, and I thought 'oh that's no good. I don't want you to quit, there's no reason for you to quit'. Because I played with him all the time in the Surrealists I knew it was coming, but I didn't understand it when it did come. I just couldn't see the reason for it. And I just thought, you're going to be irreplaceable when you go ...* (Brian Hooper)

•••

Well before Kim Salmon departed the Beasts of Bourbon, he performed with the band at the inaugural Sydney Big Day Out in January 1992. Headlining that day were a group from Seattle who, at that exact moment, were exploding to be one of the biggest bands in the world and usher in a cultural upheaval. The Grunge revolution was happening, and its music, fashion and attitude would dominate the western world, at least for a while. And it was Nirvana that were about to make it hit the mainstream. The Beasts put on a surging, powerhouse display that day and stole the show, leaving the 'audience feeling brutalised and dirty — the sign of a powerfully ugly rock band.'[2] Despite Nirvana's headline status and growing notoriety, some suggested that Cobain and co paled by comparison. Henry Rollins was witness: 'The unlucky band who had to go on after that was Nirvana. And you could see it on the faces of the band, they knew that there was no way they were going to be able to outshine the Beasts of Bourbon. Nirvana were great that day. But game, set, match the Beasts of Bourbon.'[3]

> *We were at, as they say, the height of our powers in January '92. We made the record, we were playing well and full of confidence and I don't know if we blew Nirvana off the stage but yeah it was an audience that was perfect for us to play in front of. It was going well at that point* (Tex Perkins).

Long after he came face to face with Nirvana, Kim Salmon would be associated with Grunge's evolution. So, what *is* the Formula for Grunge?

14

The Formula for Grunge

Before everybody, in the beginning, before grunge, there was the Scientists.

Kim is reflecting on comments he made about grunge. 'Boy did I get shit for that! "Oh, the Scientists reckon they invented grunge. Kim Salmon thinks he invented grunge". *I* didn't say *that*! But oh god, I'm not going to deny it … even though it's not the particular thing I would have invented, I can see where they're coming from.'

Whether he likes it or not, Kim Salmon will be forever associated with the invocation of Grunge. There are multiple narratives about Grunge — its origins, meaning and merits — but when it comes to the significant precursor influences of the Seattle Sound, the Scientists feature every time.

•••

Grunge started as a descriptor for dirty, sloppy or scungy sounds. 'The word was more of an adjective; we'd throw it around in the same way you'd say "gnarly" or "raw" or "fucked up". That's a real *grungy* guitar sound, that was how we used that word until it became the capital G, Grunge, before it became a noun' (Mark Arm). In fact, grunge was used as far back as the 1950s when rockabilly Johnny Burnette's guitar player was described as 'grungy', and repeated by Lester Bangs in a *Creem* magazine review in 1972.[1] In 1983 Kim used the term 'Grunge' to describe 'Blood Red River'. 'I don't know why this happened but it was the only word I could think of to describe the Scientists' sound. I was being interviewed on 2JJJ radio and I know that I used the term repeatedly.'[2] Not long after Mark Arm used Grunge in a self-penned parody letter of complaint about his own band Mr Ep, describing it disparagingly as 'Pure grunge! Pure noise! Pure shit!'[3] Sub Pop's Bruce Pavitt then took the term to a wider audience in his description of Mark Arm's band Green River as 'ultra-loose grunge that destroyed the morals of a generation.'[4] As the 'Seattle Sound' grew in prominence, Grunge went from an adjective to a genre, and then a popular culture revolution.

The parameters of Grunge can be recognised by a time and place, characterised by a basic sound with broadly agreed exponent bands, and accompanied by certain fashion tropes and ideologies.

The time was roughly 1990 to 1994. The place, Seattle, USA. 'Seattle at that time was a complete outpost. It wasn't as much as an outpost as Perth, 'cos that's pretty much as far as an outpost as you can get in the English speaking world!' (Mark Arm) Seattle was economically struggling, and Grunge fashion reflected a downtrodden, shiftless kind of aesthetic: flannelette, scruffy jeans or shorts, street sneakers, and long messy hair.

Grunge is known for a core group of Seattle bands, the flagships being Pearl Jam, Soundgarden, Mudhoney and Nirvana — with a second tier of Screaming Trees, Tad, Alice in Chains, Hole, L7 and maybe Stone Temple Pilots. The sound of Grunge is difficult to define, but fuzzed out dissonant guitars, dark lyrics, soft/loud dynamics and messy playing is a good start. Guitar World wrote: 'So what exactly is grunge? … Picture a supergroup made up of Creedence Clearwater Revival, Black Sabbath and the Stooges, and you're pretty close.'[5]

The orthodox history of Grunge has Seattle bands in the mid-80s slowing down punk rock by mixing it with heavy metal. Bands like the Melvins, Sonic Youth, Neil Young, Black Flag and the Scientists are credited with imprinting on Seattle bands a grunge aesthetic, which melded with the influence of older groups Black Sabbath and Led Zeppelin. The release in 1985 of Green River's debut EP 'Come on Down' is considered the first actual grunge record. As Green River separated into Mudhoney and Pearl Jam, plenty more bands piled on, and the buzz around Seattle bands gathered momentum. By 1990, the flagship bands were on the cusp of major releases, which culminated in September 1991 when Nirvana released 'Nevermind'. Produced by Butch Vig to play well on the radio, the album went berserk, and by the time they were getting towelled up by the Beasts of Bourbon in January 1992, Nirvana were the biggest band in the world. Grunge was a phenomenon, and quickly became big business. The bands that made it big were discomforted by their vast success, with Kurt Cobain and Eddie Vedder famously struggling to adapt to being poster boys for tens of millions of people they never expected nor intended their music to reach.

Despite its strong initial voice, Grunge burned itself out. The originator bands were diluted by a wave of pretenders, the movement's authenticity and anti-establishment impulse had been appropriated by the mainstream, and as the scene began to deteriorate, so did its figureheads. Lots of money was being made, but the music was diminished, and the spirit corrupted. By the end of 1994, Grunge was dead.

•••

'Well in the context of this book, what is your *definition, is what I'm kind of curious about?'*

I'm talking to Mark Arm from Mudhoney. He has taken a break from his job at Sub Pop Records in Seattle to take my call. I'd met Mark and Mudhoney co-founder Steve Turner a couple of years prior at the Tote Hotel in Melbourne before sound check at a Monkeywrench show, but somehow lost the interview recording, hence this follow up phone call. And Mark Arm, whose band actually *is* the definition, is asking *me* to define Grunge.

I first heard *Smells Like Teen Spirit* in 1991 when I was 17, but I didn't get it at first. The birth of Grunge for me was turning up at the Corner Hotel in Melbourne and seeing 300 kids in flannelette shirts, cut off army shorts and converse sneakers milling around on the street outside the pub, waiting to get in to see Bored! and the Cosmic Psychos. Although neither band strictly fits the definition of grunge, the spirit of their music fits perfectly with Mudhoney's template. It was an exciting time, a wave of fervour all for the same cause: music that suggested an intoxicating combination of apathy and righteous revolution. Mark sounds amused. 'When most people think of that term they think of a handful of bands that came out of Seattle at a particular time, and then other bands around the world tried to sound like that. I think most people are going to think more about Silverchair than the Cosmic Psychos though!' (Mark Arm) I finally admit to Mark that the most accurate definition of grunge, *I* think, starts and ends with Mudhoney's *Touch Me I'm Sick*. Grunge was a big deal after they released their first single, but it never sounded better than right then.

•••

Mark Arm started out in Mr Ep and the Calculations, which he describes as 'mostly an imaginary band without instruments. We didn't know about tuning, we didn't know that chords were a thing.

When we first picked up the instruments we were just jamming to make noise' (Mark Arm). When Steve Turner was added, the group morphed from the imaginary to the actual and they started writing songs based on a Stooges template. A successful gig for Mr Ep was one that cleared the room, but over time Mark noticed that they were attracting a weirdo following. 'The really odd balls, the more outsiders than just like punks. We hated the punks, 'cos they were too cool anyway' (Mark Arm). It was clear that Mark was 'developing a sound that was a radical departure from punk.'[6]

Mark's next band, Green River, formed after Mr Ep broke up and featured not only Mark and Steve, but Stone Gossard and Jeff Ament who went on to form Pearl Jam. Green River released 'Come on Down' in 1985 and history recognises this as the first Grunge record. When Green River folded, Mark and Steve teamed up again to form Mudhoney with Matt Lukin and Dan Peters. By this time, they knew exactly what they wanted to play and had a definitive sound in mind. Steve and Mark were avid record collectors and would scour record stores like gold prospectors. Tower Records had a good import section where Steve and Mark would loiter, rifling through the records to see what they could uncover. One day, an Australian import LP was revealed to them, with four shadowy, long haired freaks glaring out from beneath the band's moniker, printed in streaky, swampy red scrawl. 'This cover looked like something that could be really cool' (Steve Turner). They picked the LP up, turned it over back and forth, examining it, looking for clues. 'What the hell is this?! I had no idea. I hadn't read about it or heard anything, it probably took a few weeks until Steve decided to put down the money and take a chance on it' (Mark Arm). Steve and Mark took the Scientists 'Blood Red River' home and put it on the turntable. Right away they were transported. 'This is fucking great' (Mark Arm) — 'It didn't sound like what I expected it to, because it didn't sound like *anything*!' (Steve Turner)

By the mid 80s a few Australian imports had made their way to

Seattle. Other than the Scientists, there were records by the Beasts, Celibate Rifles, Cosmic Psychos, Harem Scarem, Died Pretty and some of the other Red Eye/Black Eye and Citadel acts. Au Go Go, however, was a front-runner, having infiltrated record stores and record players all over the world. So, blown away by 'Blood Red River', Steve and Mark returned to Tower Records and soon found the 'Happy Hour/ Swampland' and 'We Had Love' 7inch's and 'This Heart Doesn't Run on Blood' mini LP. From the late 70s Bruce Milne had been busily corresponding with guys like Larry Hardy in Los Angeles, who later formed In the Red Records, Greg Shipley from Numero, and other oddball fanatics who loved their music deeply, and wanted to share what they loved. Bruce wrote letters, sent fanzines and his cassette magazines all over the world, spreading the word about his key spine tingling band, the Scientists.

> *This was the important Australian music, there was no doubt, which was why I was documenting it with cassette magazines and fanzines and putting out records and doing radio shows, because I knew that this was the thing that was going to be around in forty years time and people would talk about. People in Seattle, Sweden, Spain, people all round the world were hearing about them and contacting me* (Bruce Milne).

Bruce Milne sent a copy of the *Fast Forward* cassette to Bruce Pavitt in Olympia Washington, outside of Seattle. Not only did Fast Forward expose Bruce Pavitt to the early Scientists (pre Au Go Go version of *Swampland*) but it directly led to Pavitt's Subterrean Pop fanzine morphing to a Sub Pop cassette and then eventually record label.[7]

> *It wasn't like I had foresight. This is what I know and love, what I believe is important. And so did ten other people in the town. And I just had to find those ten people in every town in the world. I was doing mail order a lot and building up that network of friends around the world* (Bruce Milne).

This sharing was, of course reciprocal, and through this mechanism obscure new US releases would dribble into Australia.

> *I first heard about Kim by reading an interview with Kid Congo who said they were his favourite band after touring with the Gun Club. So I got in touch with him and I made a bunch of pen pals in Australia. Bruce Milne who put their records out and I would swap stuff from America for music from Australia, but primarily I was interested in the Scientists and I became a bit of a fanatic over them* (Larry Hardy).

These intercontinental transactions led to a sprinkling of Australian records turning up on US college radio stations, hole in the wall record shops or being shared around among the small group of freaks who discovered it. Mark Arm volunteered at the local college radio station and played the Scientists and other Australian bands on the air. As Mudhoney pulled their songs together and prepared to make their debut recording, the imprint of the Scientists was strong. 'By the time Mudhoney began two of our most influential bands were Feedtime and the Scientists, along with the Stooges and Neil Young' (Mark Arm)[8]. The influence of the Scientists can most obviously be attributed to *We Had Love*, the heavy fuzz, the discordant shards of guitar, the growly vocals, the dynamics — all signs point to grunge Mudhoney style. Mark Arm also relates the 'Blood Red River' discovery as one of the 'cornerstones of Mudhoney. It was dark and creepy and had a cool groove. Everything is perfectly in its place. It's fantastic stuff' (Mark Arm).

Mudhoney catalogued their new songs to cassette tape, recorded so badly on an old boom box that it sounded like blown out fuzz to the point you could hardly decipher the songs. But Mark had established a good relationship with Bruce Pavitt and Sub Pop, who took the tape on face value, trusted its creators and immediately commissioned time in the studio. 'Sub Pop paid for us to go into the studio for a weekend, and we came out of that with our first single' (Mark Arm). *Touch Me*

I'm Sick, captured the perfect distillation of Grunge. Mudhoney had taken the Scientists' formula, infused it with their own ingredients, exposed it to Seattle air, and built the mould for Grunge.

Mudhoney talked up Kim and his music to other Seattle bands, playing them to Pearl Jam, the Melvins and others. 'Buzz Ozbourne from the Melvins is a fan, in the mid 80s Buzz and Matt Lukin would come into town from Aberdeen and hang out in these parties where we'd drink beer and sit around and listen to records, and the Scientists' records were definitely played a lot' (Mark Arm). Buzz was such a fan that years later he commissioned Mark Arm to record two Scientists songs — *Swampland* and *Set it On Fire* — for the Melvins' covers album 'Everybody Loves Sausages'. 'I assume *everybody* knows who the Scientists are. Then I thought about it and realized they were pretty obscure. Mark Arm certainly knew who they were. I always thought Mudhoney had a lot in common with the Scientists.'[9] The Melvins were in turn a key influence of Kurt Cobain, hailing from the same town and hanging out together listening to music, Buzz educated Kurt about punk and other underground music that was around at the time. In 1991, having perfected grunge at its most digestible, Nirvana released 'Nevermind' and Grunge went global.

•••

A lot has been written about the legacy of Grunge; some elevating it, some diminishing it. As a genre it is extinct, and its brief heyday was over quarter of a century ago, but at its best Grunge was potent. It came as a wake up call to a new generation, a reaction to the excess pomp of the 80s. Understated, authentic, stripped back, Grunge put music first, but few genres of music have had such an obvious impact on culture, most noticeably in fashion. Grunge fashion was everywhere, and by degrees, took over the western world. It responded directly to what the bands were wearing in a way not really seen in other genres. Punk aesthetic was religiously adopted by punks, but feared by the mainstream. Disco revolutionised fashion for those who were dancing, but the average kid wasn't aping Barry Gibb from *Saturday Night Fever* unless he really *was* heading to a disco. 1980's pop music fashion was very aligned to broader fashion trends, but the causation is less clear — the musicians were both influencing and responding to the fashion of the day. Country music lines up closely with its fan base, but it never crossed over into the mainstream. Only Hip Hop and Grunge (and perhaps New Wave) have shaped in such a wholesale way what ended up in our wardrobes.

The impact of Grunge fashion was convenient for the times. In the 1990s, youth unemployment was off the charts just about all around the world. It was a time of economic restructuring, and young people were shut out of the equation. But in musical and fashion terms, it was a good time to be poor. Grunge meant it didn't matter what you spent on your appearance. You could go down to Savers in Swan Street Richmond and get your whole grunge inspired outfit for $10. Grunge bands were real people, whereas the stars before and after Grunge were unattainable, and to emulate them meant serious consumption.

Grunge hit as young people were connecting more to each other via the internet while being channelled into tertiary education at rates never seen before. Only a few years prior, kids weren't even guaranteed to complete high school, but by the time Grunge hit, the majority were going onto further study. The Grunge generation were joining the dots for the first time since the hippies in the 1960's, finding out what was *really* going on. Grunge bands generally differentiated themselves from the gormless, superficial grandstanding of many of the big acts of the 80s. They had a view, and the driving ideological forces of grunge were anchored in progressive foundations:

> *So Pearl Jam wrote about domestic abuse, illiteracy, the maltreatment of the mentally ill. Nirvana looked at alienation, rape, stultifying conformity. Alice in Chains dug deeply into the black hole of addiction. Soundgarden pondered the search for meaning in an indifferent universe. Courtney*

> *Love wrote ferocious lyrics about misogyny, eating disorders, sexual predators.*[10]

Grunge led a brief counter culture resistance to the power structure, and the music world hasn't really organised in a way that attacks the machine since. Grunge cashed in the chips that punk bet in the 70s. It handed the power first the weirdos and freaks, then to the music lovers more broadly, and then to everyone. For a while, it really mattered. And then commerce won out, like it always does. But that's not the fault of Grunge, and it doesn't detract from the crackling excitement of hearing Mudhoney for the first time, seeing Tad on Rage, or walking over the knocked down fence at the Myer Music Bowl to see Pearl Jam for free.

> *Grunge wasn't just another musical or youth trend — it was the ultimate expression and fusion of most of the defining cultural, ideological and social threads of the modern western world. Feminism, liberalism, irony, apathy, cynicism/idealism, anti-authoritarianism, wry post-modernism, and not least a love of dirty, abrasive music; grunge reconciled all these into a seminal whole.*[11]

•••

The Scientists' influence on Grunge is a matter of fact.

> *The Scientists were the first grunge band. They were in existence before any of those US Sub Pop bands came along. It was US Sub Pop bands like Nirvana and Mudhoney that were openly avowed fans of the Scientists.*[12]

A New Musical Express review of the Scientists' 'You Get What You Deserve' LP in 1985 opined that the album 'establish[ed] them as the premier grunge merchants.'[13] The Guardian observed that 'Cobain … admitted the Australian wave was a big influence' on his music[14] while

Everett True wrote that 'there [was] more of an argument to be had for grunge beginning in Australia with the Scientists and their scrawny punk ilk.'[15] Kim's music has been endorsed not only by Mudhoney, but Sonic Youth, Jon Spencer, Nick Cave, Iggy Pop and many more. Henry Rollins was positively reverential when talking about Kim, and the White Stripes made a special request to meet him on their Australian tour. Over repeated telling, Kim's identity as the Godfather of Grunge has grown.

Initially the moniker sat awkwardly with Kim. Asked about it by Clinton Walker for the 2001 *Long Way to the Top* documentary, Kim was clearly uncomfortable and didn't know what to say. But the connection was made, and over time the questions kept coming until, 'I thought I should be more comfortable about it, so the next time somebody asked me about it on television I said "yeah I invented it, I woke up one day and thought we need to invent a sub culture and we'll call it grunge!"' At first he was uncomfortable, then sarcastic, now he accepts the attribution with good humour.

> *It seems to have attached itself to me. And I think,* oh god, that's about the best I've got ... *I can see the connections. It's what history has dished out to me, and I'm not going to say* fuck off, it's got nothing to do with me.

•••

The Formula for Grunge is comprised of some base elements. For the first constituent part, the Scientists distilled the core spirit and attitude of punk rock, but siphoned out the grandstanding (there was no room for aggrandising contaminants in the Scientists' formula — it was 100 per cent pure). The next ingredient was reminding punk rock where it came from by injecting it with early primitivism and reintroducing Creedence, the Cramps and Link Wray. The Scientists went backwards and forwards while the rest of the music world was moving towards New Wave on the one hand or American hardcore on the other. This new molecular structure gestured directly to Seattle.

The Scientists loaded the Formula with unpredictable and unstable molecules. While Punk was stripped back and do it yourself, it was often formulaic and reasonably predictable. The Scientists infused the Formula with crooked rhythms and bent time signatures until the batch was unrecognisable and un-reproducible.

Finally, they added deep fuzzed out noise, psyched out caterwauling, crunchy discordance, and loud thundering pulsation. Collectively, the Formula is better known as Nine Parts Water, One Part Sand.

I ask Kim (the technician behind the Formula) to reveal the hidden secrets of his scientific method. He considers a moment, deliberating whether to show his hand, before responding, 'It's not science at all. It's magic. It's alchemy.'

15

Ya Gotta Let Me Do My Thing

In 1991, Kim moved to Melbourne, which heralded a new era with the Surrealists. Kim's wife, Linda, and their second son, Jack, (who had been born literally in the back seat of their car the year before) arrived from Perth first to secure accommodation. Not savvy to the St Kilda v Fitzroy dynamic, they landed a house on Moor Street, Fitzroy. Kim joined a couple of weeks later with Alex to find, of course, that he lived on the opposite side of the river to all the musos.

Using whatever contacts he had, Kim chased up as much work as he could and found good support from Mark Burchett from Premier/Vamp. 'I said "can you get me some solo gigs? I need to earn some money." So I got a residency at the GB in Richmond.' The Great Britain Hotel in East Richmond was the centre of the Melbourne musical universe at that time. Perched above the train line, the GB was always dark, beer-soaked and completely minimal. There was a pool table, plastic beer pots for beer, some wooden stools and a low standing stage. In the era before cigarettes were banned in venues, you'd come home reeking of smoke even if you were there at two in the afternoon when the place was empty. For just $2 on any given night you could see Melbourne's music royalty: Spiderbait, Magic Dirt, Meanies, Christbait, Guttersnipes, Throwaways, Bored!, Warped, The Dirty Three. And Kim Salmon.

I'd lean against the back wall in the dark and watch the crowd surfing and pogoing in front of the low stage. Grunge regalia was in full swing with reverberations of Nirvana, Pearl Jam and Soundgarden on show. Flannel shirts, Doc Martens, Converse All Stars and cut off army pants were de rigour for the younger patrons. There were lots of second-hand suede or leather jackets, and the more wizened crowd wore op shop suits, shirts and waist coats. One afternoon I was there playing pool when in walked two bone fide Melbourne Mafia Maurice Frawley and Spencer P Jones. Spencer slapped a coin on the table and got two beers before proceeding to annihilate us on the pool table. Such was the destruction that he had the time and disregard to declare halfway through, 'I'm going to take a shit.' The game finished with Spencer and Maurice five balls clear.

It wasn't just the GB. St Kilda was still a strong hold with the Greyhound, Espy and Prince of Wales as the premier venues. Meanwhile, Fitzroy was building momentum with the Punters Club and Evelyn Hotel, along with the Tote in Collingwood. Richmond was perhaps becoming the epicentre with the Corner Hotel, reborn after years of neglect. These pubs were universally dark, dirty, covered in band posters and full of music. The crowds packed tightly into sweaty, smoky band rooms, all moving as one dazed but exultant organism as the band blasted from the stage. The music took root in these brutally loud, deliberately toxic subterranean hell pits.

There was a strong community of artists who played and hung out in pubs regularly, watching each other's bands. These artists were extremely niche, but for those in the know seeing Link Meanie talking at the bar or Ashley Naylor walking past were major sightings. The live music was backed up with a network of enviable record shops principally Au Go Go, Missing Link and Greville Records. And underneath all of this was community radio, perhaps Melbourne's greatest musical asset. In this town, music was everything.

Melbourne music would go through a decline in the 2000s with pokies, high rent and gastro pub culture driving some music venues to the wall. The Continental Café on Greville Street, a superb semiseated cabaret-style venue, was the first to go in an atrophy that would soon see the Richmond Club catering for polo top wearers from the suburbs; the Punters Club trading music for pizzas; the Espy fending off development and the Palais fighting off decay. Even the mighty Tote closed its doors. But the Tote fought its way back — the music industry got organised through SLAM and Music Victoria and advocated hard and smart, using data about the economic impact of live music to overturn unfavourable legislation and give the venue another chance. Today, in 2019, there are more venues than ever, and Melbourne rightly holds the title of music capital of the world.[1]

For Kim, early 90s Melbourne represented a rebirth and it started with the Great Britain Hotel.

> *Nick Wheelhouse, the proprietor, said, 'I'll give you Mondays but you 'oughta get some guests, make something special about it.' And he was very helpful. He did the mixing so I didn't have to get a mixer. I was looking for guests, whoever I could find. I got Charlie Owen, Andrew Entsch to play some bass for me, and one week I got Warren Ellis.*

Warren Ellis came from a musical house and picked up piano, accordion, flute, guitar and, most famously, violin. 'I found myself playing classical music, but listening to AC/DC, Black Sabbath, Led Zeppelin and The Birthday Party. I was playing these instruments that were seemingly disconnected to the music I was listening to.' In the late 80s, Warren started a busking holiday in Europe, developing a free form, expressive style away from the structures of a band. In the early 90s, he returned to the now flourishing Melbourne, and spent a year scrubbing toilets and cleaning dishes before running into an old friend who said, by chance, 'Hey, you play violin, don't you?' and invited him to join the band Busload of Faith. 'They stuck a guitar pick up on the violin with an elastic band, and my brother would give me effects pedals that I'd turn up to ten to see what would happen' (Warren Ellis). Tony Pola saw the band and invited himself to play drums, which led Kim Salmon to come along to one of the shows sometime later.

> *And that's when I met Kim. He'd come back to town, and it was this unusual period with people like Dave McCombe, Dave Graney, Roland Howard, Charlie Marshall and Kim — people who'd been in bands I'd followed in the 80s — they'd all come back to Melbourne. They were already elder statemen of the local scene. I arrived in Melbourne at this time when there were these incredibly talented people who'd already done something* (Warren Ellis).

After one of Kim's solo shows at the GB, Kim asked Warren if he'd join him on stage one night and before long Warren was sitting in Kim's kitchen carving out violin or flute accompaniments to Kim's songs.

> *We used to play a song* Kim's Dirt, *(a melody that Kim wrote on guitar)* Desensitised, Words From a Woman to Her Man, *a version of* Suzanne *(the Leonard Cohen cover). They were really fabulous those nights. It was fabulous for me, the fact that he was really open to embracing a violin and flute* (Warren Ellis).

Through the Monday night solo shows, Kim revisited some of his old material and reimagined it, but he was also writing new songs, songs that took him places the Surrealists didn't enable him to reach. The Surrealists had, by now, produced four albums: a substantial body of work with its own baggage, and the band by this stage exerted force over the song choices. The conditions that applied to assembling the songs for 'Essence' for instance, where any material would at least get a run, no longer applied. 'Now half the material would get stomped on by the band. They would say, "I don't want to play this." So instead I'd play them with Warren who tended to know what to do with them.' The songs ranged from the very sparse to the increasingly embellished. Kim was responding to the hyper-creative atmosphere, picking up the sparks from his guest collaborators and opening up new lines of enquiry.

A community of musicians was hanging around the Great Britain — Joel Silbersher (God, Hoss), John Nolan (Bored), Jim White (Dirty Three) and many others. And as the crowds for Kim's Monday night residency grew, his guest artists became more varied until 'one day I got a whole band up — Warren, Andrew Entsch and Jim White as well.'

> *All of a sudden we found ourselves with STM, this really fabulous band. I don't even know if he was trying to get a band together or if it just happened. There was something really unusual about the sound of that band. Andrew came from this jazz background; he was very open musically and a beautiful soul. Jim has such a unique style of playing and there was something wild and unfettered and unpredictable to what I was doing. And Kim is such a phenomenal guitar player — he has the chops but he does it in his own way. He can really rip something out but does it in his own way. Kim was the only one who was holding it all together, and then Kim would wig out! It was a really, really fabulous and exciting band.* (Warren Ellis)

Kim kept doing the solo shows while his backing band, the amorphously titled STM, started revving up. All the while, he was still busy with Beasts of Bourbon and Surrealists duties. When he wasn't playing, Kim fell in with a new crowd and hung out in Carlton with Mick Turner of Venom P Stinger and former Moodist player; Caroline Kennedy who was with the Plums; and Charlie Marshall who had been one half of Harem Scarem and was now making beautiful music with the Body Electric (another GB staple). Kim was riding on the success of 'Sin Factory', and was an underground celebrity in Melbourne. His generally reserved manner was off set by increasingly wild shirts and coats. Things had gotten to a really good point.

> *Moving to Melbourne was the best thing for me. Those Monday night gigs, it was all kind of happening. It got to be a really decent thing, bigger and bigger until eventually I said, 'I can't do this anymore. This will be my last one.' I ended with a big three-hour concert like Springsteen and it was packed to the rafters, absolutely packed. It was mental!*

As STM gathered momentum, Warren Ellis' friend bought the Bakers Arm Hotel in Fitzroy and invited Warren to 'get a band together and play in the corner instead of playing CDs.' Warren was already playing a few nights a week, but was up for anything so he contacted Jim White with the promise of a $50 payday. Mick Turner was brought in next, bearing a cassette of 'thirty improvisational minutes of Mick going absolutely batshit on guitar, and then some really beautiful chords' (Warren Ellis). The trio debuted at the Bakers shortly after. 'Kim was at that show and we played *Kim's Dirt,* because we needed a long improvisational piece because we had literally six or seven ideas and we had to fill three sets. So that's why it appears on the record. And we did Kim's song *Obvious is Obvious* as an instrumental' (Warren Ellis). And so, the Dirty Three were born.

Amongst all this musical action, Kim gathered a bunch of songs and set about making a new record. Kim characterises the result, 'Hey Believer', as not so much an STM album, but a solo album that featured a band on half the tracks. The album was recorded live at an old and now disused ABC orchestral studio.

> *We tracked the songs with Kim in an afternoon because we were playing live and we were kind of a crack group. We'd just bash it out, I don't think we ever rehearsed as such. It was all very exciting and otherworldly for me* (Warren Ellis).

> *We'd run through until we felt we had it, then commit it to tape and pick the best take. Recording this way is wonderful for bringing a band together. Having that experience recorded makes a record very special.*[2]

The album was released to a very warm reception. Linda took a great photo for the cover, and the album seemed to extend the surge of the 'Sin Factory' style Surrealists and concurrently reset Kim's identity. Creatively, the album was the natural progression past 'Sin Factory'. While that had been a band dominated product, 'Hey Believer' reintroduced the stripped-back and pointedly individual Kim Salmon, but also showcased his song writing and performance on the epic canvass of the STM songs. Long-time fan and former roadie to the Surrealists, Gareth Liddiard, loved it.

> *For my money, the album 'Hey Believer' is one of the best Australian records ever and one of the best ever in general … period. I'll never get sick of it.*[3] *Good songs, good band and production. It really is an amazing little record. It works perfectly from beginning to end. And it's as wild as it is highly evolved. It's not self-conscious, even though it's smart* (Gareth Liddiard).

The STM were on fire and they went on tour to promote the album. They were a strange amalgam of jazz, funk and folk and conjured a murky atmosphere. They were wild and theatrical, boiling up trouble on stage. At one show in Brisbane, the band was playing and the electricity went out, killing the PA. The band pulled a Kim Salmon salvage job and set up on a table in the middle of the room and delivered the remainder of the gig unplugged. They later stormed their way to Perth where Gareth Liddiard helped drive them around and unload their gear.

> *I was working with them the only time they came to Perth. They're still one of the best bands I've ever seen. It's hard to explain unless you break it into its component parts. Each part*

> *was singular, they all had really strong characters musically. Those parts were Kim, who had this malevolent voodoo kinda thing going on and a voice and style of writing and playing like no one else ever did. Then Andrew on the double bass plumbing the depths like a wooden submarine. Then Jim, one of the great rock drummers of all time. He's up there with Mitch and Bonham and all the great stylists. He is as original and as good as you can get. Then Warren, this fucking maniac on amplified violin. It's Warren Ellis for fuck sake. And they just go for it. 'Ballistic' doesn't do that band justice. They played* Susanne *by Leonard Cohen and it just kept going up and up and up and people were just standing there crying, it was so emotionally intense* (Gareth Liddiard).

There was a window where Kim and Warren in particular were working together intensely and frequently, and STM was like a storm gathering power and full of promise. And then one day, it just stopped. Kim was called for tour duty with the Beasts and Surrealists, and Warren and Jim went on tour with the Dirty Three and never came back.

> *Unfortunately for STM, the Dirty Three's sudden rise put an end to the band and now we can only mythologise these long-lost songs that are no longer around for scrutiny. And we will … they were fantastic! The best stuff ever. No one will know how good this band was unless they were there.*[4]

•••

It wasn't just in the song writing that the cracks in the Surrealists were showing. The band had been playing up hard, and doubly so as Beasts of Bourbon. 'It started to turn a bit sour because of the drug usage. Brian would carry on but he would never cross a line where he'd betray friends, but for Tony the lines got a bit more blurred. He was probably in heavier.'

The most intrusive manifestation of this was that, increasingly, Tony was letting the band down. He was never available. Opportunities were going begging and the band couldn't plan shows with any certainty that Tony would show up. As his drug use escalated, Tony ran with a harder crowd and took more liberties. Equipment started going missing, fights and drama became commonplace, and he withdrew from his bandmates. Even best mate Brian Hooper was getting frustrated with the Surrealists drummer.

> *There was a point after 'Sin Factory' when Tony wasn't turning up to gigs. He was being an unreliable thieving junkie and he had to be replaced. There was a point where it was just out of control and we sacked him. It was difficult for me because we were like brothers, but I understand where Kim was coming from because it couldn't continue the way it was* (Brian Hooper).

It was late 1993 when the band was offered a gig supporting Souixsie and the Banshees in Sydney, and Tony had gone to ground. When he finally surfaced he was in Perth — a long way from the gig in Sydney and in no position to play the show. With great regret, Kim and Brian made the decision to part ways with Tony and scrambled an emergency drum audition. Kim was not thrilled with this setback. 'By now the sound of the band was a *thing* and it was like trying to replace Brett Rixon.' They tried a couple of options, including Jim White but the honours went to Greg Bainbridge, who made an impact as much for his kit as his playing.

> *He had one of those weird drum kits, it was a fold up thing. He turned up to the audition and just played the shit out them. Even though it was a really weird drum kit and he had dreads and all of this stuff, he just seemed to work* (Brian Hooper).

Kim called Greg Bainbridge and told him to put on a fancy shirt, jump on the plane and get up to Sydney for the gig. 'So he shows up with his funny two-dimensional drum kit, wearing a fancy shirt … and shorts!' With no rehearsals and no notice, Greg played the full Surrealists set in front of a heaving crowd and absolutely killed it. He got the job.

•••

Manager Tim Pittman was in Perth, several hours behind the Eastern states, when he was awoken by the phone ringing. 'Someone says "this is Wendy from Michael Coppell's office. U2 have requested Kim Salmon and the Surrealists to support them on their 1993 Australian tour"' (Tim Pittman). Suitably shocked, Tim managed to ask a sensible question and found to his dismay that the U2 dates clashed with a European solo tour Kim had already booked in, so he regretfully declined. 'And Wendy says "I don't think you understand, U2 have asked Kim Salmon to support them on their Australian tour." And I said, "That's great but he won't be in the country, he'll be on tour." And Wendy said, "U2 *insist* on having Kim Salmon, how much money do you want?" So we made up some crazy amount of money and they just said "sure"' (Tim Pittman).

It turned out that Bono had contacted Mick Harvey, asking what bands to get for the tour: 'what bands didn't suck.' Mick Harvey told him The Cruel Sea and The Surrealists, and as luck would have it, The Cruel Sea couldn't do it, so The Surrealists were signed up. 'Our record company didn't believe it and thought it must have been for the Beasts of Bourbon!' The resultant tour played in all Australian capital cities to hundreds of thousands of fans. The U2 tour was the most rock star-ish moment of Kim's career, maybe even bigger than the rolling Big Day Out festivals of which he played a few. The crowds were massive, the perks were better and the energy was palpable. The presence of U2 was everywhere, from the stage sets to the catering, but the Surrealists didn't really cross paths with U2. 'We didn't actually meet most of the band. It was one of those situations where when they walked to the stage you have to get into your green room and you're not allowed to see them.' Bono was the exception; he posed for photos with Kim and Brian, and hung out with them behind the play. It was his first meeting with Bono that Kim remembers best. 'In the catering division one day, I accidentally tripped Bono over!' He pauses for effect. 'It was an accident.'

•••

In 1995, the Surrealists joined Nick Cave and the Bad Seeds in Europe, spending weeks on the road and playing hard. The days of dark Bad Seeds tour comportment had given way to a more ebullient experience and it was a fun tour. 'Nick liked to have dinner well after the gig so they'd find a restaurant somewhere and there always seemed be a big, long table like *The Last Supper*. The Surrealists were new so we'd always be sat up near Nick. There was lots of coke; everybody seemed to be trying to replace heroin with something and that was coke. There were some great nights going out with Nick.'

For Kim, 1995 was the year of near misses — mostly involving airports. The Surrealists were at the end of a six-week European run and due to fly out of Frankfurt, only a few hours drive from their last gig. It was their last night, so why not let their hair down? The next morning the three Surrealists woke up painfully, scraped themselves up and drove to Frankfurt airport with little time to spare. Looking for their flight number, they realised Frankfurt had the 'biggest airport in the world' with disparate terminals separated by vast distances. They were still scrambling madly for a terminal shuttle bus when their plane lifted off, bound for Australia, leaving the band forlornly handing over their tour earnings to book new flights.

Another Surrealists tour ended in London and after a long night of scotch, speed and no sleep, Kim, Brian and Greg stumbled out to meet their cab to the airport. But it didn't arrive. Wary of another missed flight, the trio flagged down a mini cab that offered them a share ride with another passenger. As Kim opened his brief case ('for some reason musos all had brief cases in those days. To hide stashes of plectrums and drugs, I suppose') the other passenger snatched out the envelope stuffed full of cash from their tour earnings and took off down the Brixton streets. Brian instantly gave chase, disappearing up the road while Kim and Greg fumed in the cab. He eventually came back panting, and said breathlessly:

> *'I've got good news and bad news.'*
> *'What's the bad news?'*
> *'He took off with the money.'*

Kim was crestfallen, but asked:

> *'What's the good news?'*
> *'I got in a couple of good punches!'*

This had soaked up precious time and after an angry cab ride they arrived at the airport with only ten minutes to spare. 'We went running up the gangway to the entrance of the plane and the guy said to me, "Excuse me sir, I can't let you in. Your breath smells of alcohol. If you choose to turn up intoxicated you are not getting on the plane."' Kim lost it and tried to argue his way onto the plane, but just proved the point to the contrary. They again lost their tickets and had to wait for another flight after Brian's dad wired over money for the fare. 'What is there to do at the airport? So we went to the bar. And then Iggy's band turned up.' Eric, Larry and Hal — not quite the Three Stooges but, being from Iggy's band, pretty close — enthusiastically joined the Surrealists for four hours drinking beer. At some point, Kim became vaguely aware of an increasingly irritated announcement blaring out, 'Will Mr Salmon and Mr Hooper PLEASE report to the departure gate!' Despite being four hours drunker, Kim and Brian managed to get on the plane. 'Maybe smelling of beer isn't as bad as smelling of whisky …'

On another 1995 trip, Kim was en route from Seattle to Spain via London. Despite horrible jet lag and another Tony Thewlis inspired night of scotch, Kim made Heathrow with time to spare. The flight to

Spain had a stopover. In Frankfurt. 'That should have sent warning bells already', but Kim navigated the airport mini city and got to his terminal without incident. 'I was quite relieved and had an hour to spare. I thought, "I'll have a read." I looked at the page of the book … and fell asleep.' Kim roused only as the gangway to the plane was pushed away, his protests met with a firm 'The departure gate is closed.' Many hours and frantic negotiations later, Kim finally boarded a plane to Madrid where a nervous-looking Spaniard escorted him to the gig he was due to play. 'The gig is hours late, but this is Spain, they don't care. I played at one in the morning.' After the show, Kim indicated he'd go back to the hotel but his host was having none of it: 'No way! This is Madrid. We party!' At some hour before sunlight, Kim was provided an envelope of cash and a firm commitment of transport to the airport for his flight to Barcelona the next morning. 'The flight was at 9am and he didn't show up. And *again* I didn't make the flight.' Kim eventually got to Barcelona, and after another late-night gig he packed up to go back to the hotel. There was no way he was missing another flight. His host looked at him reproachfully and exclaimed, 'The hotel? Are you kidding? This is Barcelona!' And I think you know how this story ends …

•••

The touring and songwriting for the new Surrealists album were set against the gloomy backdrop of the final dissolution of Kim and Linda's marriage. Having weathered many storms, their relationship ground to a halt when it became apparent to Linda that Kim and Caroline Kennedy were involved. Linda was furious and stormed out, taking Alex and Jack back to Perth where they remained. Back in Melbourne, Kim was a maelstrom of regret and self-recrimination. It was a painful time for them all.

> *I honestly think I tried to make things work as long as I could. It was a case of bridges burnt with friends, family, business*

associates, strangers ... For all the good things about her it was hard, hard work. I gave it the best shot I could and in the end she just wasn't able to see outside of her own framework. It was her way or the highway, basically. It wasn't that she was bloody minded, she just didn't have it in her to see things another way. I can't think of anybody who would have lasted that long in the relationship. I did the wrong thing, but maybe I was too lame to up and say 'fuck you, I won't put up with that shit' and I probably sabotaged things this way. There's always a lot more to the picture.

The mood of his relationship mess infiltrated Kim's compositions, and the new self-titled album was taking on a different appearance to earlier Surrealists works. 'My life was really getting into the mix; we were recording this just after I split up with Linda.' Lyrically the album contains ambiguous characters that may or may not be the composer, and the atmosphere is dark and reflects an undercurrent of pain and regret. 'This was more immediate; the songs came up in a short space of time and therefore they were closer to my life than they had been in the past.' The album presents some powerful songs with both echoes of 'Sin Factory' such as *What's Inside Your Box,* and forecasts to the album that would follow, such as *I'm Gonna See You Compromised* or *Innersense.* The piano features to great effect on the album, creating a distinctly different palette, particularly on *Dragging Out the Truth,* which also successfully outlines a new look Salmon vocal melody, and was 'as good a thing as I've ever written'.

Recorded again with Tony Cohen, the album had good airplay but didn't connect with the audience in the same way 'Sin Factory' did. Reflecting Kim's difficult personal circumstances, the album's mood attracted one infamous review — 'ugly hateful music for ugly hateful people.' Not taking this critique personally, Kim embraced the slogan and put stickers on the album cover as a promotional tool.

The band itself was having serious personnel difficulties. Greg and Brian regarded each other well and continued to play well and put on great shows, but they clashed at times and the musical partnership was not natural or satisfying. 'The chemistry just wasn't there, the sort of magic that you need to make new material work wasn't going to happen. It had run out of some kind of creative steam, even though as a machine it was running hot.' The vibe was bad and attendances were starting to falter. '"Sin Factory" was the apex. The self-titled album that followed was more of a dead-end tangent.'

The cohesion of the band eroded further during the recording process as little moving factions formed and dissipated. 'Sometimes it was the three of us. There were some real moments, but it was never the three musketeers like me, Pola and Hoops.' Reflecting this, Brian started branching out by playing with Roland S Howard, Charlie Marshall, Spencer P Jones, and writing his own material. He enjoyed playing with new people, crafting more melodic bass lines 'instead of dunk dunk dunk', and quickly progressed as a musician. The Surrealists, or the version the band had become, were starting to shit him.

> *Up until then it had been like the three musketeers, us against the world, and it just didn't feel that way for me anymore. It just didn't feel the same. It wasn't the same quirky thing it used to be. I stayed 'til the last gig of the tour of the self-titled album and I just said quietly to Kim at the end of the gig in Perth 'I can't do this anymore. We've supported every band around the world, we've done this and we've done that, travelled all over the place. I'm away from my family all the time making a couple of hundred bucks a week. I'm over it'* (Brian Hooper).

Brian's decision coincided with a big offer for the band to tour the States. Kim was aware that Brian was having serious misgivings about the Surrealists, but hoped that he could continue on for the US tour and rekindle the band's spirit. But then the pointed message came from the promoter — *any* drug use would land the band in big trouble in the States. Kim knew that this might be a bridge too far for the band in its current configuration, and the stakes were too high if things went pear shaped on tour. 'So I had to say, "Brian …" And he said, "it doesn't matter, I'm leaving anyway." So he left before I could sack him.' Kim was devastated to lose Brian and, although the separation was amicable, they were both hurting. The three musketeers were now down to one. Over the next few years, the friendship between Kim and Brian slowed to a walk and eventually a long silence elapsed between them. Kim played a lot of music with Brian, and spent a lot of time with him on the road as band mates and as friends. They'd rubbed each other up the wrong way at times, and fallen out badly, but when it was all boiled down, they were brothers in arms.

> *Brian was a complex guy really. On the one hand, he was fun-loving, but on the other hand he was really full of angst, trying to work out what was right and wrong and trying really hard to do the right thing. And sometimes the right thing might be to do the wrong thing, but he was always guided by the right thing to do! To me he was a very moral, rule following guy who totally wanted to ignore the rules, but he had a strong moral compass. He was loyal, hardworking and always up for the challenge.*

Reflecting on why the silence between them lasted so long, Kim ventilates the many, complicated twists and turns that lie within friend and family systems, but concludes:

> *There was a whole bunch of shit; it was too much of a can of worms. Look, I wussed out. I didn't do the right thing in those years, I know. But he forgave me. There was a gig somewhere and I saw Brian and met Ninevah, and she was really nice and forgiving and he was nice and forgiving, and I thought* oh, how hard was that? *And we became friends again.*

•••

Later in 1995, Kim was courted by Space Baby, a management company in the States who flew him to the US for some solo shows. Kim was increasingly aware that his international following, while niche, was significant and involved some very notable musical figures. To his surprise, Henry Rollins showed up in LA and Jon Spencer in New York, and he connected again with Mark Arm from Mudhoney. Kim and Mark hatched a plan for the Surrealists to support Mudhoney on tour in the US, and Kim returned to Australia to start making the arrangements.

But before that could unfold, Mark phoned up. The tour was off — Steve Turner left Mudhoney. This was shattering for the band and disappointing for the Surrealists. But Kim had an idea: What if he hooked up with the other guys from Mudhoney, write some new songs and do some shows with the Surrealists? 'A week later, Mark called up and said, "are you serious about that?" Before long, Mudhoney flew me over to Seattle'. He spent a few weeks there writing with the band.

> *I had hooks and things in mind, and it was going to be a record with a pop aspect to it. It was not going to be Mudhoney, it was going to be another band. Dan seemed to be quite keen for it but for Mark it was a bit too much pop music. So that got shelved, but it was a good time. Fact was we wrote about eight songs, we had a great time, I loved it.*

A few years later Bang! released the songs as *Kim Salmon and the Guys from Mudhoney.*

Back in Australia, the Surrealists found a new bass player to replace Brian Hooper. Stu Thomas was playing in no less than four bands when it was suggested to him that he should try out for Kim Salmon and the Surrealists. Stu knew of Kim Salmon. 'I had clocked Kim walking down to the milk bar when we both lived in Wellington Street, Collingwood, across the road from one another, but never having met. I remember some knowing glances being exchanged, like, "Oh, another muso".' but he wasn't that familiar with the Surrealists' repertoire. A phone call from Greg Bainbridge later, and Stu was loaded up with a cassette tape of Surrealists songs to learn.

> *And so that's exactly what I did: I locked my bedroom door, picked up the bass, and played that tape to death and just drilled those songs into my head and fingers, every waking hour, constantly for days on end. I just committed it all to memory. No notes were made. The rehearsal came around and we went through all the songs, and I think even some new stuff. Kim's early comment was 'I need more from the bass', so I turned right up. It was then I realised we were going to be a loud band. Kim really transformed before my eyes into a seething rock entity, when we began playing the music. I was impressed* (Stu Thomas).

Kim and Greg were impressed too. Stu was welcomed into the band with the instruction that he organise a passport immediately, since his first act with the band would be a thirty-six date European tour! 'This was a big deal for me, because I had never left Australia at this point, let alone been on an international rock tour. An exciting time for me' (Stu Thomas). Stu managed to land his passport in the nick of time, have one or two Surrealists rehearsals and face up to his very first show with the band at the Public Bar in Melbourne on the eve of the European tour. 'What sticks in my mind from that was a drunken fan repeatedly telling the band: "You two guys have big heads but *you* have a small head!" He meant me …' (Stu Thomas). More useful was the feedback from a friend who said 'when I hit the low E note, it was almighty loud and the walls shook. I knew I was on the right track then' (Stu Thomas).

The Surrealists had survived personal upheaval, lost one of the great Australian rock rhythm sections and watched the sales of their last recording dip. The highwater mark, in terms of commercial appeal and industry accolades, lay behind them in 'Sin Factory' in which the sound, look and identity of the band was so coherent and strong. With the changes of personnel and sound, the band had lost

HEINRICHSALLEE 2
D - AACHEN
52062

KIM SALMON & THE SURREALISTS EUROPE 1994

18.01	GERMANY	AACHEN	AUTONOMES ZENTRUM
19.01	GERMANY	BOCHUM	BAHNHOF LANGENDREER
20.01	DENMARK	COPENHAGEN	BARBUE
21.01	GERMANY	HAMBURG	KL. MARKTHALLE
22.01	GERMANY	BREMEN	WEHRSCHLOß
23.01	GERMANY	BERLIN	HUXLEY'S JR.
24.01	TSCHECH REPUBLIC	PRAG	BUNKR
25.01	GERMANY	DRESDEN	STAR CLUB
26.01	OFF DAY		
27.01	GERMANY	MÜNSTER	ODEON
28.01	GERMANY	KÖLN	UNDERGROUND
29.01	BELGIUM	KORTRIJK	DE KREUN
30.01	FRANCE	ST. OUEN -PARIS	LES COLONNES
31.01	GERMANY	FRANKFURT	COOKY'S
01.02	GERMANY	ULM	KRAATHALLE
02.02	OFF DAY		
03.02	AUSTRIA	EBENSEE	KINO
04.02	ITALY	FIRENZE	AUDITORIUM FLOG
05.02	ITALY	VALENZA PO	PALOMOR
06.02	ITALY	MEZZAGO	BLOOM
07.02	TRAVEL DAY		
08.02	AUSTRIA	WIEN	SCENE WIEN
09.02	GERMANY	MÜNCHEN	KULTURSTATION
10.02	SWITZERLAND	BERN	ISC
11.02	SWITZERLAND	LA CHAUS DE FOND	BIKINI TEST
12.02	SWITZERLAND	ZÜRICH	ROTE FABRIK
13.02	SWITZERLAND	BASEL	KULTURWERKSTATT
14.02	OFF DAY		
15.02	GERMANY	WEIKERSHEIM	W 71
16.02	GERMANY	PASSAU	ZEUGHAUS
17.02	GERMANY	STUTTGART	RÖHRE
18.02	GERMANY	KREFELD	KULTURFABRIK
19.02	GERMANY	ENGER	FORUM
20.02	GERMANY	HILDESHEIM	VIER LINDEN
21.02	OFF DAY		
22.02	GERMANY	NÜRNBERG	KOMM
23.02	AUSTRIA	SALZBURG	ARGE NONNTAL
24.02	AUSTRIA	INSBRUCK	UTOPIA
25.02	AUSTRIA	DORNBIRN	SPILEBODEN
26.02	FRANCE	MÜLLHOUSE	NOUMATROFF
27.02	GERMANY	SAARBRÜCKEN	BALLHAUS

momentum. But there were European and USA tours booked so Kim, Greg and new bass player Stu picked themselves up and hit the road. And something started to happen …

> *They were just fluid and wonderful shows! What a place to debut a band, off on a big tour. It was just a big party! Stu totally went for it and it was great to see Greg flourish and not be stultified by whatever the band had become. And that's when it started. I found there was all these songs that I had lying around that were going nowhere and once Stu was in there it all fell into place. Greg and Stu just lapped it up and there was a whole repertoire there to take to Europe and we found that with every sound check there was a new song.*

As the tours went on, the band freed up and bounced off each other. They collected new grooves at each new city, and on the tour bus between gigs Kim would come up with lyrics and melody to lay over the top. Each new song was simply referred to as the name of the city in which it was created. Stu added an element of classical music training to the band and helped Kim with arrangements, broadening the palette to include horns that the new songs seemed to scream out for.

> *When I joined I definitely brought more of a funk element into the Surrealists, as well as backing vocals, and knowledge of other instruments, like horns. I also liked odd rhythms, as did Kim, although I came at it from a different angle. I felt the three of us were individually breaking new ground musically on our chosen instruments, and more so when we came together* (Stu Thomas).

After the Europe tour, they set off quickly for the USA. It was Stu's second overseas trip and an eye opener. He felt like he was stepping into the set of a sitcom, but it was all real! The tour commenced with drama as their tour bus — a green Mystery Mobile style van — broke down in the desert between LA and San Francisco. At risk of blowing their first gig, Greg, Stu and tour manager Kirsten desperately rang tow trucks and mechanics to fix the van when they saw 'Kim sail by in the promoter's coupé, but she has spotted us and now has to turn around somewhere, double back and squeeze us all in. We're running real late, but with some speed-racer driving on her part we just make the gig in San Francisco' (Stu Thomas). In the audience was Jon Spencer who said to Stu, 'You sound like you're playing reggae basslines', which pleased the Surrealists bass player no end.

The Surrealists US tour was a break out for the band, and cram packed full of memorable moments. They rolled into Detroit and located the cleverly named venue, The Magic Stick (aka The Majestic) only to realise it doubled as a bowling alley. A bunch of the bowling lanes had been removed to make way for a stage and some pool tables, but four alleys still operated and the whole venue retained the late night carnival atmosphere of an oldschool ten pin hang out. Illinois held an even more unlikely setting: a venue that doubled as a laundromat. 'People watched the band while waiting for their tumblin' clothes!' (Stu Thomas). For a band founded on surrealism and deconstructionism, it all made perfect sense.

They mingled with some notables on the tour as well. In Chicago they met Bill Callahan from Smog and hung out with Fred Scheider's band, The B-52's, while in Tucson, Arizona, the Surrealists walked into the hotel's downstairs lobby and who else did they see 'working some teenage jailbait, but the suavest of all — Tav Falco!' (Stu Thomas) The Salmon/Hooper/Pola Surrealists had supported Tav Falco back in Australia, and Kim was over the moon to once again connect with the very oblique artist. Back in LA they supported and met Southern Culture on the Skids, and in New York, they were 'invited to a Rollins book launch, where Henry is visually floored at the sight of Kim. "Kim Salmon" he says with gravity and admiration, in that voice of his, when we appear' (Stu Thomas).

There were close calls too. In New Orleans, Kim, Greg and Stu were walking around Louis Armstrong Park, not far from the French

Quarter. A casual glance at any US travel guide will tell you that the Louis Armstrong Park is one of the most dangerous places in the Western world. The unassuming Surrealists stumbled across a guy trying to sell them 'weed', but on closer inspection it was clearly dodgy looking crack. The Surrealists awkwardly declined and set off down Dumaine Street in search of some coffee and beignets. But it wouldn't be that easy. Offended at the rejection, their wannabe drug dealer, proceeded to scream:

> *YOU'RE LUCKY I'M NOT A BAD N***ER. IF I WAS A BAD N***ER I COULD SHOOT YOU MOTHER FUCKERS RIGHT HERE AND NOBODY'D EVER KNOW!*

Rattled, Stu pulled out a $5 bill to try and appease him. Unsure of the going rate for purchased-under-duress New Orleans crack-masquerading-as-weed, Stu bleakly asked for change, sounding a little like Oliver Twist requesting more slop for dinner. The dealer's associates started to march over towards the three Australians, all swagger and menace, before 'Greg yanks us all out there quick-smart, as a large dark and threatening presence hovers in the distance' (Stu Thomas).

The touring was hard work, with long drives, bad accommodation and not much sleep, but the music was happening effortlessly, and it was clear there was a new record to make. Initially Jon Spencer was signed on to record the album, but at the last minute he was forced to pull out. But big deal! 'We'd had a gutful of labels and studios, we don't need them telling us what to do, fuck 'em! We can do this ourselves!' It was only natural that the album would be called 'Ya Gotta Let Me Do My Thing'. They tried out the recording conditions in Kim's house on a four track, and the first thing they played — with no rehearsal — was *The Zipper*, the version of which made it to the final album. 'We thought that was so easy, let's do an album of it!' A few calls later and Kim's weather-beaten house in Carlton was filled with recording gear. A reel-to-reel recorder in his bedroom would capture the singing in the hallway, the guitars in the bathroom, the bass in the kitchen and the brass and strings wherever else there was room. Manager Tim Pittman made a mercy dash from Sydney to handle logistics and oversee the mixdown of brass and strings onto one or two of only eight analogue tracks available.

The songs that they had gathered from sound checks around the world felt very at home in Carlton, and they fell into place effortlessly. After the more rock oriented 'Sin Factory' and 'Self Titled' albums, this collection of songs was a return to the wild, varied, kooky and unexpected tunes of the Surrealists' first album. *I Wont Tell* kicks off with a distinctive Greg Bainbridge drum beat — cool, relaxed and cruisy. Kim introduces a staccato, modern soul kind of guitar line while Stu's bass strolls along underneath it all. Kim gives one of his greatest vocal recordings, ranging from baritone night club sleaze to unhinged falsetto and all manner of growls and inflections in between. *You're Such a Freak* uses the *Freak* motif in an ambiguous, one-sided conversation that is both amusing and somehow touching, set to mildly funky, jangling guitar.

You've Got Layers is a misshapen blues-ish stomp with deranged slide guitar; *The Zipper* peels off into three sections of outer space organ, disjointed timing and robotic bass lines; *The Connoisseur* is plaintive cry from a fictitious, narcissistically deluded but damaged rock star underscored by emotive violin; and throughout the album there are sections of weird, Scientist sounding drum patterns or bursts of atonal, dissonant guitar. The songs were as strong as they were varied, and the week of recording in the Carlton house had been as affirming as it was productive. Next, they just had to find someone to get the homespun recording ready for release. Tim Pittman suggested Jim Dickinson.

> *Now Jim Dickinson is Alex Chilton's producer for 'Like Flies on Sherbet' and the third Big Star album and in my mind was as legendary as Alex. He had this anarchy that had kind of driven me in this particular direction. So I just thought 'wow, let's do*

> *it'. When the album was presented to Jim, he declared 'I hear so much of myself in Kim's music, that I think I must, I* have *to produce this' ... So everything we'd recorded in our kitchen with all our grandiose ideas, I dumped it into his lap and said 'here'. I spent a week in Memphis with Jim Dickinson, and it was one of the best experiences of my life. Jim said that anybody who plays rock and roll should come to Memphis, and in a way that's what that was about, him mixing it and everything was like him bringing it home in a way, to get treated properly.*

'Ya Gotta Let Me Do My Thing' benefited from its time in Memphis. It was a stellar record, one of Kim's best, and a validation of the new Surrealists configuration. Larry Hardy declared it the template of how all records should sound.

> *If you listen to the 1997 album 'Ya Gotta Let Me Do My Thing', each of us is pushing the envelope, and it's us having fun with it too. That was a really creative time. I felt like my joining had reignited Kim in some way, and he was enjoying the band a bit more, after the apparent trials of the previous self-titled album. I was so green and my wide-eyed wonder must've rubbed off a bit — when it wasn't annoying the shit out of them* (Stu Thomas).

The album both reinvented the Surrealists and honoured the origins of the band, with the feel of the new recording seemingly connected to 'Hit Me With The Surreal Feel', the Surrealists first record. 'It's very much those two albums are the ones, they are the moments when things were caught rather than rendered. Captured fleeting moments, and that's what I was really looking for. It's all going to fall apart at any second but it's there, it's incredible. It sounds wild and untamed.' A new form of the band had emerged too, this was not the transitional Surrealists of the self-titled album but a whole new thing. And it worked.

The Surrealists with Stu Thomas and Greg Bainbridge, if ever there was a band with chemistry going on it was that version of the Surrealists. I'd get an idea and think 'oh I've got to get it past Stu' who wanted to be the rugged individualist on every level, and Greg who was very sardonic. But when we'd get together and play it was something special.

In 2017, 'Ya Gotta Let Me Do My Thing' was reissued on vinyl and the band launched it at the Gasometer Hotel on Smith Street, Collingwood.

We had a jam to rehearse for the show, the first time in decades. Greg has got really bad tinnitus and he wanted to see how it would go. And it was fantastic! He played like I've never seen someone play, with such a hunger and he had all the chops. He was on. Totally metronomic, really just going for it and the songs came to life. You just added water and there they were. We were just grinning the whole time. Then a day or so later he said, 'it's crap, my heads aching, I just can't do it'. That was very disappointing. There was something really special about that band, that line up, the travels we did and things just happened organically. It took my playing, what I was doing, to a whole other level.

16

Caught in the Zipper

In August 1997, Kim met Sandra at a bar, and struck up an attraction based on 'alcohol and hygiene', according to Sandra. Sandra was from Perth, a literate character with affection for Italian Opera, bossa nova and P-funk. But when she saw the Surrealists she was taken with this 'contemporary band', and soon after, it's singer. Kim had recently broken up with Caroline Kennedy, and after a few adventures together, Sandra came from Perth to move in with him.

Around this time, Kim had rekindled his friendship with Dave Faulkner. The Surrealists had just done a tour with the Hoodoo Gurus, when Dave suggested to Kim that he'd like to get a new project off the ground together. 'He said he wouldn't mind getting involved in some dance stuff. At the time I was pretty interested in electronic music. I always had a bit of an interest in that path because of Suicide and Kraftwerk. He said he knew some guys — Justin Frew and Stuart McCarthy — who'd done remixes of the Gurus.' Kim's interest in drum machines and electronica stretched back to his experimental solo shows in London at the end of the Scientists, but he had never fully explored its potential, so he signed up immediately.

Kim flew up to Sydney and with Dave, Justin and Stuart, he 'basically pushed squares around on a computer screen', creating songs on a computer-based music program. Over the next few months, the quartet delved deep into song writing and recording, assembling a collection of songs that felt like an album, splitting the credits equally no matter who *actually* wrote the song. 'It was a very laborious day-to-day thing, a lot of discussion about where things should fall into place. All of the things on the album were sampled and sequenced, even my guitar lines — I'd play it until we got a decent bar of something and I've already mentioned Dave's exacting ears — so everything was in time and on the beat'.

While in Memphis a couple of years prior, Kim had tied one on at the Antenna Bar, a wild night that capped off a perfect stay in Memphis. This seemed a good moniker for the new band, and so the project became Antenna. Featuring vocals by Dave and Kim and guests Matt Thomas (The Mavis's) and The Divinyls' Chrissy Amphlett, the album 'Installation' made a splash. Released on Mushroom Records, the band's debut gig was a huge stadium based *Concert of the Century* to celebrate twenty-five years of the label, followed by the Big Day Out festival shows. It was an auspicious start.

> *It was a band on a level way beyond anything I'd been used to, it wasn't garage rock that was for sure. We had guest backing vocalists and strings, really professional playing. I look at that performance on Recovery and think 'God, how did I manage to sing that in tune?!' Dave really coached me well, he was really on my case!*

The signature song from the album was Kim's composition *Come on Spring*. It charted, was a radio staple and made the Triple J Hottest 100, the national broadcaster's youth oriented radio vote for the best songs of the year. 'It's the song that people remember. It struck a chord with people. It's that perennial thing, every year its spring again. The spring racing carnival. Gardening. There's a whole lot of connections. So my twenty-five per cent of that has done me well over the years.'

•••

One night, Kim and his current partner Maxine invites our family to her house party in Northcote, with Kim and his good friend Mike Stranges as entertainment. My daughter Hannah, and Kim's daughter Emma watched the duo's performance from Maxine's mezzanine balcony, looking down past the large art works on the expansive walls to the stage — a Persian rug on the polished concrete floor — below. Between sets, Sharon says to Kim, 'I love *Come On Spring*, it gets me through the winters. What's it about …?'

> *Originally I had this idea for a knock off of Serge Gainsbourg, you can sort of hear if you listen to the chords it's vaguely like* Bonnie and Clyde. *But when I brought it to the band Antenna, Justin and Stu put a beat to it and it had this curious sound. I played it over the phone to Sandra who suggested that it sounded like spring was going to happen, that we'd had enough of winter and it was time for spring. And I thought it does have this crisp vibe to it. It's since been suggested that maybe this song is about always being the bridesmaid and never the bride. But I think that was Dave Faulkner projecting that onto the song. Anyway, you can make up your own mind.*

Come on Spring was the most accessible song Kim had ever written and released, and with the attention it was attracting, it seemed that Kim would at last land a big fish. The industry, however, had other ideas. Some of the suits didn't believe Kim's efficacy in dissonance qualified him for a hit record and didn't get behind the project. Meanwhile, the record company was taken over by a Murdoch-owned company. In the transition, key parts of the machine failed to fire for Antenna, most critically the distribution of the record into record shops. The songs were on the radio but there was nowhere to buy the album. Without all the parts lining up, the record didn't perform, and regrettably, Antenna was soon put to bed.

•••

In 1999, Kim and Sandra were preparing to get married, and as a pre-wedding honeymoon they set off to Berlin with a theatre company.

> *Kim was doing the music for a play and there was a big international theatre festival in Berlin in July 1999 and they were invited to represent Australia. Kim did the music for the play, it was a bleak study of share house politics. Kim was a musician living downstairs in the apartment building, creating music and annoying the other residents. It was just Kim playing his Telecaster, creating very atmospheric music* (Sandra Salmon).

Kim had been commissioned by Ranter's Theatre Company to create a live soundtrack for their play, *Features of Blown Youth*. He was paid well to write and perform, and when the play debuted he found himself on stage in a car wreck, atop an elaborate scaffolding system representing share rooms. 'I was meant to be a neighbour, a bum kind of guy with a guitar disturbing the peace. I was kind of like a cast member but playing guitar music'. The play had seasons in Melbourne, Sydney, Perth and a run in Berlin and gave Kim a taste for this mode of creation. 'Somehow I got involved in another production around

2003, a play called *The Wall* and they wanted something electronic this time.' Kim set to work creating an atmospheric, electric sound scape using a state-of-the-art AKAI S5000 sampler. 'It was a brilliant piece of machinery. I loved it. I recorded a whole bunch of loops, stuff off my record collection, live samples, I got Stu to play his P Bass, some synth and organ stuff, a 'croc-a-phone' — my son Gene's baby crocodile toy with a xylophone in it.' This conglomeration of samples still lurks somewhere in Kim's music room, and you wouldn't bet against it re-emerging into his work again one day.

•••

While Kim was entering the theatre, the Surrealists continued to write and perform. With the introduction of horns and the emergence of a shonky, urban soul and funk sound, the band's identity started to mutate and morph. By mid 1999, Kim announced the end of the Surrealists, and with Leon de Bruin on trumpet and Michael Redman on saxophone joining Kim, Greg and Stu, Kim Salmon and the Business were born. 'At some point, I had the idea let's just change the name because we're not very surreal anymore. And I wanted to write some pop music because I had the thirst for it from Antenna.' Kim instructed the band to put on suits and they hit the road, touring hard. The song writing flood gates that had opened for 'Ya Gotta Let Me Do My Thing' remained wide open, and soon another album was in the pipeline.

Dave Faulkner was brought in to produce The Business album, but his exacting approach clashed with the feel of the band. Dave was critical of the horn players who he thought were full of pretension, playing bum notes and prone to repetition, and Greg's 'overplaying' on drums caught Dave's attention too often. After Dave told Kim to 'get some players', they amicably agreed that it wasn't going to work, and Kim finished off the record without him. The album, 'Record', again caught the attention of Triple J and Kim was getting more airplay than ever before. 'I had all of the chances handed to me. The Business was the most successful thing radio-wise I'd ever been involved in.' When Kim landed a big new publishing advance, it seemed commercial success was knocking on his door.

But the Business were not an easy band to keep under control. Kim tried to accommodate his new horn playing band mates, but the morays of the jazz world seemed an uneasy fit. Demands for better hotel rooms, complaints about pay, unreliability, a tendency to showboat and a rotating cast of players kept Kim on edge and the band struggled to coalesce. Keeping them on the road was proving expensive, and Kim had soon sunk his publishing advance down the drain. 'Things kind of imploded with the band. It wasn't a good time. I had to take charge … and didn't go about it in the right way. I offered deals to everyone … and there was sort of a thought that because I was offering them something I was trying to rip them off, but I was trying to give them a good deal.' Kim's endeavours to run the band like a business resulted in a mutinous band meeting to which Kim was not invited, and marked the beginning of the end for the band. The first casualty was Greg, then Leon and Michael. 'It was like I sacked the whole band, I felt like some sort of dictator, despot.'

They regrouped with new drummer Tarrick Smallman, and added horn players Paul Williamston and Ben Grant. Tarrick, however, was a bit *too* metronomic, and the horn players were too unhinged. Worse, the crowd numbers were retreating. 'People weren't really getting into it and I could see this was going to take lots of time and money. Sandra was pretty dark on the fact that all the money had gone on the band.' Kim assessed his situation and concluded the unthinkable. 'So I kind of thought "oh I'll just get a day job", and I kind of just gave up on having a band at this time.'

•••

During the rise and fall of the Business, Sandra and Kim tied the knot. Sandra reflected on the early stages on their marriage: 'We were so poor when we got married. We didn't have heating, didn't have

a car. We were like church mice.' When Sandra fell pregnant, expecting baby Gene, she got behind the notion that Kim get a day job. So, while she returned to university to get a teaching qualification, Kim started working in a warehouse. 'I ended up working at a place called Stomp, a record distribution company. I had a day job, and just made music 'cos I wanted to more than anything else.'

Gene Salmon was born in 2000, named by Clare Moore after genius jazz drummer Gene Krupa. True to his namesake, Gene would go on to be a good drummer in his teens, as well as a flute player and artist. In the mornings, Kim would hang out at the nearby Ray's café and spend time with Gene, before heading to Stomp.

> *He said he didn't like working because he had less time for music. But the interesting thing is, in the years he was working he produced more music than at any other time in his career. He produced a Hoodoo Gurus album, produced the Cassanovas and Mach Pelican, recorded SALMON, 'Wallpaper', Surrealists,*

> *'Earnest', the Business, all the licencing deals overseas, and did some work with Nick Cave ... he was a busy guy. He went overseas quite a lot while we were together, always writing songs, playing gigs, doing recordings* (Sandra Salmon).

In fact, over the next decade, Kim would release albums of new original material with no less than ten different groups in a sustained period of creative output. It started with 'E(a)rnest'. 'I had some wacky idea about share house folk music. When I was living with Caroline, most of the indie scene of Melbourne had come through our house. I'd be trying to sleep and she'd be bringing people home from the Empress and every one of them was a songwriter. I heard a bunch of songs on the Yamaha G60, they were always like diary entries.' Thus inspired, Kim started writing what were effectively parodies of the North Fitzroy share house scene. All played on the nylon string acoustic, the songs had funny titles like *Diary Entries Over a Major 7, L'Exhumation D'Yves Montand*, and *Hey There Little Lightbulb*. It also presented a reimagining of *Cool Fire*, first recorded by the Beasts. The end result was both a curiosity and prescient. 'But then folk came in not long after that with Julia and Angus Stone, Iron and Wine and all these folk things came out of Sub Pop and irony was out of fashion. I thought, "once again I'm doing something at the wrong time!"'

•••

The packing crew on the Stomp Shock warehouse floor was chock full of musos, including Ashley Naylor, Anton Ruddick and Michael Stranges. Naylor, guitarist for Melbourne band Even, thought of it as 'one of those warehouses where it was like a sheltered workshop for semi-retired or out of work musicians'. Mike Stranges was playing drums with Mark Murphy in the latter-day Ripe, one of Melbourne's finest introspective shoe gazing bands of the 90s, when he worked in the office at Stomp. 'I knew who Kim was and why he had a reputation. I thought he was this huge rock star — I was amazed he needed a job to start off with. I thought he'd be really rich' (Mike Stranges). A self-confessed 'dork for punk rock and old punk', Mike enthusiastically delved into Kim's recollections of the era. 'He would just tell me stories and shit he used to get up to. I thought it was hilarious' (Mike Stranges). Kim shared the sentiment.

> *Mike wore unusual hats. He had a big personality ... he'd say what was on his mind. I got to appreciate that. I found Mike fun to work with and he played drums and bass and guitar and a bit of everything. And he seemed to know what was what, and I was just thinking he'd be a good guy to get in a band with.*

The 2001 Stomp work party provided that opportunity. As nearly all the staff were musos, naturally a band was put together. They played Stooges, T Rex and Ramones and had a blast, triggering an idea. 'I was hanging out with Mike and Ash and I had this idea which I'd always had about a band that was heavier than all the rest.' What Kim imagined involved four guitarists, two drummers and no lyrics. High concept, hysterical but deadly serious — just the riffs and beats and everything else taken out of it. Mike was like, 'Oh, fuck, yeah, I wanna be in that', and was signed up as one of the drummers. Kim didn't have to look far for his guitar ensemble.

> *We all got to chat about things we liked and didn't like, and for whatever reason, Kim chose us to play in SALMON. The concept grew out of Kim's vision, and they were the kind of things he knew we'd go for, things we'd be happy to play. It was a concept we lived out for him and with him'* (Ashley Naylor).

Ashley Naylor has been in bands since he was seventeen, forming his first band, The Swarm, with drummer Matthew Cotter before they hooked up with Wally Kempton from the Meanies in 1994 to launch Even. Even was in the top echelons of 1990's indie bands, playing perfect 'pop and roll' and regularly landing their album 'Less is More' in various 'best Australian albums of all time' lists. Even have achieved a rare kind of success in Australia, evolving from a band to an institution with their annual 'Xmas Even' shows. Ash always has a million musical projects on the go, as well as being the go to guitarist or musical director for just about everybody.

Ash was into SALMON, and the idea took flight. Soon, Kim had assembled a cast of Ashley Naylor, Anton Ruddick, Dave Graney, Matt Walker and Penny Ikinger on guitar, and Clare Moore joining Mike Stranges on drums. Kim programmed all the drum parts on a Dr Rhythm 250, wrote all the guitar lines and assigned each band member their parts. When they took the stage in matching black SALMON tee shirts (Dave complementing the tee with leather chaps and a bowler hat) they were a sight, and generated a wave of distorted sound like nothing most punters had ever imagined.

> *Playing live was pretty amazing. Two drummers and at one point we had six guitars. It was pretty exciting and pretty confronting. It became a social experiment. Plenty of so-called open-minded indie rockers found it hard to stomach at times 'cos it was pretty full on. It was a great experience; it was structured and daunting and I hope we get to do it again* (Ashley Naylor).

In SALMON, nothing was more important than the riff. Kim's job in SALMON was conducting, peeling off a few guitar licks, and setting of samples. Singing and lyrics would be a distraction, so instead Kim turned to his collection of electonric noises. 'I thought it would be funny to trigger the samples and not have a microphone and lip synch to these dead doomy voices two octaves lower saying "*Satan!*" We'd blow peoples minds and scare the shit out of them! It was a really strange to watch.'

A SALMON rehearsal at Soundpark Studios was recorded and added to a recording of a Sydney Metro gig, and the 'Rock Formations' double album came to life. Ash Naylor described the result as 'prog punk'.

> *It could have been complete cabaret but it wasn't. There was a real exhibitionist element to it and we all got to live out some rock fantasy that we couldn't do in other bands — do the duelling guitars, the 'guitarmonies'! — preposterous hard rock posturing and then flat out punk rock in the same breath. It was multidimensional* (Ashley Naylor).

SALMON was out of this world, the most impractical but high minded project conceived from Kim's creative war chest. But if the Business was hard to keep on the road, SALMON was impossible, and the brilliant but oddball venture was retired.

•••

In 2004, Emma, Kim's fourth child, was born. Now a teenager, Emma can cite international artists and art movements, has sophisticated taste in books and cinema, and has already written, recorded and performed her own album. Her arrival didn't slow Kim down for long: he debuted yet another project — the Darling Downs — with Ron Peno the night after Emma was born. When Sandra returned to work, Kim quit Stomp and enjoyed time looking after Emma and Gene and taking every opportunity to see Alex and Jack over in Perth. These were happy times.

> *My memory of the marriage, it was a terribly productive time for Kim. I saw a lot of Mike, and Ron was an interesting character — I used to do Ron's ironing in the lounge room. Mark Arm stayed with us when Kim did a tour with Mudhoney and Mark would put baby Emma's socks back on when they fell off. Jack White's manager contacted Kim's manager saying that Jack and Meg would love to meet Kim at the Big Day Out, and Jack was star struck. Henry Rollins came and played and the only person who was allowed backstage was Kim* (Sandra Salmon).

But there were hard times. In 2005, Kim had finished a gig at the Empress Hotel when he was mugged, badly hurt and his car stolen. Inside the car were Emma's pram and baby seat, and Kim's guitar. 'I tried to get back into the car but all I could think of was the fact that this was my new family car. It's our main possession and it had the tool of my trade in it.'[1] Kim gave chase in a taxi but was outrun, and although the car was eventually found and the guitar located in a Northcote pawn shop, the assault shook Kim to his core. The costs compounded the stressors that were building up between him and Sandra. Over the next few years, financial pressures and the strain of their competing lifestyles — Kim being away on tour or working at night, Sandra forging a career in education — took its toll. 'We gave it a good go for thirteen years, and we managed to do some good things together but finally separated in 2011.' Kim moved to a flat nearby, looking after Emma and Gene on weekends, working when he could, and trying to keep his head and heart above water. 'It was a bad, bad time.'

17

Between the Forest and the Trees

Blues music in Perth, 1976 was bland and overcooked. But pretenders from Western Australia were a very different proposition to the original masters in America, and Kim soon discovered *actual* blues. The ring master, according to Kim, was Howlin' Wolf.

> *... there are so many people out there, but for my middle-class white boy one stop shop, Howlin' Wolf has it all covered. He had this show biz thing, it shares as much with vaudeville as it does with the Mississippi folk thing. The glint in his eye, crazy ideas about a song and it's like a 'wink-wink, nudge-nudge' to the audience. He reminds me of Ron Peno.*

In 1982, after a show on the Scientists never ending Vulcan Club residency, Kim ran into fellow musician Brett Meyers. 'He introduced me to this little guy and said "this is Ronny from the Hellcats".' The Hellcats could be seen in Sydney during the 70s supporting the Birdman, before Ron headed north and formed the Screaming

Tribesman who became mildly famous for their song *Igloo.* 'Ron had that Howlin' Wolf glint in his eye and he asked me, "so what's that song, eight parts water?" He immediately latched on to the idea of the formula, with a Benny Hill kind of humour. I took a shine to him immediately.' Not long after, Kim looked down from the stage as the long-haired Scientists blasted away. And at the front of the stage, there was Ron, trashed as always, wearing a long red wig, mocking and admiring the Scientists. Kim soon discovered that Brett and Ron had a band, Died Pretty, who were slotted in to support Salamander Jim — Kim, Tex and Richard Ploog's short lived trio.

> *Richard and I were trashed off our tits on hallucinogens and poor Tex didn't know what hit him. Before that I saw Died Pretty and they just mopped the floor with us. They were wonderful. Ron had all these moves, and he understood what made singers great. This guy was so good, he's kind of Dylan, Roger Daltry, he's Iggy, he's got them all there in this strange kind of package that combines a bit of everything without being any of them. He understood the medium. It was art what he did.*

For years after their initial meeting. Kim would catch up with Ron in Sydney, and Ron would announce that they would one day make a country album together. In 2002, 'Dave Faulkner rings me up and says "Kim you got to help Ron out. He's down in Melbourne and doesn't have any friends down there. He needs someone to go have a coffee with." I was touched by Dave, so I got in touch with Ron and we decided we'd get together every fortnight, no pressure.' So, every two weeks, Kim would drop by Ron's apartment to talk, drink coffee and share ideas. Kim would capture these musical ruminations on his tape player, and after a few of these visits, he gave Ron a cassette with some of the song ideas to listen to. 'We'd never even look at a song after we'd record it, we'd do a different song the next week, rather than work on the songs we'd written. We'd just leave them in a heap.' After a year or so of this, Ron suggested that they should play some shows. 'I said, "we need more songs, we've only got four or five", and he said, "No we have about twenty", and he played them all back to back, and I was sitting there and my jaw dropped. These were all beautiful, perfectly formed songs, and I could hear it. Everything was there. The magic was intact. What I just heard was really wonderful, I didn't want to change a thing.' The melodies were intricate, taking unusual pathways but always finding satisfying resolution. Even in these rough sketches Ron's voice was stunning, and the artistry and sophistication of Kim's song design leapt of the tape.

Ron loved it too, but he was pushing to form a band that could birth the imagined strings and embellishments he could hear around these sparse songs. 'And I said, "if you can hear them, we don't need to put them in." So he would sing to me what he imagined cellos would play and I transposed it to guitar.' In a song writing approach reminiscent of his experience with James Baker, Kim would listen to Ron's vocalisations and explanations and bring the songs to life on guitar or banjo.

> *So that if it was C, G, D, I'd hardly feel I'd written anything as prescribed by Ron's beautiful melody, so I'd put a D with a F sharp bass and a slash chord, suspended 4th and things. I'd do as much of that as I could, take the music as far as it would go. It's quite simple, but I'm working hard. A lot is going on. The actual harmonic structure is classic, more Mozart than Shostakovich.*

As the songs took shape, a gig opportunity presented: supporting Ed Kuepper. Still in duo format, Ron and Kim compiled a show from the tunes on the cassette. Ron suggested they wear suits, believing the atmosphere of the project demanded the more formal appearance. 'Ron had some theory about country and western and the further back you went the sharper dressed they were. It was urban and sophisticated. Because they alluded to something more, the showbiz! People like to look back and think it was all about dirt farmers, but in actual fact they were looking into the future.'

When asked by the promoter for a band name, Kim recollected the scribble on the old cassette cover, K and R, short for Kim and Ron, which Ron would extrapolate to KR Darling Downs, a regional, small goods company and household name. The KR gave way, leaving the perfect band name: Darling Downs. Divergent views remained as to whether the act should be a duo or expand in personnel. Kim was adamant that the true magic lay in the powerful, but somehow delicate intricacies of just the two of them: Ron's voice working in with Kim's inventive guitar. He loved the basic form, the stripped back sound and spontaneous approach that the duo enabled. And besides, 'I didn't want a band for selfish reasons 'cos I knew I'd be part of the backing band behind Ron. I'd be absorbed into it. You don't think much about Brett Myers in Died Pretty even though he's twice Ron's height and a really good guitarist. It's all Ron. He uses up a lot of space, that boy. I want to be an equal share in it, even If I'm going to be the straight man. I'm Ernie Wise to his Eric Morecambe.'

The first show was at the Corner Hotel in Richmond in May 2004 with Ed Kuepper. Kim played a nylon string guitar, which would not be repeated often in his career. The response was electric, and the new outfit was on its way. Soon after, the Darling Downs scored a residency at the Victoria Hotel in West Brunswick where Kirsty Stegwaski was establishing a new scene. 'The indie folk really responded. The scene at the Vic — Joel Silbersher, Mike Noga, Kirsty and others — it was an indie club going on, and there was a bit of a vibe going on for us.'

In 2004, the Darling Downs recorded their first album, turning to Dave Graney and Clare Moore as producers. Dave and Clare have created a sanctuary studio called Ponderosa in the hills of outer east Melbourne, where they create most of their own prodigious output. Despite their camaraderie, Ron and Kim can argue like wild cats and push each other's buttons. They had a bitter fight about what to call the first album, with Kim eventually triumphing. From this, 'How Can I Forget This Heart of Mine' was born. There seemed to be something about the unlikely pairing of the two, and the unconventional performance mode that captured the attention of the music world.

The album demanded great critical response. It was described it as 'an almost impossible album: a record of nuanced beauty, a subtle masterpiece',[1] while the Sydney Morning Herald contrasted the album favourably with conventional country: 'When country music falls into the hands of Kim Salmon and Ron Peno, and Dave Graney and Clare Moore do the engineering, you can expect something different. The result will never win hearts and minds in Tamworth. It is simply too daring, too deeply felt and far too experimental.'[2]

It fell primarily to Kim, now the de facto manger, to do the publicity for the first album and therefore the logistics. This reignited some of the sparring between them, making the union difficult for a time. Ron had someone in his ear, raising his hackles, and concurrently he was juggling the territory of having been in a successful band like Died Pretty, and having to re-establish himself from ground zero.

> *Ron had a different trajectory to me. He was a lead singer from a different time. I had to go from the Scientists and lose my way and find it again with the Surrealists. I had lots of years being brought back down to earth, but Ron was up in the air with Died Pretty. Going from Died Pretty to Darling Downs was a shock for him. I'd already realised that success in one thing isn't necessary transferred to another. You've got to create the need for something else.*

These niggles and deviations aside, the friendship between Ron and Kim continued to deepen, so they carried on their regular coffee and idea generating sessions, securing another cassette worth of mumbled, hummed or sung melodies. In 2007, Kim and Ron took the collection of song ideas on cassette to Ponderosa and set to work. 'We were trying to decipher what was sung in the guide vocals on tape. Dave was encouraging us to go with the weirdest interpretation, which came to a head on the song *Circa '65*, an incredibly surrealistic, eerily creepy song straight out of a David Lynch film. Dave was going "that's really cool, that's great. What did you sing there Ron? Was that 'I'm a naked old man roll over?'"'

The resulting record, 'From One to Another' ('for the second album title, I let him have his way') was darker, more obscure, and showed off the duo's rougher edges and murkier sides. Somehow, the second album didn't deliver what people wanted, as though the audience was expecting more of the tear jerkiness of the first album rather that the 'share cropping, dark, sinking into depression mood' of 'From One to Another'.

2013 saw the release of their third album, 'In the Days When the World was Wide'. It was another stunning album, not just for its songs, but the presentation of the duo through the album cover art, with stunning photos of the pensive and besuited Kim and Ron against a plain white background. The art work captured the unique proposition of the Darling Downs and matched the commanding performances on the album. The song writing had progressed too, with Kim finding new and intriguing ways to embellish his playing and Ron soaring or whimpering as the mood dictated. Remarkably, both Kim's musicality and Ron's lyricism were elevated on 'When the World Was Wide'. The collection of songs were more completely realised and ethereal, but retaining their earthen quality.

For Kim, working with Ron Peno has been an eye opener. Ron's singing and melodic sense provides a unique foil for Kim to design his songs and guitar playing around, and it has extended him. With Ron, Kim isn't shredding solos, but he is inventive, oblique and works incredibly hard to sustain the momentum and power of the song with deceptively simple guitar motifs. Ron also surprised Kim with his approach to lyrics.

> *He doesn't really think about his lyrics, just sort of sings whatever comes into his head and it's kind of rubbish actually, but it sounds really important. I've heard Nick Cave say to Ron 'oh your lyrics are amazing' and I'm thinking to myself 'that's gobbledegook what Ron's singing, bizarre shit that doesn't mean anything.' But then again, you listen to it another way and it's kind of very bizarre and dreamlike and he's just making it up*

off the top of his head. Because he thinks it's easier, he actually thinks it's easier to make lyrics up than to learn them. You'd have to be incredibly smart on some level just to do that.

Much is made of the surprising combination of the Darling Downs, and that an artist like Kim, who has basically spent his career trying to make as much dissonant noise as possible, would make country music. But Ron and Kim are not such an odd couple. Both are charming, funny, articulate men whose sensibility veers seriously off the beaten track. They are creatives capable of sinking into their art and not at all interested in conforming to expectations. In Kim's estimation, 'Darling Downs is very much part of something that I would do. But people think that it's really different because of the ways it's delivered and the way it's put across, and I just think of it as being another part of the same thing. I don't think it's that surprising, I particularly don't think it's that different to the Scientists in a lot of ways. It's stripped back and the minimalism is there.'

•••

In December 2017, the Darling Downs headlined a Christmas show at the Grandview Hotel in Fairfield, featuring Brian Henry Hooper and Charlie Marshall in support. Charlie's solo set, with his beautiful voice and earnest, academic like stage persona transported me straight back to the early days of 90s Great Britain. It was all smoothness and grace, in contrast to Brian Henry Hooper who — along with pianist Daniel Tuccera — planted a chair on the stage and smashed the audience in the chest with high-impact, emotionally-charged material. His battered guitar literally had a gash punched into the body, and Brian tested every ounce of his instrument's construction with his heavy, passionate playing. He put on an epic show, which was, very sadly, his last solo performance.

By the time the Darling Downs arrived on stage, the energy in the room was popping. Kim and Ron put on an extraordinary display.

Ron lunged and lurched, microphone in hand, doubling over as if in pain to singing exultantly at the ceiling. Kim's guitar playing broke new ground, delivering subversive melodies with surprising twists and turns. Ron would put his arm around Kim's neck, singing to him playfully, and Kim would return the humour, but would always play the straight man to the flamboyant Peno. The lively songs were hectic and inspirational, the quiet songs reverent and hushed. The performance, was peerless. It was like a night at a gospel church. We were wrung out and moved, sure that something significant had occurred.

The Darling Downs play irregularly, but their scarcity makes them even more exceptional. Kim and Ron are like two conspiring high school kids when they are together, full of mischief and always close to a hilarious argument about something trivial. The affection between them is obvious, as is the admiration. 'I found Ron to be possibly the most musical person I've ever worked with. He could compose parts and didn't realise how incredible he was, and he is such an incredible singer.'

Ron and Kim are survivors, and they are thinking big. 'Next for the Darling Downs? I don't think we should do anything unless we do it on a massive scale, 'cos we've done the stripped back thing. Like orchestras and violins and mellotrons, everything. Grandiosity. Over the top. Push all the tear-jerking buttons.'

18

Loose Ends

In 2008, Michael Stranges returned to Melbourne from a failed mission to relocate to Canada. Kim was short a Surrealist drummer for a show supporting Gareth Liddiard's band the Drones, and on hearing of Mike's return asked if he would fill in. During rehearsals for the show, Mike heard a new song and was absorbed by its lyrics and intent. Feeding back to Kim his interpretation — 'it sounds like a Greek chorus in a Greek play' — Mike was struck by Kim's emphatic affirmation. 'I could see that he worked out that I *got* what he's doing. I saw something and made him realise what he was actually doing'. The penny had dropped for Kim; he had found in Mike a kindred spirit, someone who was on his page. Someone he would like to produce the new Surrealists record. 'I didn't even know how to work a fucking tape deck! He's got a sense of adventure. He could get an *actual* producer, but he probably thought that he knows what he is doing, but he could use another set of ears that gets what he does' (Mike Stranges).

The album Mike was wading into would become the Surrealists

seventh, and to this stage, final album: 'Grand Unifying Theory'. It had been a decade since 'Ya Gotta Let Me Do My Thing', and although Kim's output during the intervening years had been prodigious, the Surrealists had — other than accepting some cool supports and overseas festivals — been quiet. Now, with the tightly ordered guitar onslaught of SALMON behind him, Kim had been hard at work creating something more free form.

> *The early training for the 'Grand Unifying Theory' album went for several weeks, with just myself and Kim. I would go over to Kim's house on a regular weekday evening and we convened to his back room. Kim laid out ideas that he'd been thinking up, and I learnt them, took notes and added my own. We practiced incredibly quietly, so as not to wake children and/or disturb neighbours. After quite a few of these sessions, Phil became involved, carrying out his parts on Kim son's toy drums. The songs began to take shape and I guess we took it to rehearsal rooms later, to get loud and out there* (Stu Thomas).

Phil Collings had joined Kim in the latter stages of The Business. 'Phil was a fantastic guy, that was the thing that struck me about him, he's so sweet, you couldn't not like him'. Not long after Phil joined, Kim rested the band for a six-year hiatus. It wasn't until they were invited to perform at the Azkena Festival in Spain that the trio reformed. The layoff gave the audience time to adjust to the format without Brian and Tony and allowed the Surrealists to be reborn. Phil brought a very different spectre to the band. Having come from the jazz world, he was sharp and agile, making him ideal for the new bent shapes that Kim and Stu were cooking up. 'Since Phil and Stu have been in the band it's taken it to another galaxy. You start following Phil and you just hang on for dear life. We did this version of *Melt* and it was fantastic, in danger of falling to pieces but it somehow hung together beautifully'. Kim was trying out some new tricks, using a handheld cassette recorder/player to record his guitar, then rewind it, play it back and then more guitar over the top of it. 'All while Phil and I are creeping in with a sort of minimalist evil blaxploitation groove. One drum track was recorded on that tape recorder as well, then slowed down. Some of the grooves shifted into other songs, and some songs were almost a summation of all the various grooves' (Stu Thomas). Kim was grabbing elements from the cracks in the floorboards and using them on tape.

> *It was initially a couple of segments from a 'solo' electronic piece I worked up a couple years back. When I was looking for material for 'Grand Unifying Theory' I realised that this could be modified for a band and really fit the bill. Also, one of the segments used to always elicit extreme reactions, like walkouts and abuse, so I thought it really deserved a guernsey. The second half of that piece is in effect an ending that we couldn't end, and some of the concise short songs are really just bits of Grand Unifying Theory Parts 1 and 2 that I've focussed on and turned into songs.*[1]

The song writing process had been hard boiled creativity, and now 'the plan was to record us all playing together in the rehearsal room, as was done with the first album. Except this time it wasn't a four-track recording, but straight to two-track. I guess some would say that's a brave move, but really for us that's just the same as playing live and making stuff up in a room instead of on-stage. We're good at that individually, and as a band' (Stu Thomas). Mike had a portable mini disc player which he took to some Surrealists rehearsals at Soundpark and recorded the band using just two microphones.

> *We congregated and recorded for a number of days and got a lot of versions of songs down, improvising a fair amount of it, changing sound levels on the go, tweaking grooves as required. At some point, after a million takes, I didn't know what was good or bad, but we ploughed on. I remember Mike once suggesting that we extend an already lengthy jam, and get*

> *really far out. This became the album's centrepiece, eventually running for around 28 minutes. At the end of the sessions, I certainly wasn't sure what we had, but I knew there was a lot of it to choose from* (Stu Thomas).

Mike consolidated the recordings on the mini disc player for presentation to the band. 'I didn't know what I was doing. It sounded like fucking shit, but you could hear the music and that's enough'. He played what he captured on tape to Kim who said 'Hey, we could make an album with that!'. This was Kim's salvage operation in full swing — take the resources you have at your disposal, use what you find lying around, if things are broken, see what you can rescue. Salvage something whole and good from the opportunities you find. Or, as Mike puts it, 'If you've got no money, you make an album the way you can'. Mike was cautious but up for the challenge and took the recordings back to his place, introducing them to his rudimentary Pro-Tools skills. Every Saturday night he and Kim poured over the recordings, doing overdubs and introducing new elements before finishing off the vocals at Ponderosa with Dave Graney at the helm. Finally, 'Grand Unifying Theory' was done, the most far out record Kim has produced. The mini disc recording rendered a cool, remote, lo-fi production. Some of the songs are completely unstructured, the rest following their own rules. Dissonance, tension, space and movement contribute more to the album than singing or guitars. It is both a total deviation from their previous recordings, and a natural evolution. If some critics were unimpressed, judging the album as unworthy to bear the Surrealists name, the band were pleasantly surprised at what their collection of performances had mutated into.

> *To hear it full-blown with the vocals, added handclaps, percussion, etc takes some getting used to, but I did eventually, and I have to say, it is a fine chunk of space-rock; equal measures improvisation versus arranged parts, clean sounds versus frighteningly raw stuff. It looks back and forward at the same time and lives up to the Surrealists moniker* (Stu Thomas).

•••

While the Surrealists negotiated their re-emergence, and in the wake of the SALMON bombast, Kim returned to minimal solo shows. But when he was offered the support for Japanese punk band Teengenerate, Kim drafted in Mike on drums and played the show as a duo.

> *After that, he and I started doing gigs together, just me accompanying him. I kind of learnt how he constructs songs and just realising how fucking talented he is — It's like insane. His understanding of song construction is just crazy* (Mike Stranges).

The more they played the stronger the musical affinity between them grew. They connected on a shared knowledge and fascination of obscure musical facts, theories, opinions and ambitions. And most importantly, on dress sense.

> *We don't rehearse, but we talk about what we're going to wear. We kind of wear outfits that complement each other. We were wearing bandannas for a while, denim and that kind of thing, kind of like a punky, glammy sort of look. For me, that's more important in a band. Once you've got the look, the music will sort itself out* (Mike Stranges).

As Kim and Mike played together more, Andrew McGee from the Stomp/Shock music days had them as guests in his Nagambie studio which had witnessed Gareth Liddiard, Brian Hooper, Mick Harvey and many others make records. 'We ended up with an album's worth of stuff that we co-wrote. I didn't want to have another band with my name at the start, so Precious Jules is the name we came up with because it's the opposite of my first punk band's name — Cheap Nasties'. The Precious Jules album, featuring cover art by Emma Salmon, was one of Kim's most enjoyable and easiest records to make. A cross between punk rock and glam, it would capture a reworking of the Cheap Nasties theme song (*Cheap 'n' Nasty*) as well as an ode to his former band the Beasts of Bourbon (*Pearls before Swine*). The experience of working with Mike would have a substantial impact on Kim's career, and Mike would be a feature in most of Kim's artistic output thereafter. The song-writing chemistry between them was as great at their live shows, and they drove each other to reach for a funnier line, a more obscure reference or an outlandish rhyme. Mike understood the conceptual basis for Kim's work, and was therefore able to offer tangents and embellishments that were on Kim's level, not a distraction. Kim affirms 'I kind of view him now as being my band.' Mike became Kim's musical confidant and great friend, dropping over to Kim's each week for a cup of tea and song writing in the front room, Mike playing Kim's electric drum kit. Planning for something big …

> *My own personal dream is to make something orchestrated and really slick, with loads of hooks, awesome lyrics and it sounds good on the radio and dudes want to hear it and want to hear it again. That's what I want. I know Kim's capable of it and willing to give it a go. I'd love Precious Jules to — just to write — I'd love us to write a number one hit song* (Mike Stranges).

•••

Leanne Chock, now Leanne Cowie, had eventually returned to Australia from London, but didn't play any more music. She had her memories of the Scientists tours to sustain her, but she focused on her role as a truancy officer with the New South Wales Education Department. In 2002, the Scientists toured for the reissue of the 'Blood Red River' album using a fill in drummer given the tragic death of Brett Rixon from an overdose in December 1993. When the tour hit the Annandale Hotel in Sydney, Kim invited Leanne up to play some songs. Instantly the penny dropped once again — Leanne held the key to the intangible Scientists sound.

> *The Scientists played a reformation show and we invited Leanne up for the encore, and it was back to that feeling of being the*

> *Scientists again. There was no doubt in anybody's mind in that room that 'oh that's the Scientists'. Her demeanour, not doing some of the things that drummers think they have to do. So she was involved every time there was a reformation after that.*

Leanne was thrilled by the experience, but rattled at the same time. Out of practice and low on confidence, she hardly felt like she qualified as a drummer any more. Grateful for the opportunity, she returned to her life — the drums still packed away in the spare room.

> *I didn't think any more of it, but then in 2004 he asked if I was interested in doing a European Scientists tour as a three piece with Stu Thomas because the others couldn't do it. I said, 'yeah sure, but you'll have to give me six months-notice'. And he said, 'I am'. So I practiced and practiced and we did this tour as a three piece* (Leanne Cowie).

This was just one of many 'one off' Scientist reformations. In 2010, the band was invited to the All Tomorrow's Parties (ATP) festival in New York to play alongside the Stooges, Sonic Youth, Nick Cave and the Bad Seeds and Mudhoney, and then they moved onto the European leg too. Fellow Australians the Drones were also at the ATP festival, and Gareth Liddiard enjoyed connecting again with Kim.

> *It wasn't until we started doing lots of ATP festivals that we saw him regularly again in the UK and in the US. Those were really cool times ... We were playing with and meeting all our 'fave bands, and The Scientists were doing the same thing as were the Dirty Three. It was a lot of fun being in the actual world playing along side bands we actually had stuff in common with. It's mainly a blur of back stage boozing and English pubs and seeing that second incarnation of The Scientists up there with the Sonic Youths and Nick Caves of the world. They were a super modern machine band that crushed you with its mind. They shat all over 90 per cent of the ATP bands because they were designed to* (Gareth Liddiard).

Twenty years after leaving the Scientists, Leanne was again playing drums for the band on the international stage — and loving it. So when Kim called her up in 2011 and asked her to join him as a duo to fulfil a gig booking she, of course, said yes.

> *Kim got a support playing Big Day Out side shows with The Jim Jones Revue and asked if I wanted to play with him. He wanted me to learn Precious Jules songs, and again no rehearsal, just a sound check. We made this whole thing about not rehearsing but just learning songs in sound check and playing them. So we did that ... And it got a good response* (Leanne Cowie).

The drum/guitar duo combination that Kim started in London in 1986 with Nick Combe and perfected with Mike in Precious Jules also served him well with Leanne. 'Kim got the idea that maybe he and Mike together could do some songs that were more like Scientists songs for us to record' (Leanne Cowie). So Kim and Mike began assembling songs for an album.

> *It was amazing, over two months we wrote and demo-ed a whole album. It's probably the most fun thing I've ever done in my entire life. I was living on High Street, just up the road. So he'd come up with a song in the lounge room and then go into the kitchen and write the words. It was like a hit factory! We haven't made any money out of these songs, that's the difference!* (Mike Stranges)

The album would be called 'True West', and it was immediately clear that Kim and Mike in combination were a potent — and hilarious — song writing force. Lyrically, the album is littered with one liners, double *entrendres* and pop culture references while musically it manages to capture the spirit of the Scientists without being a facsimile. *Carry on Baggage*, 'oh matron won't you ask me how I can carry on while we're still bruising. Is there a limit to this carry on, we've really got to get it checked ...' *Freudian Slippers*, 'get your Freudian Slippers off my couch and into my brain' and *Ow! Baby, Baby* — 'what's the matter inya, makes me wanna ring you next. But I'm just a cheapskate, all I did was send a text' — these songs are all clever and funny, line after line. But my favourite is The Science Test:

Now and then you will have to think of me
And it won't matter how hard you try
CBT may rid you your anxiety
But this one time it won't make me a lie
One day when something will come over you
Maybe even on the day that you die
How you greet me is all yours and yours alone
Embrace me maybe laugh, maybe cry

In January 2012 Kim sent Leanne a disc of the compiled songs, and the two of them recorded the final product in April 2012. The first time Leanne played the songs live was at a gig, eschewing the ideas of rehearsing yet again. 'We had two shows and then we recorded it! Just like 'Hit Me with the Surreal Feel'. But I always feel like one day someone's going to shout at me you're such a fraud get out of here' (Leanne Cowie). It seems unlikely that anyone will yell such a thing any time soon.

•••

The emergence of Mike and Leanne as Kim's Melbourne and Sydney based drummers respectively was the origin of his 'pick up bands' in each capital city. Kim would fly into town, maybe do a quick rehearsal at soundcheck with his interstate rhythm sections, play the gig, and then fly off to pick up another band in another city. The different iterations of these ensembles became known as the Kim Salmon Power Pop Trio, or to use its preferred name, the KSPPT. The core of the KSPPT was based in Melbourne, with Mike Stranges on drums and Loretta Wilde or Jeff Hooker on bass. In Perth Kim drafted local art and music identity Pete Stone on bass and the multi-talented Todd Picket from Kill Devil Hills on drums. There were less regular versions in Sydney and Brisbane, but it was the Adelaide charter, featuring Shakey McGee and Pete 'the Stud' Howlett that really made its mark. Pete the Stud explains:

> *I was in this band Bloodsucking Freaks in '93 and we were big fans of the first Scientists album. We cut our teeth to those early records so we were disgustipated when Kim came out with the uni-kid palatable and smooth as sickening silk Rose Coloured Windscreen, especially after we were angry about all the upper middle class championing of his celebrated swampy Scientists stuff while his earlier stuff was snobbed off as trash. So we wanted to release something to upset the phonies. We wrote and recorded this song, Kill Kim Salmon Now …*

The album cover pictured a doctored Scientists photo, and the song title emblazoned with three exclamation points. Pete the Stud meant business. The song made its way from Adelaide to an unsuspecting Kim Salmon in Melbourne. 'I freaked out!' Kim lived with this hilariously ominous threat hovering somewhere in his unconscious for a decade when, playing the River Rocks Festival in Geelong, a drunk stage invader took off with his set list, only to return it minutes later — 'one that I wrote out in the front bar ten minutes earlier of *my* choices!' (Pete the Stud)

Another decade passed and the original Scientists reformed and needed a support for their Adelaide show. Pete the Stud lobbied hard, begging Kim's forgiveness and even declaring his love for 'Rose Coloured Shitscreen'. 'And guess what — he gave us the support!' (Pete the Stud) Pete's total disregard for convention appealed to Kim — 'I just love the guy. His band was pretty cool, and we stayed in touch and naturally enough at some point I asked him to be in my band'.

Pete the Stud was overjoyed and started dreaming of all the unnecessary guitar parts he would play over his favourite Kim Salmon classics.

> *Instead he gleefully forces me to play bass and sends me a list of twenty songs — all from the Kim Salmon era I despised. At first rehearsal he reveals half the songs he told me to learn were all lies and we are actually going to play the ones I love. He made me suffer and painstakingly teach myself twenty songs we weren't going to play just to teach me a lesson from something I did twenty years ago. Truly the act of a depraved sadist* (Pete the Stud).

•••

The Standard Hotel in Fitzroy is a venerable Melbourne music institution, an appropriate setting for Kim Salmon and Spencer P Jones to reconnect. Kim and Spencer hadn't crossed paths that often since Kim left the Beasts. Sometime in 2012 Kim was doing a series of solo shows at the Standard when Spencer showed up with his partner Angie. Spencer had moved north side with Angie, away from St Kilda and was purporting to be free of old influences. 'It was just nice to reconnect with him. And Mike suggested "why don't you do something with Spencer, do some gigs with him it would go down a bomb". I suggested it to Spencer, and we never did any rehearsals, we just got a run of shows at the Old Bar and they were massive'. The Kim and Spencer shows at the Old Bar saw them each doing a set of their own material before joining forces for a bunch of songs. The first show was 'a complete train wreck', with Spencer quickly drinking his nerves away to the extent that, unscheduled, he joined Kim on stage and launched into a song Kim didn't know in full ramshackle glory. 'He got totally trashed and started paying whatever the fuck he wanted!' The audience loved it, and the shows got bigger and bigger.

They started spreading their wings with song choices too. Kim suggested anything from Kanye West to Peggy Lee, and Spencer was happy to go there. 'He would often just go off on his own tangent. He showed that he could definitely go out of his comfort zone if you pushed him, he could come up with amazing stuff 'cos he's very quick and clever'. When Spencer pulled out a chord progression that referenced Sonny Sharrock Kim fired up all his jazz licks, and 'a little bit of that appears on *Loose Ends*. I had some lyrics that I jotted down at an airport, you know, just loose ends. And I thought let's just sing one note. I've *played* one note, so let's just *sing* one note'. As the collection of songs took on coherence, Kim invited any courtiers willing to fund a recording to come forward, which flushed out Adrian Ackerman from Incubator Records. Adrian offered to record an album in his studio for a cut of the publishing, and suddenly Kim had another project on his hands. 'I thought, let's just go into the studio unprepared 'cos all of our shows were unprepared, it's the ultimate salvage job. Let's take that ethos in to the studio and see what happens'. The result was spectacular, a combination of uniquely interpreted covers and really strong originals, played authentically, with heart.

'Runaways' was the third album that Kim delivered in twelve months, across three different projects, Darling Downs, Kim and Leanne and this one with Spencer. In the same year, the course of Interferon he was taking delivered a hard won cure for hepatitis C, the contraction of which remains a mystery for Kim — 'People might not believe me, but I was never an intravenous drug user. In twenty five per cent of cases they don't know why people get it. You can't have been a member of Beasts of Bourbon and not had it. Maybe I got it from sharing a tour van rather than needles'[2]. The treatment that made him better was ravaging, producing horrible anxiety, and it was a painful year while he endured the side effects. The illness was on the heels of his divorce from Sandra, the end of his time at Stomp, and an existential collapse. In the aftermath, a new batch of songs were percolating, songs of illness and healing.

19

My Script

Maxine Pryce loves the Labour in Vain in Brunswick Street Fitzroy. To this day, it is the venue she is drawn to more often than any other to see music. In February 2013, Maxine walked into the Labour in Vain feeling happy with her life. She had a new job and was catching up with good friends. Life changing events were not on her radar that night, she was just there to watch Tex Napalm and Dimi Dero. It was only when she noticed Kim Salmon looking at her as he entered the bar that she realised he too was playing that night. Between sets, Maxine was upstairs in the beer garden when Kim joined her table and introduced himself. They talked, each sharing a brief life history before 'he asked for my phone number to catch up for coffee. He was open, honest, a nice guy so I said yes but I never thought anything would occur. My rule was never go out with a musician! I was sitting most of the time, so if he had seen that I was taller than him maybe he would not have asked me out!' (Maxine Pryce)

Kim watched Maxine as they talked. 'I noticed she was really open and expressive, and that she had a lot of friends around her and that she was good to them. She was taking care of everybody. She was pretty stylish, I thought she was really attractive. There was really something about her.' Kim and Maxine scheduled some dates, all of which were disastrous. They endured bad food, bad art presentations, and bad movies but saw the funny side of it. 'I think the only reason that he asked me on further dates is he asked me to choose music in my car and I chose Television and Big Star to put on, and they happen to be two of his favourite bands' (Maxine Pryce). Further dates turned into spending most nights together, and after twelve months or so, Kim moved into Maxine's house in Northcote, with Gene and Emma taking week on-week off residency soon after. The house is open and warm in spirit, naturally creative and a combination of rustic (the fire wood stacked on the front verandah) and modern (huge gallery like glass sliding doors opening onto decking). As an allied health manager and physiotherapist with post graduate neuroscience qualifications, Maxine balances a busy work schedule with an impulse for soaking in as much music as she can, and is an avid supporter of Melbourne's music scene. Kim remains impressed: 'To find somebody like that you'd be crazy to let it go, she is really a wonderful warm beautiful person and a lot of fun.' And most importantly, she loves guitars.

•••

The front room of Kim and Maxie's house is a relaxed jumble of musical oddments. The old Fenders, a new Yamaha, an SG and a Col Clarke acoustic recline together on the guitar rack. They are joined sometimes by a five-string banjo which, when not in use, rests in its case atop the high book shelf, causing Kim the occasional back injury as he fishes it down. A couch that is both cosy and lumpy sits next to the gas fireplace over which hang framed posters — Darling Downs, Beasts of Bourbon, Surrealists — Kim's own work mainly, but peppered with other bands. The book shelf is groaning under the weight it carries, volumes of music biographies and books on art, and stacks of cassettes and CDs which, along with a crooked pile of electrical tape reinforced boxes holding neat rows of vinyl LPs, comprise Kim's merch desk arsenal. Music stands, a practice drum kit, sheet music and guitar cases accompany a duo of gold fish who alternately keep an eye on the gear and look out the window to the wild, enchanting garden overhung with a luxuriant tangle of trees through which I walk each Wednesday evening for my guitar lesson.

I always inhale deeply before knocking on the door, hearing the Epiphone muttering accusingly under its breath as we prepare to enter for the lesson. It's 2016, and by now I know Kim relatively well. We've gone drinking, been to gigs, I've been his guest at dinner parties and we've talked for hours over many absurdly menu-ed inner city breakfasts, interviewing for this book. But before every guitar lesson, I'm nervous. Kim Salmon remains to me, at some level, an otherworldly rock 'n' roll figure inhabiting the indistinct memories of my youth.

But here I am, learning guitar with him. Some lessons might be about *Ramblin' Man* by Hank Williams, or *Blues for Alice* by Charlie Parker. We spent a few weeks on *The Girl from Ipanema*, learning it at Kim's urging in case I needed 'a good party trick'. Often, I would lose track completely as Kim delved into the mysteries of music theory.

My favourite parts of guitar lessons though, were when fragments of new Kim Salmon songs would escape and I would hear, by degrees, their gradual birthing. This would happen with increasing frequency, as Kim would demonstrate a point with lyrics like 'I take all the treatment 'cos it's making me better, one day I'll look back and just think what was that? All this *defeatment* is like an old sweater, it once kept me warm but it's now off my back ...' explaining that sometimes he would simply make up a word like 'defeatment' in service of a good rhyme and the best meaning. As the lessons went on, I realised I was hearing a new album taking shape.

In March 2016, not too far off forty years since his first album, Kim released 'My Script', a sweeping double LP of songs that at once bear no resemblance to each other, yet make perfect sense together. Stomping New York inspired post punk glam sits happily next to quiet acoustic deliberations; pure pop cohabitates comfortably with investigational dissonance, all punctuated with five tracks of numbing guitar and ambient noise.

'My Script' fell out of upheaval. A few years earlier Kim had lost his job, was recently divorced, and battling serious illness.

> *To get through it all I would write songs whenever I could ... collecting separate musical sketches. I'm not one of those songwriters that has to get the muse right ... I don't need a set of conditions and I don't like limiting myself that way. It's just a stage in my life where I don't sit around writing songs very often. If I need a song, I write it. But occasionally, I get these moments of insecurity and think — 'can I write a song? Can I just do it like that?' So, sometime around 2011, probably not that long after my marriage break up and all of that, I was on my own thinking — 'can I write a song? Can I actually do this anymore? Have I still got it?' I didn't think I couldn't. I just wanted to make sure I could.*

•••

Meanwhile, in Swaziland South Africa, Melbourne producer Myles Mumford was assigned by Australian Volunteers International to develop a community radio station and deliver health promotion initiatives. He built an entire recording studio with little more than 'one circular saw, one electrical drill with no drill bits, a pencil, some chalk, a ruler and a piece of string', and began producing records for an entrenched underclass of disenfranchised rappers, none of whom had the means to pay for the recording time. When he returned to Australia after this transformative experience Myles was glum. 'People were making songs about inner Melbourne culture and getting a good coffee, and I'm like, "fuck, I'm bored"'. So he called Kim Salmon.

Years earlier, Myles had produced a track for the 'Key of Sea' project, which pairs a local musician with musicians from migrant and asylum seeker backgrounds to raise money for the Asylum Seeker Resource Centre. The track Mumford worked on, *Client JT89*, featured Kim Salmon paired with lecturer, journalist, and television star Waleed Aly. It had been a positive exchange, so looking for a spark, Myles called Kim out of the blue. 'He was like … "Let's go and get a coffee". And maybe a month or two later, we were in my lounge room making music'.

The recording was governed by a few simple principles. While guitars would be central, anything else they could get their hands on would be incorporated. It would feature a mish-mash of new versus old technology, with iPhone drum machines recorded through old school valve tape players. Unusual AKGC34 stereo microphones sat on coffee tables soaking up the ambient sounds in the room to be fed to the hungry recording desk. And of course, there was Kim's Dictaphone.

•••

It's March 2015, and I'm at the Yarra Hotel in Abbottsford to see Kim and Mike Stranges. An old, battered Dictaphone dangles from a lanyard around Kim's neck dancing around the microphone set to capture its output. With Mike half hidden behind the drum kit, Kim stands at the front of stage and tunes the Dictaphone, getting the right pitch. An eerie chorus of ghostly strings float out, unseen atmospheric conditions sustaining the gentle, contemplative guitar below. Kim leans into the microphone: 'Pathologise me if it makes you feel better, eulogise me, you got me to the letter'. The Yarra Hotel falls silent. As the song trickles to a breathless end, Mike launches the floor tom and snare into a flat-out sprint. Kim's right red boot hits the pedal and the Fender snarls into life, a pneumonic drill battering out a G chord. Just one chord. And it just stays there … for the whole song! My friend Jim, a genuine guitar nerd, fidgets and shuffles in his seat

as the tension of the sustained note continues unrelentingly. After two break neck minutes the song snaps shut. Jim throws his hands in the air and exclaims … '*It just never changed!*'

•••

The Dictaphone on *Pathologise Me* is one of the first things heard on 'My Script', but it's not the quirkiest instrumental device used on the album. *Fucking Shit Up*, the first song recorded, uses smart, funny lyrics set only to minimal drums and atonal bursts of noise — 'just sharp of G' — created by Kim pressing his thumb on his amplified guitar lead. Despite its sparse production, Kim characterises it as 'quite a sophisticated jazz thing. It's a weird pastiche really because it's got a glam rock kind of shuffle beat along with experimentalism and a jazz melody. You know, Michael Bublé could have sung it. So, it's got a few things going on, but because of the nature of the song, there's not much there, which to me is kind of like something I've strived for my whole career. Minimalism.'

On *Animal Man* Kim reproduced a corrupted version of the drumbeat from the Stones' *Honky Tonk Woman* by bashing a toy piano and stomping his foot on the floorboards of Myles's lounge room. 'When I first heard it on the radio, about 1970 or whenever, I thought that was the most primitive thing I'd ever heard. I just imagined a bunch of cavemen sitting around banging rocks. So I made myself write lyrics and came up with the idea of somebody that was an embarrassment to us all. Back in the '90s, when I still hadn't moderated some behaviours I was a bit of a piss head sometimes and could drink to the point where people would be telling me stories the next day, and they'd be quite incredible stories of things that I would *never do!* And my old manager Tim Pittman would say to me, "Don't let Animal Man come along, please." I thought when I was writing this thing "Oh this is a solo album. I should bring Animal Man in the picture."'

Kim also had ambition to record a long, completely improvised piece that didn't rely on conventional instrumentation. Years earlier, Kim and his friend David Brown had performed like this at the Make It Up Club and at international jazz festivals. David Brown had played multi-tonal bass in 'free jazz/punk/metal/art' group Bucketrider, and now plays what he calls 'prepared guitar'. Kim remembers all the various 'contraptions rigged to it, alligator clips and egg whisks and it makes a great sound, and we would basically just make it up on the spot'. Taking this concept into 'My Script', Kim set about creating sound textures: distant notes, sustained throbbing resonances, and wispy atmospherics and recorded a twenty three minute piece that, for 'My Script', is cut into five segments and inserted carefully into the song list.

Another song, *Client JGT683*, was repurposed from the *Key of Sea* project in 2012. When informed that he would be working with Waleed Aly as the 'migrant half' of the team, Kim's first thought was 'he follows Richmond. I don't even have a footy team … he's more Aussie than I am!' Mindful of Waleed's guitar shredder chops and general erudition, Kim prepared carefully, and crafted the bones of a story about the dehumanisation of Australia's immigration processing. 'People were called clients. They were given numbers rather than names to enable some of what goes on', and together, Waleed and Kim gave life to *Client JGT683*.

'My Script' was a success. Rolling Stone gave it a four and a half star review and featured Kim in a living legends article and series of live shows. Henry Rollins, a vocal Kim Salmon fan declared 'it might be Kim's best record. It is *so damn good*'. Kim toured it for months from one end of Australia and back again, through Europe, and then back and forth across Australia again — and he loved the record. 'My Script' held something special and stood out from the rest of his work. Reflecting on the album, Kim writes:

All I have done with this record is just make music and write songs without any criteria other than 'do I like this idea?' and 'does it sound good?' I've never really done that. In the past, I've approached my music from a conceptual art perspective. The Mark 2 *Scientists was all about minimalist primitivism, the Surrealists was about deconstruction and salvage, Salmon was about all kinds of HEAVY, 'E(a)rnest' was about the glut of singer — songwriter 'share-house folkies' around the place, The Darling Downs was the search for uplifting but simple beauty, Precious Jules' was punk/glam hooks; even a project like the Beasts of Bourbon had conceptual elements.*

I will continue to create in this way. I dropped out of a Fine Arts degree all those years ago to get a 'real job'. I soon realised that playing music took up the head-space I had for making art … so I've always approached it as though I was making art.

•••

My reward for ordering an advance copy of 'My Script' during the crowdfunding campaign was an original Kim Salmon drawing, penned during the recording of the album. As it turns out, he *does* have the head space for both music and visual art. Drawings poured out of Kim during the creation of 'My Script', initially nondescript everyday items like Selley's glue tubes, playing cards, or the musical equipment scattered around Myles' studio. These scribbles in black ink morphed and grew and demanded their own forum, so Kim brought to life his *Rock 'n' Roll Visual Diary* — a tiny black sketch book in which he started mapping the things around him while on tour — a drinks shelf at a bar, a seedy Sydney Street at night, fish 'n' chips on butchers paper …

It was the emergence of these drawings that led to *Salmon for Breakfast: Kim Salmon in Story, Sketch and Song*, a show I produced for the 2016 Darebin Music Feast at the Northcote Town Hall. Narrated by the wonderful Brian Nankervis, *Salmon for Breakfast* told the story of how I came to be writing this book and some of the things I found out about Kim. Part narration, part rock show and part art exhibition, it featured a curated display of over sixty of Kim's drawings from the *Visual Diary* that my friend Ross had painstakingly captured in photographic form. We projected selected artworks onto a colossal screen behind the stage to depict the scene that was unfolding under Brian's expert care, while on stage I drummed, and Kim played his songs, told stories, and read his lines from the script — playing himself in a show about, himself.

Kim started painting and sketching in earnest, no doubt making the ghost of Henry Hall back at the Art Faculty of the WA Institute of Technology very happy. In November 2018, the Brunswick Street Gallery opened *Lexical — a survey of artwork by Kim Salmon* featuring a mix of old and new paintings, plus a large collage of Ross' photographs of the original *Visual Diary* sketches.

The exhibition was the creative full stop on the 'My Script' era which Kim had entered in upheaval and ended on an artistic high. 'My Script', with its mix of songs both challenging and super catchy, had landed him firmly in the present tense and reasserted his credentials. The visual art spawned from the album's creative process both closed a loop that had started in high school and opened a new field of vision to the creative quests ahead. 'My Script' had delivered on its promise. It was, after all, a healing record.

20

Perpetual Motion

On the dashboard of Kim's car is a small rose made of Blu Tack, moulded into shape by Spencer P Jones. Spencer's health had been in decline for some time, and on a bad day Kim dropped round to his house with a bunch of flowers to lift his spirits. They sat for hours having 'a good old yarn', Spencer happy to be talking about anything except liver cancer. While he talked, Spencer was looking down, fiddling with something — not distracted, just purposeful. When Kim got up to leave Spencer thanked him for the flowers; he was touched and wanted to reciprocate. The Blu Tack rose was passed from Spencer to Kim as a simple but elegant act of friendship and appreciation.

Spencer would soon be in and out of hospital, but doing his best to fight it off. Angie Jones, Spencer's partner, recounts a night in 2016 when Spencer became very ill with severe build up of fluid in the abdomen that clearly needed treatment. But Lydia Lunch was in town, so Spencer suffered through the pain and swelling, watching the first half of Lydia's set before finally Angie ushered him to hospital. In

March 2018, the stakes were raised substantially when Spencer was diagnosed with cancer. Even then, after vomiting blood all over the floor, the typically stoic Spencer, who never took things too seriously, said he felt better after the spew and was going back to bed. Angie's better judgement again prevailed, and Spencer once again found himself at the hospital.

He did not, however, expect to be across the road from one of his band mates, in the hospital opposite. In November 2017, Brian Henry Hooper went to the doctor at the insistence of his wife Nineveh. He'd had a persistent cough for a couple of months that needed checking. When an x-ray was produced, the doctor couldn't hide his alarm — Brian had advanced primary lung cancer. Brian absorbed the news for a moment, then turned to Nineveh and said, 'I'm going to kick its arse, I'm the man for the job'. Typical Brian. Within days he was in treatment, fighting for his life. After battering courses of chemotherapy, radiation therapy and immunology treatment, Brian's prognosis only worsened, and in February 2018, while Brian lay in intensive care, Nineveh braced for his imminent passing. Yet somehow, a couple of months later, Brian Henry Hooper was again on stage playing bass in the Beasts of Bourbon.

In April 2018, a benefit show for Brian was arranged at the Prince of Wales, with a long line up featuring Kim Salmon and the New Scientists (Clare Moore, Mike Stranges and Boris Sujdovic) and a rare performance by the Beasts of Bourbon. Brian was gravely unwell but entered the Prince stage from his hospital bed in a wheelchair, accompanied by six nurses, an oxygen tank and an IV drip. 'The fact that he made it to the benefit was a miracle, he's a fighter. He had two wishes, to play again with the Beasts of Bourbon and to go home to his girls. We couldn't make that second wish come true though' (Nineveh Hooper). Brian played sitting in the wheelchair, as a sombre but still compelling Beasts of Bourbon played for the last time in support of their bass player. 'It was cathartic, and so highly emotional. People were amazed. It was like a miracle, most of the audience was crying'

(Nineveh Hooper). As the rumble of *Chase the Dragon* faded, Brian gave an emotional address to the teary crowd, saying 'My ship is sinking, I don't know how long I've got, and I'm not the only one …' looking across the stage at Spencer P Jones, whose time was also running out.

The morning after Brian's benefit, Kim picked up the phone to a reflective Tex Perkins. Tex was on his way to the airport and had resolved to get all of the Beasts of Bourbon band members, past and present, back into a recording studio.

> *Brian and Spencer played at Brian's benefit and it was such a triumphant, incredible, inspiring thing the next thing was let's go to the studio for one last time. It was more a case of let's just be there together. It was just to enjoy each other's company, in that way, for one last time* (Tex Perkins).

The Beasts all answered the call enthusiastically, with Brian pushing to record some hard and fast punk rock songs. But tragically, they had cause to come together sooner than they expected. Only six days after the magical show at the Prince of Wales, Brian Henry Hooper passed away. Brian, who had already faced a life destroying back injury but recovered to work full time, continue to play music, buy a house, marry Nineveh and be a proud father to his new twin daughters, couldn't fight on anymore.

In early 2019, I return to Brian's house to talk with Nineveh, sitting at the kitchen table where I interviewed Brian, only now his guitars are displayed instead of in active duty. As she recounts her life with Brian and his painful death, her daughter Ava approaches and shows me a CD, saying 'Daddy's album'. In November 2018, Nineveh held a launch for Brian's solo record, *What Would I Know*, a dark, miraculous record, the cover art of which is a haunting image of Brian's fatal x-ray. A second posthumous Brian Henry Hooper album, made with Mick Harvey, JP Shiloh, Kim and others at Thornbury's Incubator Studios, will be released too. There will be plenty of music for his family to hold on to. But it's Brian's compassion for others that Nineveh returns to as we talk, 'He would sit in the street and talk to a homeless man, he was amazing how he related to people at all levels. He really connected with people and he was so open'.

Kim was in Perth preparing to play a second benefit show for Brian the day he passed away. They had known each other for nearly forty years, and been through the mill together. In the final months of visiting Brian in hospital, Kim saw yet another side of his former band mate and friend.

> *He was truly inspirational in how he dealt with the situation. I watched him face his future with hope, humility, graciousness, courage and finally acceptance. Those last months were a lesson for me that I'll never forget. Brian was the teacher. I'm a better person for having known Brian, but from my own selfish point of view, all I can think is I've lost the person with whom I can share all those specific memories.*[1]

Brian's presence looms large in Kim's story, so I ask Nineveh what she thinks we should capture for the book. 'The key things for me are Brian's determination to live a well-balanced, stable life after his accident. His determination to keep going with his solo music. His compassion. He loved the Beasts of Bourbon and the boys. And he loved Kim' (Nineveh Hooper).

•••

The remaining Beasts of Bourbon returned to Melbourne for Brian's funeral. 'So that night I just booked a couple of days in the studio' (Tex Perkins), and the next day Kim, Tex, Boris, Tony, Charlie and Spencer all landed at Soundpark Studios. Spencer was gravely ill. No one really knew how he'd got through Brian's benefit show. But he spent as much time at the studio as he could, sitting in a comfy chair with a guitar amp nearby. 'We got a song out of him, and we got a few laughs. He just sat on the couch for many hours as well, just soaking it all in and occasionally giving his opinion. I'm really glad that all of us could be there. Kim was probably there the most, he was the most dependable, he was someone to lean on' (Tex Perkins).

Not really intent on recording an album as such, the Beasts brought in a couple of covers and some outlines of new material. Ideas were thrown around and then thrown together, the band working in together with the same ease as they did for the 'Axemans Jazz' recording. Charlie Owen says 'It didn't take long for the old chemistry to kick back in. We had a show in Spain where Spencer was meant to go but couldn't, so I played with Boris and Kim there'[2]. Before long another album was taking shape, with songs by Kim, Tex, Boris, James Baker — who couldn't be there for the recording due to his own ill health — Spencer and Brian. A couple of new songs materialised in the studio, or in the case of *Your Honour*, were formed over a text message exchange between Tex and Kim. The shadow of Brian's death, and the looming fate for Spencer forged a reflective and appreciative atmosphere in the studio. 'I really enjoyed the interesting new mix of players. Mostly it was really enjoyable working with Kim again. Just bombing ideas off each other, it was great to be doing that again' (Tex Perkins). The recordings captured the easy by play between the Beasts, the effortless performances and rekindled connections between the players. The songs were strong and the production by Andrew 'Idge' Hehir at Soundpark fit the occasion perfectly.

> *Tex and I were saying 'jeez, it came up better than we both expected didn't it — and yes it did! And part of the beauty of that is we weren't expecting anything. We were just going in as a bunch of mates to honour our mates and it was kind of the end of an era, but it was the birth of a new one in a way.*[3]
> (Charlie Owen)

The sessions at Soundpark would be Spencer's last outing with the band. Not long after he returned to hospital, but this time in palliative care. As word spread, the Melbourne music community gathered around him. Inexplicably in the last month of his life Spencer had taken to listening to harmonious Irish folk music, enjoying it because it was 'lovely, and pissed off all the people next door!' (Angie Jones)

On the 21st of August in 2018, late in the day, a friend sang softly to him in the hospital. 'And to the sound of an Irish tune Spencer's breathing changed, and he left us' (Angie Jones). Kim was shattered, weathering the death of another close friend. 'What a patient, quirky, thoughtful and meticulous fellow my friend was despite the rock and roll legend that followed him everywhere. So sad is the loss of this truly unique and inspiring person. He was my bro, my comrade, my other bookend in the Beasts of Bourbon and he will be missed by me and countless people all over the world'.

Reflecting on Spencers' life in and out of music, Mick Thomas views him as anarchic and courageous:

> *He led by example in that he was prepared to go out on a limb stylistically. He was such a laconic character, he was prepared to let situations play out and not intervene. I reckon he had this pretty anarchic position in everything, in his playing and in his personality. If there was a road he'd just charge down it and he was musical enough he could get away with it* (Mick Thomas).

Spencer and Angie had paid their respects at Ross Hannaford's funeral at Blackwood only months earlier, and loved the setting. Spencer, having spent much of his life in dark, urban music venues was charmed by the open sky, tall trees and damp grass of the quiet, country spot. He declared to Angie that it was where he wanted to end up too, so she laid him to rest there with the simple inscription, 'All the way with SPJ'.

Spencer's death transformed the Soundpark recordings from a final Beasts of Bourbon record to a noisy ode by a bunch of old friends to their fallen comrades. 'The Beasts of Bourbon is over. The Beasts of Bourbon was a band I started with Spencer. But we accidentally made this record' (Tex Perkins). So, it was just the 'Beasts', not the Beasts of Bourbon, who went out on the road.

•••

It's only early, but the room is full, and the sense of occasion almost drips off the walls. The crowd is a mix of bearded old rock dogs, the well-heeled young and many in between. The merch desk is already on rations, and the bar is churning thirsty customers at pace, like Beasts of Bourbon crowds of old. The band room is dark, and the stage soaked with dim, otherworldly blue light and thick fog from the smoke-machine. Through the indistinct haze walk the five shadowy Beasts, looking purposeful as guitars are slung on, microphones clenched, and drums positioned. The lights shift, and the band is revealed; Charlie Owen, Tex Perkins, Tony Pola, Boris Sujdovic and, to the right of stage, Kim Salmon. Tex leans forward and addresses the crowd: 'Thanks for having us. This one's for Brian' — and Tony and Boris open up *On My Back*. Charlie and Kim shoot a glance across the stage, and in unison their guitars kick in. Tex grabs the mic stand with both hands. 'Lying here. Feeling queer. All my fears, reappear …' The Beasts — still here — are back.

'Ladies and gentlemen, we have Kim Salmon here!' announces Tex, pointing over at Kim who, on cue, peels off the opening riff of *Pearls Before Swine*, his self-appointed Beasts theme song. Kim looks charged, sharp and crackling with energy. Tex is all fluid movement, potent as ever. Charlie is hunched over his guitar, shifting back and forth like he's sizing up the assignment. Boris looms over his bass, immersed and monolithic. Behind them, Tony is visible through the smog and lights due only to his Santa Clause-esque beard and whirling drum sticks. The band look and sound great — life's rough edges leaving maybe a little less swagger but greater resolve and authority — a little bit of danger mixed with a safe set of hands.

Brian Henry Hooper and Spencer P Jones are missed, but not absent. Tex talks about them, gives thanks to them, sings for them at times. Brian's song *What the Hell Was I Thinking* is an emotive guts punch, a great song already and elevated by these Beasts paying tribute to him through its performance. Spencer's *At the Hospital* is delivered as a solemn, late night, smoky jazz-hymn; the quick humour of the every-day hospital drama unfolding in the lyrics not masking the band's deep sadness for the song's departed creator.

The on-stage transformation from the Beasts of Bourbon to the Beasts unfolds with warmth, respect and class. Only the cool physical and spiritual presence of Boris Sujdovic could stand alongside the space left by Brian Hooper and assemble a complete picture. Kim's return looks so natural. He summons the voodoo that made the original Beasts such a grand puzzle, while introducing a whole new palette of chicanery. Any questions about how he and Charlie would operate together in the wake of Spencer P Jones are answered immediately. Neither try to replicate Spencer's role, but instead create their own complementary lines to recast the Beasts in a new light. It works incredibly well.

Most of the 'Still Here' record is represented in the set, the new songs sounding at home amongst Beast's landmarks like *Chase the Dragon, Low Road* and *Drop Out.* The show culminates with Spencer's *Execution Day*, played to an eerie, subdued on-stage landscape and atmosphere. Spencer and Brian could just about be alongside the Beasts still here as the song's last note rings out. The band embrace and line up arm in arm, leaving the audience with a heartfelt theatrical bow and the dissonant rumble of guitar feedback.

•••

It's like surfing on the edge of a black hole sometimes.

Kim is describing a recent show with the *Mark 2* Scientists at Geelong. Momentum surrounding the 1985 line up of the Scientists — Leanne, Tony, Boris and Kim — has been building for years, and finally, they have launched. In 2018 the Scientists did a full Australian tour in April and a long European tour in June. In September, over thirty years since Mark Arm and Steve Turner fished 'Blood Red River' out of a Seattle record store import rack, the Scientists finally embarked on their inaugural US tour. Starting with dates in Portland and Seattle with friends Mudhoney, the tour went to San Francisco, LA, Austin, Chicago, Brooklyn, Jersey City and more. Put together by Emmett Kelly from Ty Segall's band, the tour was a major success. 'Every show was sold out, and loads of people didn't get to see us. We stunned people, and they said all kinds of crazy shit about us! I got accolades that I've never had before, like I could start a cult!' The tour was so successful that the band were asked to return straight away, and in April 2019 they conducted a blitzkrieg assault on Chicago, Cleveland, Detroit, Toronto, Brooklyn, Philadelphia, Durham, Atlanta, New Orleans and LA.

The shows were free and wild, the Scientist machine was fuelled up and indestructible. Kim put down the guitar each night, dancing, swinging his arms around directing the band and cajoling the audience. 'Tony can handle the guitar! I don't need to play that much with him around. Tony is a very sophisticated guitarist, he's up there with Robert Fripp'. Each night the crowds got more intense, pushing forward to see the band not shrinking in shock to the back of the room as they did when the Scientist first unleashed their ungodly din on the Sydney Trades Union Club in the 80s.

The legend of the Scientists had percolated all those years, and their arrival was heralded as destiny fulfilled. 'The biggest thing I got from that tour was not that it was sold out, it was that every support band we played with came up to us said, "man, it's an honour to play with you guys" and shook our hands. I thought "fuck, how good is that". We hadn't played in thirty years and still people were coming up and saying it's an honour to play with you. It was full on respect everywhere we went' (Boris Sujdovic). The Scientists had proved themselves many times over and were now playing with full throttle enjoyment, not the morbid battles and hostilities of their former years. Only the audience in New Orleans were treated to the antagonisms of old after Kim literally jumped off the stage ready to fist fight each and every one of them in response to a sharp heckle! No longer focused just on survival, the Scientists could appreciate their achievements. 'I guess when everyone comes up and says it's an honour to play with you, you think maybe I *have* done something in my life' (Boris Sujdovic).

The Scientists are out of this world. They have remained as confounding and peculiar in their renaissance years as during their formative years. The US tours accentuated just *how* atypical the Scientists are. 'It's like we're a parallel to rock 'n' roll really. I don't think we actually *are* a rock 'n' roll band. We're something from a completely other dimension and galaxy, that's the Scientists.'

To coincide with the European tour and first US tour, the Scientists released 7-inch singles: *Mini Mini/Perpetual Motion* and *Brain Dead/SurvivalSkills*. The idea to return to the studio arose after Tony, based in London, recorded a musical telegram for a friend's birthday, adding Kim's vocals and Boris' bass to his initial effort by overdubbing in Melbourne. It worked so well that the same method was applied to the new singles. It's risky bringing a classic band back to record new material, and for a long time Kim was reluctant, but the audiences' appetite for the singles made him reconsider.

When Kim had finished promoting 'My Script', he contemplated how he would repackage himself for the next assault. To sustain a career in music for as long as Kim has, presenting the audience with a new idea or proposition was essential, and this time round he was considering a 'weird 70s folk thing, like Cat Stevens'. In Canberra 2017, Kim played Sam Worrad and I a sneak preview of some new acoustic numbers before our show later that night — *Hey Sydney, Whats this Game,* and *SurvivalSkills*. They were scratchy, but immediately appealing. Different, but somehow recognisable, like something the Scientists might do. Kim played the songs to Tony and Boris, and they loved them. For now, we won't know what Kim Salmon channelling Cat Stevens sounds like, for these new songs chose a different life, forming the back bone of the new Scientists EP '9H2O. SiO2' — released while in the thick of their 2019 US tour. Kim took the creation of the EP seriously, knowing that a wrong move could diminish the band's revival. 'It's a process of scientifically putting it together to try and preserve those things that happened in 1981 when I first heard Tony in a room with Brett and Boris … and I thought, "I want that sound!" You can't write just any old shit for this band.' The formula remained the same. As the songs were presented to the band, the salvage operation swung into gear.

> *I put down a bass line and Kim was saying 'nah I don't like that', 'it's a bit too … nah I don't like it'. So after the third time I thought I'll just ignore the structure of the song, the rhythm and everything and I'll just play fucking anything. So it did that, and I said 'there, is that what you wanted?' And he said, 'yeah that sounded great!* (Boris Sujdovic)

•••

The US tours have been life affirming for Kim. 'I found myself on that trip in so many ways, I found that I *was* the person I thought I was in the first place!' After forty three years of music, he remains fired up, continues to push boundaries, and still puts on a show. 'I've been in front of his amp for forty years and some of the stuff I still hear him play blows me away. He's just doing his thing and I think, "where the fuck does that come from?"' (Boris Sujdovic)

And it keeps coming. The band returned to the States for a third time in July 2019, followed by a Kim Salmon solo tour to promote the LP reissue of *Hook Line and Singer*. The hectic touring and new recordings have given the opportunity for the band to exist again. The band that formed Kim's very identity back in Perth, have affirmed his life long, unwavering, intrepid commitment to making *his* art, *his* way. 'I came back from the tours thinking "what a band"! It was like in the mid 80s, everyday I'd wake up and think "at least I know I was in the greatest rock band in eternity". I knew that nobody came close. And I felt that again'.

Kim once railed against being defined by the Scientists, but the analogy the band provides — transforming from contrary outsiders to aging international artists who will not compromise their creative ideals and keep doing things their way — defines Kim as much as anything. His entire adult life has been dedicated to this journey into the dark matter of art and music, and he shows no sign of slowing down or playing it safe.

> *I always had a feeling that I was a late starter. Who cares about how old we are? I think I'm well equipped to be an old person rock star.*

21

Essence

This story is told by a long-time fan who became a biographer by accident. It's an appreciative tribute to an artist who has dedicated his life to music, and my experiences as Kim's fan of nearly thirty years, as his guitar student, occasional collaborator and eventually, friend, informs the narrative. Kim's story is rendered here, but its telling gifted me much more than the publishing of a book.

In guitar lessons Kim coaxed me to learn Carole King's *Too Late Baby* by promising, if I nailed it, he would get up on stage and play it with me. Duly challenged, I mastered Carol King's wonderful chords and my bandmates Jim, Paul and Maddy worked the song up ready for debut on stage. After I invited him to join us on stage, Kim responded 'Well I promised didn't I, so I better do it'. In one of the best nights I've had in music, Kim played three songs with us, and with Sharon, Hannah and Maxie there to watch the night felt like a triumph.

Another favourite moment was during the *Salmon for Breakfast* shows. Aside from working with Brian Nankervis, the most naturally confident and effortlessly charming person I've ever met, something incredible happened each night on stage. I got to sit behind the drums, on stage with Kim Salmon, and watch him perform in a show I wrote, about a book I was writing, about him! An audience member and fan, from the vantage point of co-performer on stage — it was surreal.

When I first knocked on Kim's door, I was timorous, not knowing what to expect. The Kim Salmon stage persona — aloof, fierce, absorbed and slightly contemptuous — didn't suggest an easy social presence. But the Kim Salmon I've come to know is courteous, self-effacing, curious and very, very funny. He's also stubborn, proud, determined, genuinely artistic and one completely abstract cat. Kim Salmon has been taking the hard path all this life. He's endlessly toured, played, recorded, written, drawn and sung, never deviating from the course his artistic impulses set. He's made and lost money, been in and out of fashion, had lucky breaks and major setbacks, and muddled through health and family travails like the rest of us.

Kim knows what he's best at: distilling concepts from the nebulous to the applied, embracing ambiguity, creating with integrity, salvaging curious remnants to construct a powerful and unique whole, and enduring. That is, Kim's strengths are writing great songs, putting on killer shows, and working really, *really* hard. How he continues to perform and create with such vitality, to such an exceptional standard and in such a rarefied field after more than four battering decades, is a riddle this book sought to resolve. What *is* the essence of Kim Salmon?

It was always clear that Kim was not interested in fitting in. He was an *individual,* and set out to do things his way, with the psychological push and pull of deliberative determination and sub conscious imperative. The Scientists set the template. 'He was really going it alone, there was no road map for what he was doing — you can't really see the parallels elsewhere in the world where they fitted in' (Bruce Milne). His innate commitment to individualism has struck a chord with artists all over the world, inspiring others to follow.

> *He's not looking outwards, he's going with what's coming out of him. He's on the record as saying that listening to Alex Chilton gave him permission to be "more like himself" and that's beautifully put. And the writers and the musicians that I love give me that permission, not to do something like them but to go off and be utterly myself. And an audience picks up on that at a very, very deep level. So that's why I think he's such an important musician. He's gotta do—and completely commits to doing—his own thing. It gives you enormous courage as an artist to see someone doing that'* (Andy Griffiths).

Kim's *inventiveness* has produced an incredible array of music. A Kim Salmon 'best of' album would be a wild ride. With such a wide bandwidth, he is impossible to categorise. Henry Rollins has followed Kim's career passionately, keeping track of every new release. 'Kim is obviously wired into a signal very strong and strange. One of his great strengths is that he has evaded definition for decades. The only way to describe one of Kim's records is to put it on' (Henry Rollins). Few artists can claim such a diverse range of music as their output — post punk, power pop, swamp, glam, acoustic, dissonant noise, jazz, rock, country, and of course grunge … it's all there in the Salmon catalogue. 'His legacy is tough 'cos he's done so many different phases, and different styles and sounds. He helped kick start grunge, but he did a lot more than that' (Larry Hardy).

Performance, as well as creation, is central to Kim's proposition. In the Scientists, his primary motivation for writing songs was to give the band a reason to perform, to help define and redefine the concept the band was offering. While song writing took on increasing significance for Kim, he has never stopped playing guitar, singing, performing. In fact, his performance is becoming more liberated. His presentation is carefully considered, particularly the constructed appearance of the band. His singing is idiosyncratic, identifiably Australian, and versatile — from wavery falsetto to growling baritones and everything in between. 'He's got one of the great shouts in rock' (Tex Perkins). His guitar playing is blistering, inventive and one of a kind.

> *He's a really instinctive player, he can play off anything, he's one of the top players in Australia. It's vicious when it needs to be, sweet when it needs to be, droning when it needs to be, he can do it all. Just his attitude, the way he fucken tears it up. When he gets in that frame of mind he plays like a maniac! He has got some power within him, he's just definitely got it* (Brian Hooper).

Unpredictability is central to Kim's work. He has confounded audiences and industry observers with his choices — walking away from the Beasts of Bourbon at their height, touring the Human Jukebox Scientists instead of the all-conquering *Swampland* line up — and moving from project to project as though trying to throw off a close tail. Kim mines opportunities, follows leads, and responds to signals most humans can't detect. 'You can't predict what he's going to do, but he's going to be three steps ahead of you on that and as a fan it's really fun to follow. And you know it's going to be good and interesting and intelligent' (Larry Hardy). In performance, Kim refuses to toe the line of expectation. 'If you're going to see him play live, he will wilfully experiment, and if you're not ready for it … if you're expecting to see him play songs and instead he's connected pickups to his body and producing various loud squealing noises, you're in for a shock!'(Bruce Milne)

Kim is no prima donna. Work ethic and *endurance* sit hand in glove with his creativity. Time on the road touring, long hours sound-checking and loading gear, and late nights performing are the most obvious intrusions. More insidious is the quiet percolation of a creative impulse, an artistic knot that needs to be untied, that keeps an artist in their head and absent from the present tense. The dedication to reach for that perfect composition — no matter how many rewrites are required. 'The dude can't stop. It's kind of amazing, it's like he doesn't even have time to just stay at home and get depressed. He just works even harder' (Mike Stranges).

Living with this *dedication f*or the arts is not complementary with life in the 'real world', and Kim's art has, at times, come at personal cost. He has war stories and regrets, relationships compromised or lost. His vocation gives no guarantees, no secret tricks, and plenty of evidence that failure is much more likely than success. Yet the arts are not only Kim Salmon's calling, he's managed to make it his career.

> *Kim has swapped out life for music. Any musician who was any good has to make this choice. One suffers at the expense of the other. He's the real thing. You know it when you hear it. I've always been amazed at how Kim keeps it going, decade after decade. I still keep getting the records and they remain great. When you look at how much music he's generated, how many people he's collaborated with, it's beyond impressive* (Henry Rollins).

I ask Dave Graney, who has been Kim's friend from just about the beginning, how Kim should be categorised.

> *He probably sees himself as a type of 'in action artist'. I think his music has gotten better and better over the years. I think he would probably like to be approached via his work and there are songs of his that express a lot of complexity and silliness/simplicity all at once. Great as a band leader and polemical art songwriter* (Dave Graney).

Everyone I talk to about Kim identifies him as an artist of high and unusual order. The early talent he showed in the visual arts morphed into music, and the mysterious landscapes of his wild, swampy childhood implanted a twisted impulse, a propensity to find the dirt not the flowers.

> *He's an artist. It doesn't matter what you play or what you do. If you're one of a kind, if you have your own lexicon or turn of phrase and you're off the beaten path or subverting or perverting something and doing it in a way that actually*

connects with people — like a force of nature — then you're an artist (Gareth Liddiard).

As with all art, there are hits and misses, but it's never boring. 'If you're interested in Kim there's going to be things you're going to hate and things that will astound you, but overall you're going to say well the guy is a fucken artist and no one told Pablo Picasso that he had to keep doing cubist painting, and if they were this size, they'd sell better than that size!' (Bruce Milne)

The *humour* that is so evident in Kim the person is now immediately recognisable in his work. There were always sharp witted gems hidden amongst the swamps, fire and cockroaches — songs with a sense of danger, but a sense of humour. But Kim's recent output has been ripe with confounding rhymes and sharply funny lyrics. Kim's funny bone is seriously bent. He pops out abstract gags and funny, obscure references like a tommy gun, peppering every conversation with oddly comic remarks that have you half in stitches and half on guard in case you let one fly past without detecting it. The intrusion of this spirit into Kim's lyrics has elevated his work, enhanced the deconstructionist underpinnings, and transitioned his style to a rich, new phase at a stage of his career where many artists are recycling their former glories. New Scientists songs, still unmistakable, are infused with clever asides and satisfying rhymes. On his song *100 Points of ID*, he assigns identity points according to value: 'the first born son of a drummer from a rival band — ten points. DNA from your gran's favourite pet duck — five points. Bailey and his latter-day Saints — forty points. Michael Hutchence — seventy points', and then puts a full stop on it with an exuberant 'oawwwaah!!'

Kim's knowledge of song construction and constant endeavour to *push the boundaries* is definitive. 'It's just like being in a band with Paul McCartney or someone. Someone that's always trying to do something new and different' (Mike Stranges). And key to everything he tries is anchoring it in a concept or totem. 'Just the way he thinks about things is from an artists' perspective. Kim has got that artistic edge where the music has got that theme or high concept' (Ashley Naylor). Every song, every clothing choice, every lyric carries meaning. 'It's never a nothing. It's always *something* that he's presenting because everything is *conceptual*' (Mike Stranges).

Kim's likens his approach to performance, song writing, creation as a *salvage operation*. The evidence of this is strewn all through his career — adapting *Mark 1* Scientists to James' lyrics and melodies, forging *Mark 2* Scientists out of the raw elements his band mates possessed, the multiple identities of the Surrealists that responded to the new personnel, and Kim's adaptability in making different music in *so* many different formations. It all requires the capacity to hunt and gather, salvage what can be found lying in the wreckage.

> *If all he had was red paint, he'd paint a red picture. The idea is to make something out of what you have. And if you want something for your book, that's a metaphor for his career and the type of artist he is. He's making something out of what's around him at the time* (Mike Stranges).

Kim's salvage operation affords respect to his collaborators. It shows empathy for the strengths and skills of others, understanding of limitations, and demonstrates flexibility to adapt and reorganise. Each new salvage moves the narrative forward to another interpretation, another definition. In Kim Salmon's artistic world, there is no treading water. 'It's all about growth, it's all about moving forward. Kim knows that very well. He doesn't stand still' (Brian Hooper).

Whatever his essence, Kim has left his mark.

> *He writes unusual stuff from a particular angle and on top of that he's a really interesting, special guitar player. Combine those two and throw in all the projects he's been involved with and he's a really important figure ... He's got a compulsion to be pretty eccentric and when you channel that you get an amazing result, something pretty special* (Mick Harvey).
>
> *He is viewed as an incredibly important part of the*

Australian music industry, the world music industry. His influence continues to grow. His influence will be remembered in a hundred years time and there'll be people playing his songs in a hundred years time (Bruce Milne).

•••

Kim Salmon may have had the formula for Grunge, but his whole career is a mystifying non-formula. Kim is incapable of choosing the safe road. He confounds expectations, assumptions, and obstacles not to prove a point, but just because he knows no other way. He is a genuinely misshaped creative mind. He has been at the frontier over and over again, way ahead of the rest.

I ask Gareth Liddiard from the Drones, 'What do you think is the most important element that a book about Kim should contain?'

Just that he is an artist in a country where that's not okay. There are plenty of great performers, but there's always a shortage of great artists. It's usually the artists who inspire the performers to inspire the people ... and all the artists usually get for thanks are those same people writing off artists as being difficult wankers and snake oil salesmen. Kim is not always great. Sometimes he overshoots and sometimes he undershoots, but that's what you get for being an artist. Kim chose the hard road because he has integrity. Integrity may not be in fashion this week or decade or whatever but it will come back around. It always does because integrity is right in all situations, always (Gareth Liddiard).

What I've really learned is that Kim takes people with him, he gives people a chance. He's generous with what he knows, and he adapts to give others the opportunity to participate. He challenges you to try, and makes you believe you've got something to offer.

Todd Pickett, Kim's Perth drummer quietly concludes:

> *Kim is inspiring because he makes me think its okay to follow my gut and do music … It means the world to me 'cos I constantly doubt myself, and I guess Kim makes me a little bit softer on what could happen. 'Cos if Kim can still do it, after all the ups and downs, and he still gives it everything, it makes me feel like I'm going be alright* (Todd Pickett).

Even with these insights, there remains something intangible about Kim Salmon. He is still at the edges, making art where others rarely venture. I ask Tex, who has known Kim for over thirty years, how he would describe Kim, to sum him up.

> *'Sum him up? No, I haven't summed him up. I'm still getting to know him'* (Tex Perkins).

•••

It's my last interview with Kim for the book. We sit at his dining table, drinking coffee as the evening turns cool. Maxie is floating around, getting dinner ready and chiming in with the occasional observation. Emma arrives home, quietly alerting Kim to her presence, and soon after, Gene walks in. It's getting late, and I want to leave Kim to his Sunday evening — but just a couple more questions. I feel a faint nostalgia for this moment even though I'm still in it, aware that these long and winding conversations are at their end. Kim's story, at least the version that I've uncovered, has been told.

I ask Kim to reflect on his journey through music, the choices he has made, the paths he has travelled, and the things he's achieved.

> *I am in the position of being able to make a living out of playing music. Being able to still create music. That in itself is an achievement and I think it's a lucky position to be in. You can't just go regretting what didn't happen. I did what I did. And I can't imagine having done it any other way. It's a path I've chosen to take.*

What has been the meaning, the key thing?

> *I just think the joy of making music, and the fact that I once wouldn't have thought I had a musical bone in my body, but suddenly found I could learn to play an instrument. The thrill of learning to make music, singing, learning to write lyrics. It's something I'm still doing, I'm learning the drums now. Learning to manipulate sounds into art is really the journey. I still think I'm never going to be a natural at it and that's going to be the thing that I've got to give to it. 'Cos it's still a mystery to me and I'm still trying to work it out, and that's why it works for me.*

And what is next for Kim Salmon?

> *I'd like to keep playing music, and I'd like to do more art. I think I've still got things to say. There's still a lot of exploring to do.*

I put away the Zoom for the last time, and ask one final question. Do you think you and Mike will write that number one hit?

> *[laughs] Yeah. That would be great!*

POSTSCRIPT

This book was first published in November 2019, launched with a sold out show at Memo Music Hall in St Kilda. We brought out Kid Congo Powers to headline, and he teamed up with the Near Death Experience (Harry Howard, Edwina Preston, Clare Moore and Dave Graney) to deliver a set of Cramps, Gun Club and Kid Congo songs which we recorded, and Kid later released as a live album. It's a nice memento.

In the years since, the pace of Kim Salmon's creative output has not slowed.

Over the summer of 2019/2020 there were terrible bushfires in Australia, and the music industry were front and centre of the community response, raising money and good spirits for those effected by the fires. This outpouring of good will would soon be tested by the COVID-19 pandemic which almost completely shut down the creative industries, but at the time Kim Salmon enthusiastically joined the throng of artists contributing by forming a new outfit, **Smoked Salmon**, to play some fund raiser shows. With a mission statement to play the hits, Smoked Salmon focused on the poppier numbers from Kim's output, and eventually grew into an international cast, as Kim assembled players in Perth, Brisbane, Sydney and France to augment the original Melbourne based line up. A Smoked Salmon album of all new songs was released in March 2025, and with shows all over Australia, a tour of France in 2023, Japan in 2024 and broader Europe tour in 2025, the band moved at pace. At the time of writing the band are about to release a new compilation of Salmon songs called Totally Sick.

Kim's connection with Japan garage rock was fostered on the tour, and subsequent hosting of garage punk legends The Fadeaways for shows in Australia in 2024. This led to a collaboration with **Masami**, with a totally improvised live show at the Make it Up Club in Collingwood that was later rendered to vinyl called Blossoming and released in 2025.

The Scientists were busy during this period too, with the classic mid 1980's line up of Salmon, Boris Sudjovic, Leanne Cowie and Tony Thewlis touring Australia and Europe several times and a long-awaited return to the USA. The band released an album of all new material in 2021. In the most recent of some very sad events, Leanne tragically and unexpectedly passed away in March 2025. Kim, Boris and Tony are currently planning a repackaging of the Scientists with legendary drummer Clare Moore.

The Surrealists, who also starred at the 2019 launch of this book, have played sparingly over the last few years, but notably featured in two peculiar on line events during the pandemic when proper live shows were off limits. One of these events produced an album of mostly improvised music, with the process live streamed to viewers watching safely at home.

The Beasts of Bourbon transmuted to simply **The Beasts** after the passing of Brian Henry Hooper and original member Spencer P Jones in 2018. The band was shaken up further with the passing first of Tony Pola in 2021 and then the legendary James Baker in 2025. In late 2025 the Beasts celebrated the 35th anniversary of their classic Black Milk album, now with Evan Richards on drums.

In the book we describe a **Darling Downs** show from 2016. It turns out that was the last ever performance of the duo. Ron Peno, who had been riding high with his band The Superstitions, became ill and was forced to cancel a series of shows with the reformed Died Pretty. He eventually passed in 2023, and although he and Kim had discussed plans for their next album it did not have the chance to eventuate. The song, A Little Bit of Rain by Fred Neil was recorded on the Smoked Salmon in honour of Ron.

In the Red Records in LA are planning the 2026 release of our **Haunted Grooves** double album, a co-production and performance between the artist and this author, presenting live recordings of tales and songs capturing how some of the now deceased characters in Kim's life impacted his music. It is the most realised production in a series of performances that have seen Kim weaving story telling amongst the songs.

Miles Davis is credited with saying 'A painting is music you can see, and music is a painting you can hear.' Perhaps in this vein, Kim Salmon has, over the years since the first edition of this biography, forged a serious and satisfying career as a **visual artist**. With multiple solo and group exhibitions, an artist's residency and a healthy sales record, Kim is now rarely far from a watercolour sketch book or canvas.

Kim Salmon is, as I write this, nearly 69. He lives in Northcote, an inner north suburb of Melbourne, with his partner Maxine and their cat Zoro. He continues to write, paint and perform.

November 2025

NOTES

Chapter 1. 'So, you written my book yet?'

1 Cass, Dan (1 July 2013). 'What Happened When I Learned to Play Guitar with My Idol Kim Salmon', *The Guardian*, 1 July, 2013.

Chapter 6. Cheap & Nasty

1 McFarlane, Ian. 'Whammo Homepage', *Encyclopedia of Australian Rock and Pop*. St Leonards, NSW: Allen & Unwin 1999.
2 Salmon, Kim. 'Kim Salmon's Perspective on the Early Perth Punk Era', *Perth Punk, www.perthpunk.com/personal-perspectives/kim-salmon/*
3 Salmon, Kim. 'Kim Salmon's Perspective on the Early Perth Punk Era', *Perth Punk, www.perthpunk.com/personal-perspectives/kim-salmon/*
4 McFarlane, Ian. 'Beasts of Bourbon' entry at the Wayback Machine, *web.archive.org/web/20040420012412/, www.whammo.com.au/encyclopedia.asp?articleid=84*, (Archived from the original on 20 April 2004).
5 Salmon, Kim. 'Kim Salmon's Perspective on the Early Perth Punk Era', *Perth Punk, www.perthpunk.com/personal-perspectives/kim-salmon/*
6 Bungle, Ross. *www.perthpunk.com/personal-perspectives/kim-salmon/*
7 Salmon, Kim. 'Kim Salmon's Perspective on the Early Perth Punk Era', *Perth Punk, www.perthpunk.com/personal-perspectives/kim-salmon/*
8 Stratton, Jon. 'Pissed On Another Planet. Perfect Beat', *The Pacific Journal of Research into Contemporary Music and Popular Culture*. 7 (2): pp. 36-60, 2005.
9 Davidson, Eric. 'Legendary Australian Band, 'Scientists' Reveal Their Secret Formula!', *Please Kill Me* (20 September, 2018), *pleasekillme.com/australias-scientists*
10 *Hozac Records* (2018), *www.strangeworldrecords.com.au/products/cheap-nasties-s-t-lp*
11 Salmon, Kim. 'Kim Salmon's Perspective on the Early Perth Punk Era', *Perth Punk, www.perthpunk.com/personal-perspectives/kim-salmon*

Chapter 7. Pissed on Another Planet

1 DNA Fanzine, issue 7 (February 1980), *https://ozmusicbooks.com/product/dna-issue-7-february-1980/*
2 DNA Fanzine, issue 7 (February 1980), *https://ozmusicbooks.com/product/dna-issue-7-february-1980/*
3 Salmon, Kim. 'Kim Salmon's Perspective on the Early Perth Punk Era', *Perth Punk, www.perthpunk.com/personal-perspectives/kim-salmon/*

4 DNA Fanzine, Issue 13 (July 1980), *https://ozmusicbooks.com/product-category/australian-and-new-zealand-music-books/fanzines-and-magazines/dna-fanzine/dna-issues-11-21/*
5 McFarlane, Ian. 'Lethal Weapons - 1978 And Melbourne Punk', *Third Stone Press* (2007), https://*www.thirdstonepress.com.au/archive-blog/2018/5/1/lethal-weapons-1978-and-melbourne-punk*
6 DNA Fanzine, Issue 3 (December 1979), *https://ozmusicbooks.com/product/dna-issue-3-december-1979/*
7 DNA Fanzine, Issue 34 (January 1984), *https://ozmusicbooks.com/product/dna-issue-34-january-1984/*
8 Ibid.
9 McFarlane, Ian. 'Beasts of Bourbon' entry at the Wayback Machine, *https://web.archive.org/web/20040420012412/http:/www.whammo.com.au/encyclopedia.asp?articleid=84, (Archived from the original on 20 April 2004).*
10 DNA Fanzine, issue 7 (February 1980), *https://ozmusicbooks.com/product/dna-issue-7-february-1980/*
11 DNA Fanzine, Issue 13 (July 1980), *https://ozmusicbooks.com/product-category/australian-and-new-zealand-music-books/fanzines-and-magazines/dna-fanzine/dna-issues-11-21/*
12 DNA Fanzine, Issue 34 (January 1984), *https://ozmusicbooks.com/product/dna-issue-34-january-1984/*
13 Salmon, Kim. 'Kim Salmon's Perspective on the Early Perth Punk Era', *Perth Punk, www.perthpunk.com/personal-perspectives/kim-salmon/*

Chapter 8. This is My Happy Hour

1 Numero Group, 'A Place Called Bad' Scientists box set, *www.numerogroup.com/d/the-scientists-a-place-called-bad*
2 DNA Fanzine, Issue 13 (July 1980), *https://ozmusicbooks.com/product-category/australian-and-new-zealand-music-books/fanzines-and-magazines/dna-fanzine/dna-issues-11-21/*
3 Livingston, Alistair. 'Scientists – Au Go Go Records – 1983 / 1984'(May 3, 2010) *https://killyourpetpuppy.co.uk/news/scientists-au-go-go-records-1983-1984*
4 Delibašić, Aleksandar. 'Blood Red River: 1982-1984, Citadel' (November 2000), *https://badmusicforbadpeople.com/blood-red-river-1982-1984-citadel-november-2000/*
5 (DNA)
6 Irwin, Tom. 'Tav Falco's Panther Burns' (May 23, 2019) *https://illinoistimes.com/article-21253-tav-falco%25E2%2580%2599s-panther-burns.html*
7 Delibašić, Aleksandar. 'Blood Red River: 1982-1984, Citadel' (November 2000), *https://badmusicforbadpeople.com/blood-red-river-1982-1984-citadel-november-2000/*
8 Livingston, Alistair. 'Scientists – Au Go Go Records – 1983 / 1984'(May 3, 2010) *https://killyourpetpuppy.co.uk/news/scientists-au-go-go-records-1983-1984*
9 Ibid.
10 Stratton, Jon. 'The Scientists and Grunge: Influence and Globalised Flows'. *Australian Rock: Essays of Popular Music*. Perth, WA:

Network Books. Department of Communication & Cultural Studies (Curtin University), 1 December 2007.

11 Emery, Patrick. 'Kim Salmon of the Scientists Talks About *Blood Red River*'. I-94 Bar, *https://web.archive.org/web/20130926034111/http:/www.i94bar.com/ints/bloodredriver.html*

12 DNA Fanzine, Issue 33 (October 1983), *https://ozmusicbooks.com/product/dna-issue-33-october-1983/*

13 b92 Forums, *https://forum.b92.net/topic/15323-the-scientists-australia/*

Chapter 9. Save Me a Place

1 Walker, Clinton. 'The Ugliest Band On Earth', *www.clintonwalker.com.au/beasts-of-bourbon.html*

Chapter 10. A Place Called Bad

1 Brokenmouth, Robert. 'Tony Thewlis and stories of Weird Love, Blackadder and a re-possessed TV', *www.i94bar.com/interviews/tony-thewlis-and-stories-of-weird-love-blackadder-and-a-re-possessed-tv.*

2 Ibid.

3 Delibašić, Aleksandar. 'Blood Red River: 1982-1984, Citadel' (November 2000), *https://badmusicforbadpeople.com/blood-red-river-1982-1984-citadel-november-2000/*

4 Livingston, Alistair. 'Scientists – Au Go Go Records – 1983 / 1984'(May 3, 2010) *https://killyourpetpuppy.co.uk/news/scientists-au-go-go-records-1983-1984*

5 Andrews, Mark. 'You Only Live Twice: An Interview With The Scientists' (September 18, 2018) *https://www.loudersound.com/features/you-only-live-twice-an-interview-with-the-scientists*

6 Ibid.

7 Andrews, Mark. 'You Only Live Twice: An Interview With The Scientists' (September 18, 2018) *https://www.loudersound.com/features/you-only-live-twice-an-interview-with-the-scientists*

8 Falling, James. 'The Scientists Finally Discover America After 40 Years Of Searching And Destroying', *LA Weekly* (October 2, 2018), *www.laweekly.com/the-scientists-finally-discover-america-after-40-years-of-searching-and-destroying/*

Chapter 11. If it's the last thing that I do

1 Delibašić, Aleksandar. 'Blood Red River: 1982-1984, Citadel' (November 2000), *https://badmusicforbadpeople.com/blood-red-river-1982-1984-citadel-november-2000/*

Chapter 13. Non-Stop Action Groove

1 McFarlane, Ian. 'Whammo Homepage', *Encyclopaedia of Australian Rock and Pop*. St Leonards, NSW: Allen & Unwin 1999

2 Casimir, John and Shane Danielson. '25 years on - a long, hot day's play at the first Big Day Out', *The Sydney Morning Herald* First published December 9, 2016. Updated January 25, 2017) *www.smh.com.au/entertainment/music/25-years-on--a-long-hot-days-play-at-the-first-big-day-out-20161209-gt7kyf.html*

3 Rollins, Henry. 'Nirvana vs Beasts Of Bourbon at first Big Day Out

– Henry Rollins reflects', *ABC Double J* (13 July 2014) *www.abc.net.au/doublej/music-reads/features/nirvana-vs-beasts-of-bourbon-at-first-big-day-out-henry-rollins-/10273188*

Chapter 14. The Formula for Grunge

1 Cross, Charles R. *Here We Are Now: The Lasting Impact of Kurt Cobain.* It Books. 2014.
2 Stratton, Jon. 'The Scientists and Grunge: Influence and Globalised Flows'. *Australian Rock: Essays of Popular Music.* Perth, WA: Network Books. Department of Communication & Cultural Studies (Curtin University), 1 December 2007.
3 Northwest Passage. 'The origin of "grunge"', *www.revolutioncomeandgone.com/articles/1/the-origin-of-grunge.php*
4 Cross, Charles R. *Here We Are Now: The Lasting Impact of Kurt Cobain.* It Books. 2014.
5 Guitar World. "*Seattle Reign. The Rise and Fall of Seattle Grunge. By Jon Wiederhorn (pp. 1–12)*'. Guitar World Presents Nirvana and the Grunge Revolution, 1998.
6 Stratton, Jon. 'The Scientists and Grunge: Influence and Globalised Flows'. *Australian Rock: Essays of Popular Music.* Perth, WA: Network Books. Department of Communication & Cultural Studies (Curtin University), 1 December 2007.
7 Ibid.
8 Ibid.
9 Murphy, Tom. 'Buzz Osborne of the Melvins on how the band chose covers for Everybody Loves Sausages', *Westword (15 July 2013), www.westword.com/music/buzz-osborne-of-the-melvins-on-how-the-band-chose-covers-for-everybody-loves-sausages-5687742*
10 McManus, Darragh.'Just 20 years on, grunge seems like ancient history', *The Guardian* (1 November 2008), *www.theguardian.com/music/musicblog/2008/oct/31/grunge*
11 Ibid.
12 Stratton, Jon. 'The Scientists and Grunge: Influence and Globalised Flows'. *Australian Rock: Essays of Popular Music.* Perth, WA: Network Books. Department of Communication & Cultural Studies (Curtin University), 1 December 2007.
13 Ibid.
14 Dubrow, Chris. 'Nirvana had nothing on Australia's Lubricated Goat', *The Guardian* (7 April 2014) https://*www.theguardian.com/music/australia-culture-blog/2014/apr/07/australia-grunge-nirvana*
15 True, Everett. 'Ten myths about grunge, Nirvana and Kurt Cobain', *The Guardian* (25 August 2011) *www.theguardian.com/music/2011/aug/24/grunge-myths-nirvana-kurt-cobain*

Chapter 15. Ya Gotta Let Me Do My Thing

1 Wood, Gretchen. 'Down Under Punks and Dixie Rock: Reflections on Making the Documentary Film Chinese Whispers-Southern Roots in the Australian Swampy Sound', Dissertation, The Unviersity of Mississippi (2018), ISBN: 9780438066311
2 Liddiard, Gareth. 'Kim Salmon –

By The Drones' Gareth Liddiard', *Australian Musician, https://australianmusician.com.au/kim-salmon-by-the-drones-gareth-liddiard/*
3 Ibid.
4 Ibid.

Chapter 16. Caught in the Zipper

1 *The Age* (9 June, 2005), 'Singer tells of carjacking' *www.theage.com.au/national/singer-tells-of-carjacking-20050609-ge0bix.html*

Chapter 17. Between the Forest and the Trees

1 *www.carrottoprecords.com/media/darlingdowns/saki039-DDHow-PRESS.pdf*
2 Zuel, Bernard. 'CD Reviews', *The Sydney Morning Herald Blogs* (13 October, 2005) *blogs.smh.com.au/entertainment/archives/club_metro/002620.html*

Chapter 18. Loose Ends

1 Pejic, Dan. 'Kim Salmon Shares His Grand Unifying Theory', *The Dwarf* (15 March, 2010) thedwarf.com.au/interview/1521/kim-salmon-shares-his-grand-unifying-theory
2 Northover, Kylie. 'Lunch with ... Musician Kim Salmon', *The Age*, (29 March, 2014) *www.theage.com.au/entertainment/music/lunch-with--musician-kim-salmon-20140327-35jlh.html).*

Chapter 20. Perpetual Motion

1 Salmon, Kim. 'Thunderous Groove: Kim Salmon Remembers Brian Hooper', *RRR* (21 August, 2018) *www.rrr.org.au/explore/news-articles/kim-salmon-remembers-brian-hooper)*
2 Australian Rock Show Podcast, 'Episode 107 – Charlie Owen Interview', *Australian Rock Review* (16 February, 2019) *https://australianrockreview.com/2019/02/16/episode-107-charlie-owen-interview/*
3 Ibid.

BAND LINE UPS

Moulin Rouge

1975

Dave Faulkner (*keyboards*)
Kim Salmon *(guitar, vocals)*
Neil Fernandes (guitar, vocals)
Tony Ellison (sax)
Rob Moncello (keys, guitar, vox)
Chris Leech (bass)
Steve Gordon (guitar)
Stuart Davies Slate (drums)

Troubled Waters

1975

Kim Salmon (guitar)
John Farley (vocals, bass)
Frank Shannelle (drums)
Chris* (vocals, guitar)
* Surname unknown

The Cheap Nasties

1976

Kim Salmon (guitar, vocals)
Mark Betts (drums)
Neil Fernandes (guitar)
Ken Seymour (bass)
Robert Porritt (vocals)

The Invaders

late 1977 – early 1978
Kim Salmon (vocals)
Roddy Rradalj (guitar)
Boris Sujdovic (bass)
John Rawlings (drums)

The Scientists

May 1978 – August 1978

Kim Salmon (vocals)
James Baker (drums)
Roddy Rradalj (guitar)
Boris Sujdovic (bass)

The Scientists

January – April 1979

Kim Salmon (vocals)
James Baker (drums)
Roddy Rradalj (guitar)
Dennis Byrne (bass)

The Scientists

May 1979 – January 1980

Kim Salmon (vocals)
James Baker (drums)
Ben Juniper (guitar)
Ian Sharples (bass)

The Scientists

1980

Kim Salmon (guitar, vocals)
James Baker (drums)
Ian Sharples (bass)

Louie Louie

April – June 1981

Kim Salmon (guitar, vocals)
Brett Rixon (drums)
Kim Williams (bass)

The Scientists

September 1981 – mid 1985

Kim Salmon (guitar, vocals)
Brett Rixon (drums)
Boris Sujdovic (bass)
Tony Thewlis (guitar)

The Scientists

mid 1985 – mid 1986

Kim Salmon (guitar, vocals)
Boris Sujdovic (bass)
Tony Thewlis (guitar)
Leanne Chock (drums)

The Scientists

mid 1986 – early 1987

Kim Salmon (bass, vocals)
Tony Thewlis (guitar)
Nick Combe (drums)

The Scientists

1987

Kim Salmon (bass, guitar, vocals)
Tony Thewlis (guitar)
Nick Combe (drums)
Brett Rixon (bass, guitar)

Scientists

2004

Kim Salmon (guitar, vocals)
Stu Thomas (bass)
Leanne Cowie (drums)

Kim Salmon and the New Scientists

2018

Kim Salmon (guitar, vocals)
Boris Sujdovic (bass)
Clare Moore (drums)
Michael Stranges (guitar)

The Scientists

2017

Kim Salmon (guitar, vocals)
James Baker (drums)
Boris Sujdovic (bass)
Roddy Radalj (guitar)

The Scientists

2017 – present

Kim Salmon (guitar, vocals)
Leanne Cowie (drums)
Boris Sujdovic (bass)
Tony Thewlis (drums)

Salamander Jim

1983

Kim Salmon (guitar)
Tex Perkins (vocals)
Richard Ploog (drums)

Beasts of Bourbon

1983 – 1991

Kim Salmon (guitar, vocals)
Tex Perkins (vocals)
Spencer P Jones (guitar, vocals)
Boris Sujdovic (bass)
James Baker (drums)

Beasts of Bourbon

1991 – 1993

Kim Salmon (guitar, vocals)
Tex Perkins (vocals)
Spencer P Jones (guitar, vocals)
Brian Henry Hooper (bass)
Tony Pola (drums)

Beasts

2018 – present

Kim Salmon (guitar, vocals)
Tex Perkins (vocals)
Boris Sujdovic (bass)
Tony Pola (drums)
Charlie Owen (guitar)

Kim Salmon and the Surrealists

mid 1987 – 1993

Kim Salmon (guitar, vocals)
Brian Henry Hooper (bass)
Tony Pola (drums)

Kim Salmon and the Surrealists

1993 – 1995

Kim Salmon (guitar, vocals)
Brian Henry Hooper (bass)
Greg Bainbridge (drums)

Kim Salmon and the Surrealists

1995 – 2000

Kim Salmon (guitar, vocals)
Stu Thomas (bass)
Greg Bainbridge (drums)

Kim Salmon and the Surrealists

2000 – present

Kim Salmon (guitar, vocals)
Stu Thomas (bass)
Phil Collings (drums)

Kim Salmon and STM

1994

Kim Salmon (guitar, vocals)
Jim White (drums)
Andrew Entsch (bass)
Warren Ellis (violin, flute)

The Business

1999 – 2000

Kim Salmon (guitar, vocals)
Stu Thomas (bass)
Greg Bainbridge (drums)
Michael Redman (Tenor) Saxophone)
Leon De Bruin (Trumpet)

Antenna

1998

Kim Salmon (guitar, vocals)
Dave Faulkner (vocals, keys)
Justin Frew (guitar, programming)
Stuart McCarthy (guitar, programming)

SALMON

2004

Kim Salmon (guitar, samples)
Ashley Naylor (guitar)
Dave Graney (guitar)
Anton Ruddick (guitar)
Clare Moore (drums)
Michael Stranges (drums)
Matt Walker (guitar)

Precious Jules

2010 – present

Kim Salmon (guitar, vocals)
Michael Stranges (drums)

Kim and Leanne

2013 – present

Kim Salmon (guitar, vocals)
Leanne Cowie (drums)

Kim Salmon and the Guys from Mudhoney

2010

Kim Salmon (guitar, vocals)
Mark Arm (guitar, vocals)
Guy Maddison (bass)
Dan Peters (drums)

Darling Downs

2004 – present

Kim Salmon (guitar, banjo, vocals)
Ron Peno (vocals)

Kim Salmon Power Pop Trio

2015 – present

Melbourne
Kim Salmon (guitar, vocals)
Michael Stranges (drums, vocals)
Loretta Wilde (bass)

Perth
Kim Salmon (guitar, vocals)
Todd Pickett (drums, vocals)
Pete Stone (bass)

Adelaide
Kim Salmon (guitar, vocals)
Shakey McGee (drums)
Pete the Stud Howlett (bass)

Salmon Wilde Stranges

2018

Kim Salmon (guitars, vocals)
Loretta Wilde (bass, vocals)
Michael Stranges (drums, keys, vocals)

SELECTED DISCOGRAPHY

Scientists – Frantic Romantic/Shake (Together Tonight) 7"

The first Kim Salmon single, written with James Baker – the first of Kim's drumming cowriters. Frantic Romantic is still one of the live staples.
Released: June 1979
Produced: Produced by Chris Tuna and The Scientists.
Recorded: Sweet Corn studios, Perth
Label: D.N.A. Records

Scientists – EP 7"

The self-titled EP featured Last Night which the group played on Countdown and which was featured on the *Classic Countdown* compilation record.
Released: 1980
Produced: Produced by Chris Tuna and The Scientists.
Recorded: Sweet Corn studios, Perth in October 1979.
Label: White Rider Records

The Scientists

Also known as the Pink Album, this is the first full length release by Kim. Effectively recorded after the band broke up and funded by passionate fans, the Pink Album was the final document of the Mark 1 Scientists, capturing their punk/pop sound.
Released: 1981
Produced: Produced and mixed by Peter Simpson
Recorded: Shelter Recording studios, Perth between January/March 1981.
Label: EMI Custom

The Scientists – demo tape

The Scientists reappeared in Sydney as the *Mark 2* second coming. The band sent this promotional demo tape, featuring an early version of *Swampland*, out across the country and handed it out at gigs. One of the cassettes ended up with Bruce Milne in Melbourne, who went on to sign the Scientists to his Au Go Go label.
Released: 1981
Produced: Chris Logan
Recorded: @ 2SER studio (Sydney university radio station), Sydney one afternoon in May 1982.
Label: self-released

Scientists – This is My Happy Hour/Swampland 7"

Swampland was the breakout release for the Scientists. Initially attention for the double A side single was stuck on Happy Hour but when *Swampland* emerged the band was big news. A huge selling single for the Australian underground, featuring a different coloured cover on every repressing.
Released: 1982
Produced: Chris Logan and Kim Salmon
Recorded: Palm studios, Sydney in August 1982
Label: Au Go Go

Scientists – Blood Red River (mini album)

Recorded to perfection but marred by unsympathetic mixing, Kim ordered the album be done over and supervised the final mix to deliver a masterpiece for the band.
Released: September 1983
Produced: Chris Logan and Kim Salmon. Mixed by Mark Nutney and Kim Salmon
Recorded @ Richmond Recorders, Melbourne
Label: Au Go Go

Scientists – We Had Love/Clear Spot 7"

The Scientists most grungy recording. Kim described Tony's guitar as sounding like a vacuum cleaner.
Released: December 1983
Produced: Produced by Peter Watts and Kim Salmon
Recorded @ ABC studios, Sydney in August 1983 for a 2JJJ-FM Radio session
Label: Au Go Go

Scientists – When Worlds Collide/Ghost Train 7"

Given away for free at gigs in Sydney and Melbourne and not released elsewhere. Dave Faulkner donated a riff that became the bass line for the A side.
Released: September 1983
Recorded @ recorded live at the Trade Union Club, Sydney and the Prince Of Wales, Melbourne by Ross Giles.
Label: Au Go Go

Scientists – This Heart Doesn't Run on Blood, This Heart Doesn't Run on Love

Another of the Au Go Go recordings in the Scientists purple patch with the label. Featuring the ultra minimal Nitro from the legendary Parramatta Leagues Club show where the band were bottled off stage.
Released: 1984
Produced: Produced by Peter Watts and Kim Salmon.
Recorded @ A.T.A. Studios, Sydney
Label: Au Go Go

Beasts of Bourbon – Axeman's Jazz

Thrown together in one boozy session, the Beasts debut was a stand out in Australian alternative music circles for high sales and low preparation.
Released: July 1984
Produced: Tony Cohen & Roger Greirson
Recorded @ Paradise Studios, Sydney
Label: Green/Big Time

Scientists – Demolition Derby 7"

Whisked off to Belgium to record after the Scientists wowed it at a Festival in Amsterdam, the Scientists mixed a week of drinking, eating and arguing with time in the studio to produce this release. The first appearance of a Scientist stand out Murderess in a Purple Dress.
Released: February 1985
Produced: Paul Delnoy
Recorded @ Soundwor Studios, Brussels
Label: Soundwork Records

Scientists – You Only Live Twice 7"

A cover of the Nancy Sinatra sung James Bond theme song which the band made sound just like the Scientists. Also featured If It's the Last Thing That I Do – Kim's ode to Travis Bickle from Taxi Driver.
Released: September 1985
Produced: Peter Watts/Richard Mazda
Recorded @ Falconer Studios, London & Berry Street Studios, London
Label: Karbon Records

Scientists – You Get What You Deserve

The album that pulled together a bunch of songs in the shadow of the Au Go Go dispute. This was Brett Rixon's last recording session with the band.
Released: 1985
Produced: Peter Watts/Paul Delnoy
Recorded @ Berry Street Studios, London & Soundworks studios, Brussels
Label: Karbon Records

Scientists – Atom Bomb Baby 7"

An example of the parallel release situation the Scientists found themselves in after the dispute with Au Go Go in which new releases would often end up released by two different labels, under different titles and featuring different tracks.
Released: June 1985
Produced: Peter Watts/ Paul Delnoy
Recorded @ Berry Street Studios, London & Soundworks studios, Brussels
Label: Au-Go-Go Records

Scientists – Heading for a Trauma

Compilation taken from early singles, Demolition Derby EP and some unreleased tracks. Heading for a trauma was originally a reference to a girl from Perth who always seemed to be in some kind of drama.
Released: 1985
Label: Au Go Go

Scientists – Weird Love

A re-recording of everything that mattered to that date for their US label Big Time. Leanne's last recording with the band, and one of Kim's favourite albums from the Scientists.
Released: April 1986
Produced: Richard Mazda
Recorded @ West3 studios, London & the Falconer Studios, London
Label: Karbon Records/Big Time Records

Scientists – The Human Jukebox

A surprise third generation version of the band recorded this album quickly and cheerfully, introducing even more challenging songs and sounds that left even some rusted on fans scratching their heads.
Released: May 1987
Produced: Kim Salmon, Tony Thewlis and Nick Combe
Recorded @ Reel 2 Reel studios, Brixton-London.
Label: Karbon Records

Kim Salmon and the Surrealists – Hit Me With the Surreal Feel

The first Surrealists record, captured by two microphones hung from the ceiling of a rehearsal room. Kim's pattern of having one song as a theme running through the record was in evidence here for the first time, with various versions of the Surreal Feel featuring.
Released: 1988
Produced: Kim Salmon
Recorded @ a rehearsal studio in the north west Perth suburb Osbourne Park
Label: Black Eye Records

Beasts of Bourbon – Sour Mash

The second outing from the Beasts was a wild and varied affair, with anything on the table. Considered by some the strongest Beasts record.
Released: December 1988
Produced: Phil Punch and The Beasts
Recorded @ Electric Avenue Studio, Sydney Australia
Label: Red Eye

Kim Salmon and the Surrealists – Just Because You Cant See It, Doesn't Mean It Isnt There

The second Surrealists album was 'creepy where it needed to be, ugly where it needed to be'. Featuring Melt 1 2 and 3 – one song broken into three parts because the band sped up so much during its recording.
Released: 1989
Produced: Kim Salmon, Brian Henry Hooper, Tony Pola
Recorded @ Electric Avenue Studio by Phil Punch
Label: Black Eye Records

Beasts of Bourbon – Black Milk

The album on which Kim introduced the jazzier, intellectual and more emotive songs to the Beasts – songs like Cool Fire and Words from a Woman to her Man took the Beasts to new territory. After this record James Baker and Boris Sujdovic left the band to focus on the Dubrovniks.
Released: July 1990
Produced: Phil Punch and The Beasts
Recorded @ Electric Avenue Studios, Sydney Australia
Label: Red Eye

Kim Salmon and the Surrealists – Essence

One of Kim's favourites, Essence is a wild, tumbling collection of songs from bombastic rock to fragile compositions.
Released: 1991
Produced: Rob Grant
Recorded @ Poons Head Studio in East Fremantle
Label: Red Eye Records/Polydor Records

Beasts of Bourbon – The Low Road

Now with Brian Hooper and Tony Pola as the rhythm section, this was the Beasts most coherent and commercially successful record, honing their previously widespread sound down to a hard edged rock n roll record. Kim's last recording with the Beasts of Bourbon.
Released: December 1991
Produced: Tony Cohen
Recorded @ Metropolis Audio
Label: Red Eye

Scientists – Absolute

In a timely endorsement from the home of grunge – Sub Pop Records – this compilation selected tracks from all releases during the period 1982-1987. The cover featured Kim Salmon original caricatures of the four band members.
Released: 1991
Label: Sub Pop Records

Kim Salmon and the Surrealists – Sin Factory

The apex of the Surrealists in which the 'band was firing on all cylinders'. Commercially and critically successful, this album captured a time and place, image and sound like few other albums can. The last in the sequence of alternating Beasts/Surrealists recordings from an amazingly productive period from '88 to '93 in which seven albums were produced by the two groups.

Released: 1993

Produced: Tony Cohen

Recorded @ RBX Studio Mixed at Atlantis and RBX Studios

Label: Red Eye Records/Polydor Records

Kim Salmon and STM – Hey Believer

A solo album in which half the tracks featured Kim's organically evolving band, STM. Regrettably a one off recording for this group, Hey Believer is a standout of Kim's recorded output. Features a cover of Hank Williams Ramblin' Man – perhaps Kim's best vocal performance.

Released: 1994

Produced: Phil M McKellar

Recorded @ ABC Caulfield Studios, Melbourne

Label: Red Eye Records/Polydor Records

Kim Salmon and the Surrealists – self titled

The only album featuring the Brian Hooper and Greg Bainbridge combination of the Surrealists.

Released: 1995

Produced: Tony Cohen

Recorded @ Metropolis Audio

Label: Red Eye Records/Polydor Records

Kim Salmon and the Surrealists - Ya Gotta Let Me Do My Thing

Recorded in Kim's kitchen in Carlton and mixed by the great Jim Dickinson in Memphis, this album introduced new bass player Stu Thomas, and a broader palette of instruments to Kim's songs. Mostly written at soundchecks while on tour in Europe this album's natural style harks back to the spirit of the Surreal Feel.

Released: April 10, 1997

Produced: Kim Salmon & Jim Dickinson

Recorded @ Kim's house in Carlton, Melbourne. Mixed at Powerhouse Studios, Memphis

Label: Half a Cow

Antenna – Installation

One off recording for the band that reunited Kim with Dave Faulkner, one of his very first collaborators in 1970s Perth. Featuring a guest vocal from Chrissy Amphlett and Kim's most successful song, Come on Spring, this album was Kim's foray into producing pop and electronically inclined music.
Released: 1998
Produced: Antenna
Recorded @ Mr Chill's Flat, Darlinghurst
Label: Mushroom

Kim Salmon and the Business – Record

This was initially to be produced by Dave Faulkner but when things didn't pan out, Kim took over production duties. Record landed Kim lots of air play and several remixes. With lots of horns and keys, this album stands out from other Kim Salmon recordings.
Released: October 25, 1999
Produced: Kim Salmon & Andy Baldwin
Recorded @ Sing Sing Studios, South Yarra - Melbourne
Label: Half a Cow

Kim Salmon - E(a)rnest

Essentially recorded by Kim solo with just an acoustic guitar, this lesser known solo record was intended as a parody of indie folk music but was timed awkwardly with the rise of Angus and Julia Stonet al.
Released: April 4, 2002
Produced: Dave McCluney
Recorded @ Atlantis Sound
Label: MGM

Kim Salmon - Wall/Paper

Home made electronic ambience that Kim created for a theatrical production. A rare and little known Kim Salmon recorded artefact.
Released: 2004
Produced: Kim Salmon
Recorded @ Max Grille
Label: Ecstatic Peace/My Mind's Eye

The Darling Downs – How Can I Forget This Heart of Mine?

Kim and Ron argued about the title for their first album, which started life as a collection of intimate audio sketches the pair created over coffee at Ron's place. Kim won the album title debate.
Released: November 5, 2005
Produced: Kim Salmon
Recorded @ Ponderosa, Melbourne by Clare Moore & Dave Graney
Label: MGM/Carrot Top

The Darling Downs – From One to Another

A darker follow up album featured some 'gobbledeegook' Ron Peno lyrics that amazed Kim and co-producers Dave Graney and Clare Moore. This time Ron's preferred title prevailed.
Released: November 1, 2007
Produced: Kim Salmon with Clare Moore, Dave Graney, Ron Peno
Recorded @ Ponderosa, Melbourne by Clare Moore & Dave Graney
Label: MGM/Carrot Top

Scientists – Sedition

Recorded at Shepherd's Bush in London this is the definitive live set by the Scientists. The next day they played the All Tomorrow's Parties festival as guests of curators Mudhoney.
Released: 2007
Produced: Recorded by (fan and live taper) Shane Browne. Mastered by Greg Wadley and Kim Salmon.
Recorded @ Shepherd's Bush Empire, London
Label: ATP Records

SALMON – Rock Formations

Six guitars, two drum kits, live activated samples and no vocals. This unusual combo was captured in two halves for the album, a studio rehearsal recorded to mini disc on side A and a live recording on side B.
Released: May 17, 2007
Produced: Kim Salmon/John Olson
Recorded @Tracks 1 to 9 recorded live to Pro-tools at Soundpark Rehearsal Rooms in August 2004. Tracks 10 to 22 recorded live at the Sydney Metro January 2006 (live sound at that show by Jordan Briebach).
Label: BANG!

Kim Salmon and the Surrealists – Grand Unifying Theory

With the 2006 reunion of the Surrealists, for the Spanish Azkena Festival, Kim was re-acquainted with the free jazz/noise/ fusion bug and resolved to get the band back together …
Released: March 27, 2010
Produced: Michael Stranges
Recorded @ Soundpark Studios, Northcote - Melbourne
Label: Low Transit Industries/BANG!

Precious Jules

Kim's collaboration with good friend and musical all-rounder Michael Stranges which grew out of their shows as a drum/guitar duo. Shock founder Andrew McGee caught them one night and invited them down to his recording facility in Nagambie to make this record.
Released: June 1, 2011
Produced: Andrew McGee
Recorded @ Empty Room Studio, Nagambie
Label: Agitated Records

Kim Salmon and the Songs from Mudhoney

The result at Kim's 1995 working holiday in Seattle.
Released: 2011
Produced: Kim Salmon/Mudhoney
Label: BANG!

Kim Salmon and Spencer P Jones – Runaways

Recorded on the hop by Kim and Spencer with Mike Stranges, this was recorded at Incubator Studios – literally a refashioned incubator shed in Thornbury. Featuring some unlikely covers by Kanye West and Peggy Lee.
Released: February 15, 2013
Produced: Adrian Akkerman, Kim Salmon, Michael Stranges
Recorded @ Incubator Studios, Thornbury – Melbourne
Label: Kim Salmon/BANG!

The Darling Downs - In the Days When the World was Wide

Ron and Kim shared lyric duties to a much great extent for the third album. This album has subtle instrumentation and beautiful art work.
Released: July 28, 2013
Produced: Ron S Peno, Kim Salmon and Andrew Hehir with Baz Williams
Recorded @ Soundpark Studios, Northcote - Melbourne
Label: Kim Salmon/Beasts Records

True West – Kim and Leanne

Written by Kim with Mike Stranges in only a couple of months, this album throws new Scientist-esque songs at one half of the Scientists to great effect. A collection of songs heavy on clever word play and sharp rhymes.
Released: August 8, 2014
Produced: Kim Salmon and Michael Stranges
Recorded @ Soundpark
Label: Kim Salmon/ BANG!/Hozac

My Script

Described as Kim's first solo record. Recorded mostly in the house of producer Myles Mumford with Kim playing most instruments. During My Script Kim rediscovered his love of visual art, taking up sketching while he waited for Myles to do the sound tech stuff during recording.
Released: March 18, 2016
Produced: Myles Mumford
Recorded @ All Tracks recorded by Myles Mumford at his home and Bakehouse Studio North Fitzroy, Victoria except for tracks 2 and 14 recorded by Jozef Grech at Underground studio Booragoon WA.
Label: Kim Salmon/BANG!

Scientists – A Place Called Bad (4 CD/LP compilation)

A monumental, beatifically curated 80 track, four CD/LP collection of all phases of the Scientists performing and recording career.
Released: 2016
Label: Numero Group

Cheap Nasties - 53rd and 3rd

The only known recording of the most remote punk band in the world. This was a rehearsal at the band's house in Perth, the tape of which surfaced and was eventually released on CD and vinyl by Hozac Records.
Released: June 13, 2016
Produced: Kim Salmon and Michael Stranges
Recorded: These songs were recorded in a dining room in 1977 at the place where the band lived: 53 Third Avenue, Mount Lawley, Perth, Western Australia.
Label: Hozac

Kim Salmon – Live at Tym Guitars

Played with Joe Presedo, who had played in the Scientists in the UK back in the mid-80s along with friends Rob and Alana, this recording captured an instore performance at Tym Guitars, who also produced a Kim Salmon Murderess fuzz pedal.
Released: 2016
Produced: Donnie Miller
Recorded @ Tym Guitars, Brisbane, August 2016
Label: Tym Records

Scientists – Mini Mini Mini/Perpetual Motion 7"

The Scientists first release since the Human Jukebox in 1987. On tour in France Kim renewed affection for Jacques Dutronc which was playing everywhere and recorded Mini Mini Mini, putting it alongside a new version of Perpetual Motion from the Vulcan Hotel days in 1982.

Released: October 2017
Produced: Scientists
Recorded @ The Lab
Label: BANG!

Kim Salmon – Hook Line and Singer

A landmark live cassette recording that Kim made at the Central Club, Richmond in 1992. In 2017 Tym Records transferred the tape to digital and released it on vinyl, giving new life to one of Kim's most complete solo performances.
Released: December 2018
Produced: Andrew Hepburn/Donnie Miller
Recorded @ Central Club Hotel, Richmond, 29 February 1992
Label: Tym Records

Kim, Sam and Doug – Clean, Friendly and Good Communicators (cassette)

Recorded live by a fan at Smiths Alternative in Canberra, this show was a one off for Kim, Sam and Doug after performing the Sydney iteration of *Salmon for Breakfast*. The title alludes to the positive AirBnB review the band got – much to their shame.
Released: February 13, 2018
Produced: Sam Worrad
Recorded @ Smith's Alternative, Canberra by Patrick Cox, Thursday 21/9/17.
Label: Damn You, Records

Scientists – Braindead (Resuscitated) SurvivalsKills 7"

An old Scientist song reimagined and sped up combined with a curious new composition.
Released: July 2018
Produced: The Scientists
Recorded @ Rolling Stock Studio, Collingwood-Melbourne by Myles Mumford
Label: In the Red Records

Beasts – Still Here

Recorded by accident after the passing of Brian Henry Hooper. With Spencer resting on the couch in the studio, the Beasts recorded songs written by nearly all members past and present.
Released: June 2019
Produced: Andrew Idge Hehir
Recorded @ Soundpark Studios, Northcote - Melbourne
Label: BANG!

Scientists – 9H2O.SiO2

The triumphant mini album return of the Scientists, released while on tour in the States. Kim, Boris and Leanne laid down tracks in Melbourne while Tony added guitar noise in the UK.
Released: April 2019
Produced: The Scientists
Recorded @ Soundpark Studios, Northcote-Melbourne by Andrew (Idge) Hehir, except "Hey Sydney" recorded @ Rolling Stock Studio, Collingwood-Melbourne by Myles Mumford
Label: In the Red Records

Kim Salmon/Scientists single – The Poison Pen/Dissonance, split 7# single

A song on which Kim plays all the instruments as part of the promotion for Douglas Galbraith's biography entitled Kim Salmon and the Formula For Grunge backed with Scientists giving a sneak preview from their 'in the can' forthcoming album to be released post pandemic.
Released: November 9, 2019
Label: Self released

Kim Salmon - Let's All Get Destroyed/Unadulterated 7"single

Two entirely Salmon performed songs initially recorded to help promote the US In The Red release of My Script.
Released: August 22, 2020
Label: Self released

Kim Salmon & the Surrealists – Rantings from the Book of Swamp

An improvised show, broadcast live to an online audience during COVID-19 lockdowns, with the purpose of recording a new album. For lyrical content Kim referred to his sketchbooks, all entitled various volumes of "The Book Of Swamp' with the intention of fitting various sketched lyrics as vocals with whatever the band came up with musically – hence the title of the show.
Released: September 4, 2020
Produced: Kim Salmon & the Surrealists
Recorded: June 13th and 14th, 2020 @ Rolling Stock Recording Rooms by Myles Mumford for 2 live streams directed by Andrew Watson @ Semiconductor media.
Label: In the Red Records

Kim Salmon – OK Commissioner

One sided limited run of individually signed red vinyl LP of an experimental improvised performance from 2015. The label features an individually hand drawn artwork. This track was heavily edited into a series of segue vignettes incorporated on the solo album My Script. This is the first time available in its original full form. Side 2 is engraved with the credits.

Released: March 15, 2021
Produced: Kim Salmon
Label: Self released

Scientists – Negativity

The album reunites the classic 1980s lineup of Kim Salmon, Tony Thewlis, Boris Sujdovic, and Leanne Cowie for the first full length album in 35 years.
Released: June 11, 2021
Produced: Scientists
Label: In the Red Records

Kim Salmon – Self Replicator/Everybody's Out of Town

Inspired by walking the deserted streets during COVID-19 lockdown, the original song Self Replicator is paired with the Bacharach classic, with Kim Salmon playing and arranging himself on guitar, vocals, fuzz bass, synth and drums.
Released: August 20, 2021
Produced: Kim Salmon
Recorded @ Headgap Studios, Thornbury by Finn Keane.
Label: Self released

Smoked Salmon – How Did They Ever Manage/Slider Street 7# single

First single from Smoked Salmon featuring the Melbourne line up of the band, which also spawned a film clip produced by Benny Ward from Pinkhouse Studios. The B-side features the Perth line up of the band.
Released: August 23, 2024
Produced: Kim Salmon
Recorded @ Rollingstock Records by Myles Mumford, and Jozef Grech.
Label: Cheersquad Records and Tapes

Smoked Salmon – Hell in a Handbasket/These Grooves are Haunted 7# single

Hell in a Handbasket is Kim Salmon's bleak appraisal of current world events, straight outa Bosch! On this second single from the Smoked Salmon album, French rhythm section and vocalists Delphine Ciampi and Dimi Dero team up with Salmon and Douglas Galbraith to deliver this blistering descent into hell. B-Side is 'These Grooves are Haunted', a maniacal slice of stomping glam rock performed by the Smoked Salmon Melbourne Chapter and recorded by Henry Hugo.
Released: November 29, 2024
Produced: Kim Salmon
Recorded @ Recorded at Stereodrome Studios Perpignan France by Sylvain Philipon; Recorded at Untuned Studios Doncaster by Henry Hugo
Label: Cheersquad Records and Tapes

Smoked Salmon – Hey Hey Narcissus, digital single

The French chapter of Smoked Salmon booked themselves into Stereodrome Studio in the South of France to wind up their national tour in October 2023. Armed with a couple of unfinished songs and a sketch, Kim asked "got any spare riffs?". Bassist Delphine provided one which the band promptly jammed into shape. Kim eventually channelled the vocal hook line of Hey Hey Narcissus, which was later sung by Melbourne mainstay Claire Birchall.
Released: January 31, 2025
Produced: Kim Salmon
Recorded @ Recorded at Stereodrome Studios in Perpignan France by Sylvain Philipon; vocals recorded at Rollingstock Recording by Myles Mumford.
Label: Cheersquad Records and Tapes

Smoked Salmon

The inaugural Smoked Salmon LP featuring the work of four separate engineers in four separate studios with nine musicians across three states and two countries.
Released: February 28, 2025
Produced: Kim Salmon
Recorded @ Stereodrome Studios (Sylvain Philipon); Rollingstock Recording (Myles Mumford); Headgap Studios (Finn Keane); Jozef Grech.
Label: Cheersquad Records and Tapes

Kim Salmon & Masami Kawaguchi – Blossoming

Stemming from their mutual admiration, Kim Salmon and Japanese guitarist Masami Kawaguchi collaborate to create these unique improvisational compositions that blend their distinct guitar styles.
Released: 2025
Produced: Kim Salmon
Recorded: Live
Label: Kasumuen Records

Smoked Salmon – Totally Sick

Unreleased at the time of writing, this record captures sickly themed songs from Salmon's catalogue.
Released: TBC 2026
Produced: Kim Salmon
Label: Cheersquad Records and Tapes

Kim Salmon – Haunted Grooves

Haunted Grooves was recorded live on stage at various venues between 2019 and 2023 with Douglas Galbraith, Mark Carson and a loop pedal accompanying Kim Salmon. With selected songs and stories, Haunted Grooves exists to bring your attention to some of these songs and the now deceased characters who helped create them.
Released: TBC 2026
Produced: Kim Salmon and Douglas Galbraith
Recorded: Live at The Great Club Marrickville, George Lane St Kilda, Bridge Hotel Castlemaine, Wheatsheaf Hotel Adelaide by Dugald Jayes, and Thornbury Picture House, Thornbury by Alan Flindell.
Label: In the Red Records

Recordings available @
kimsalmon.bandcamp.com

BIBLIOGRAPHY

(?), Eric. 'A Quick One: Kim Salmon', *Blogspot*, February 1, 2009. *http://attackingthebeat.blogspot.com/2009/02/quick-one-kim-salmon.html*

Barrett, Peter. 'Rock of ages. The evolution of rock in Melbourne – a tale of tribes, egos, revelry and rebellion', *The Sydney Morning Herald*, October 26, 2012. *https://www.smh.com.au/entertainment/music/rock-of-ages-20121016-27pdd.html*

Brokenmouth, Robert. 'Runaways - Kim Salmon and Spencer P. Jones (Incubator Recording)', *i94 Bar*, June 1, 2014. *http://www.i94bar.com/albums/kim-salmon-and-spencer-p-jones-runaways-incubator-recording*

Brooker, G. 'The Scientists, songs that kim salmon taught us', 2004. *www.youbettershutupandlisten.com/lead/%3Fp%3D111*

Buncle, Ross. 'The Dave Faulkner Song Credit Controversy', *Perth Punk*, 2013. *http://www.perthpunk.com/the-geeks-story/the-dave-faulkner-song-credit-controversy/*

Cameron, Keith. *Mudhoney: The Sound and the Fury from Seattle*. Voyageur Press, March 21, 2014.

Dorval, Sophia. 'KIM SALMON & THE SURREALISTS – Grand Unifying Theory', *Verbicide Magazine*, April 21, 2010. *https://www.verbicidemagazine.com/2010/04/21/kim-salmon-the-surrealists-grand-unifying-theory/*

Dwyer, Michael. 'Grunge City', *The Age*, February 23, 2005. *https://www.theage.com.au/entertainment/music/grunge-city-20050223-gdzni8.html*

Emery, Patrick. 'Animal magnetism: Two former Beasts of Bourbon have reunited', *The Sydney Morning Herald*, February 3, 2012. *https://www.smh.com.au/entertainment/music/animal-magnetism-20120202-1qv3d.html*

Emery, Patrick. 'Kim Salmon', *The Brag*, March 31, 2016. *https://thebrag.com/kim-salmon/*

Emery, Patrick. 'Melbourne launch for posthumous Brian Henry Hooper album'. *i92 Bar*, October 6, 2018. *http://www.i94bar.com/news/melbourne-launch-for-posthumous-brian-henry-hooper-album*

Goldberg, Aaron. 'Kim Salmon Interview', *Perfect Sound Forever*, October 1999. *https://www.furious.com/perfect/kimsalmon.html*

Hogan, J, 'Rock Star car-jacked', *Sydney Morning Herald*, 2005. *https://www.smh.com.au/entertainment/celebrity/rock-star-car-jacked-20050610-gdlhh7.html*

HoZac Records, 'Kim Salmon & Leanne Cowie', *HoZac Records, https://hozacrecords.com/kim-salmon-leanne-cowie/*

Palmer, Tahlia. 'Coming Back to Where it All Began: TP interviews Kim Salmon', *cool Perth Nights,* December 15, 2010.

Pecorelli, John. 'Transcript of 1994 interview with Kim Salmon', *atomicage.com*, 1994. *http://www.atomicage.com/notes/salmint.html*

Perkins, T. 'Tex', Pan McMillan, Australia, 25 July 2017.

Pissant! A Story of 80s Australian Underground, August 8, 2011. *https://8tracks.com/cousincreep/pissant-a-story-of-80-s-australian-underground*

Prato, Greg. *Grunge is Dead: The Oral History of Seattle Rock Music.* Toronto: ECW Press, April 1, 2009.

Rogers, Neil. "Getting the Band Back Together': Kim Salmon Chats to Neil Rogers about The Beasts' New Album, Still Here', *RRR,* February 14, 2019. *https://www.rrr.org.au/on-demand/segments/getting-the-band-back-together-kim-salmon-chats-to-neil-rogers-about-the-beasts-new-album-still-here*

Salmon, Kim. 'Spare a dollar for the maker, music doesn't play itself', *The Age,* 2011. *https://www.theage.com.au/opinion/society-and-culture/spare-a-dollar-for-the-maker-music-doesnt-play-itself-20110809-1ikri.html*

Stratton, Jon. 'The Birthday Party and The Scientists: Nihilism, Suburbia, and the Importance of Class.' *Thesis Eleven 144,* no. 1, February 2018, pp. 100–116. *https://doi.org/10.1177/0725513618755776*

Tijs, Andrew. 'Waleed Aly and Kim Salmon', *Noise11*, August 12 2019. *http://www.noise11.com/vinterviews/waleed-aly-and-kim-salmon*

Walker, Clinton. *Stranded: the secret history of Australian independent music, 1977-1991.* Sydney: Pan Macmillan, 1996.

Williams, Tom. '"Living Legends" To Be Honoured By Other Legends in New Concert Series', *Music Feeds,* June 17, 2014. *https://musicfeeds.com.au/news/living-legends-to-be-honoured-by-other-legends-in-new-concert-series/*

Yarm, Mark. *Everybody Loves Our Town: An Oral History of Grunge.* New York: Three Rivers Press, March 13, 2012.

ACKNOWLEDGEMENTS

To Kim Salmon

Thank you for your generous collaboration on this book — for your time, stories, memories, photos, songs, jokes, art, breakfasts, drinks, theories, trust and friendship.

Special thanks to

Andy Griffiths, Bob Galbraith, Di Galbraith, David Tenenbaum, Jill Griffiths, Maxine Pryce, Ross Johnston.

Thanks to

Alex Salmon, Alex Kamenev, Antoni Jach & Masterclass XVIII, Ashley Naylor, Angie Jones, Andrew Fuller, Barry Douglas, Boris Sujdovic, Brian Henry Hooper, Brian Nankervis, Brooke Munday, Bruce Milne, Caroline Kennedy, Clare Moore, Clinton Walker, Chris Pickering, Daniel Emeny, Dale Nelder, Dave Graney, Davey Lane, Dan Kelly, Dean Purkis, Diya Dey, Ellen Yan Cheng, Emma Salmon, Fairfield Primary School, Gareth Liddiard, Garry Gray, Gayle Sherwell, Gene Salmon, Geoff Reaney, Grandview Hotel, Guy Maddison, Gorka Larruzea, Harry Butler, Henry Rollins, Hozac Records, Jack Salmon, James Baker, Jaimie Leonarder, Jane Durrell, Jacqui Galbraith, Jesse Maddison, Jim Antonopoulos, John Wertfein, Juan M Iturrarte, Jon Von Goes, Joy Salmon, Leanne Cowie, Larry Hardy, Leticia Maher & Memo, Kat Amiss, Kerri Simpson-Alison Ferrier-Barb Waters-Suzannah Espie, Kid Congo Powers, Madeline Galbraith, Mark Arm, Mark Newbound, Maria Kamenev, Megan Salmon, Michael Stranges, Mick Harvey, Mick Thomas, Mitali Ross, Myles Mumford, Neil Fernandes, Ninevah Hooper, Numero Records, Owen Salmon, Paul Mameghan, Penny Ikinger, Pete The Stud Howlett, Project 33, Robert Brokenmouth, Rick Swaney, Ron Peno, Roslyn Johnson, Russell Barclay, Sam Worrad, Sandra Salmon, Scott Shaw, Sean Simmons, Steve Turner, Stu Thomas, Taylor Renee Thomas, Tex Perkins, Tim Pittman, Tim Marmach, Todd Picket, Tony Thewlis, Ursula Woods, Warren Ellis.

THE AUTHOR

Douglas Galbraith is a writer, public servant and part time musician. This is his first book.

Other Melbourne Books music titles:

Astonishing Rock Trivia
John Tait

Captain Matchbox & Beyond: The Music & Mayhem of Mic & Jim Conway
Catherine Fleming, John Tait, and Mic and Jim Conway

Cold Chisel: Wild Colonial Boys
Michael Lawrence

Daddy Who?: The inside story of the raise and demise of Australia's greatest rock band
Craig Horne

Hear Me Talking to Ya
Bob Sedergreen

I Hear Motion: Bands that soundtracked our lives 1980–89
Jane Gazzo

I'll Be Gone: Mike Rudd, Spectrum and how one song captured a generation
Craig Horne

Mick Thomas: These Are The Days
Mick Thomas

Midnight Oil: The Power and The Passion
Michael Lawrence

Noise in My Head: Voices from the Ugly Australian Underground
Jimi Kritzler

Paulie Stewart: All the Rage
Paulie Stewart

Roots: How Melbourne became the live music capital of the world
Craig Horne

Shoulda Been Higher: A Celebration of 30 Years of Triple J's Hottest 100
Tom W Clarke

Sound As Ever: A Celebration of the Greatest Decade in Australian Music (1990-1999)
Jane Gazzo

Spirits of the Hoey: A Love Letter to the Hopetoun Hotel
Liz Giuffre, Gregory Ferris & Bryan Cook

Sunbury: Australia's Greatest Rock Festival
Peter Evans

Tait's Modern Guide to Record Collecting
John Tait

Techno Shuffle: Rave Culture and The Melbourne Underground
Paul Fleckney

The Ballroom: The Melbourne Punk and Post-Punk Scene
Dolores San Miguel

The Dingoes' Lament
John Bois

The Remarkable Mr Morrison: The Virtuosity and Versatility of Australia's Master Musician
Mervyn E. Collins

The Seekers
Graham Simpson and Christopher Patrick

The Seekers: Behind the Curtain
Bruce Woodley AO

This will explain everything
Jeff Duff

You Don't Need A Weatherman: Bob Dylan for Beginners
Chris O'Connor

Wangaratta Festival of Jazz & Blues 30 Years
Adrian Jackson & Andra Jackson

Whatever Happened to Diana Trask
Diana Trask

www.melbournebooks.com.au/categories/music

Wade Street, Embleton still echoes with the sound of Kim, aged 16, practicing guitar. Photo: Joy Salmon

top: Brad, Megan and Kim, circa 1967.
Photo: Kim Salmon

bottom: Owen and Joy Salmon, Fremantle circa 1982.
Photo: Kim Salmon

top: Kim acoustic guitar, which he painted and repainted to fit his latest musical taste. Circa 1973. Photo: Joy Salmon

bottom: Salmon goes electric, complete with Army Disposals leather jacket. Circa 1975. Photo: Chris Leech

top: The Cheap Nasties, 1977. Seen here with Elvis poster. Photo: Darry Le Murcia

middle top: An early version of the Cheap Nasties, 1976, featuring Dave Flick (Faulkner) — far left. Photo: Kim Salmon

middle bottom: Between Cheap Nasties and Scientists there was Exterminators/Invadors — introducing Boris Sujdovic and Roddy Radalj, 1977. Photo: Kim Salmon

bottom: Mark 1 Scientists, circa 1978. Enter James Baker. Photo: Nigel Birch

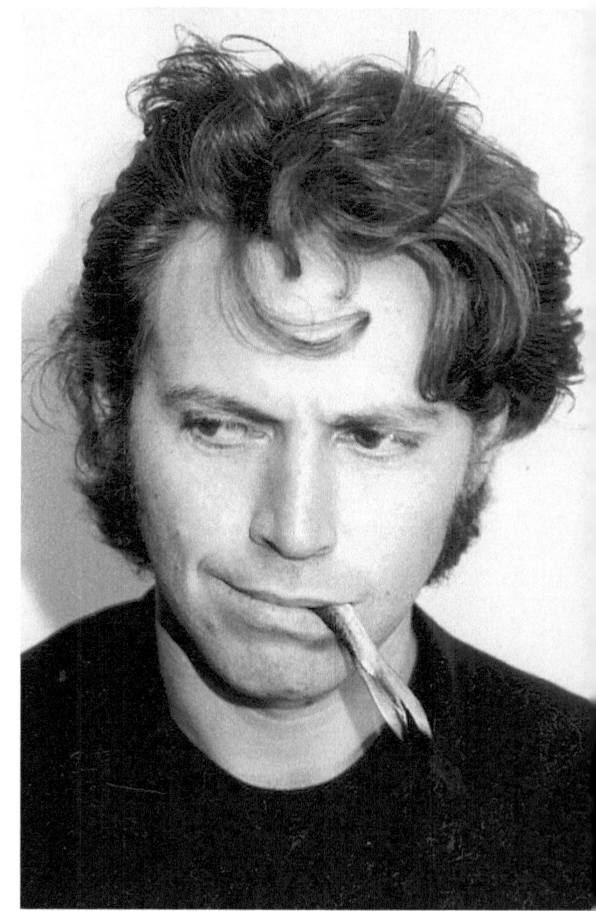

top: Original Beasts of Bourbon line up, promoting Black Milk, circa 1989. Photo: Tony Mott

bottom: 'How many surrealists does it take to change a light bulb?

A fish…' Photo: Russell Kilbey

Kim Salmon and Tex Perkins, early Beasts of Bourbon, circa 1983.
Photo: Kim Salmon

top: Brett Rixon - smart alecy hobbo and great friend. RIP. Circa 1985. Photo: Liz Dear

bottom: Kim Salmon with the 'flame guitar' circa 1985 — a customised coral (salmon) toned Fender Coronado with Kim's hand carved flaming scratch plate. Recreated by Tym Guitars, Brisbane in 2017. Photo: Kim Salmon

top: Mark 2 Scientists circa 1984. Photo: Tony Harrison

bottom: Scientists circa 1985 — dark, angry, silent & foreboding. Photo: Tony Harrison

top: Kim with Fender Thinline circa 1997. Photo: Kim Salmon

bottom: Kim's last gig with the Beasts of Bourbon, 1994. Photo: Kim Salmon

top: Kim with Andrew Entsch & Spencer P Jones at the GB residency, circa 1992. Photo: Kim Salmon

middle: Kim Salmon and STM — 'I didnt even tell the band what STM stood for', 1994. Photo: Kim Salmon

bottom: STM — 'still one of the best bands I've ever seen' (Gareth Liddiard), 1994. Photo: Kim Salmon

top: Kim Salmon and his Magic Pants (clearly the pants had lost some magic by this point). Coney Island, 1992. Photo: Kim Salmon

bottom: Kim and Brian Hooper outside Tony Thewlis' flat after another night of whisky. Waiting for Andrew Hepburn to take them to Dover, 1995. Photo: Kim Salmon

top: Kim Salmon and the Surrealists circa 1992. Photo: Piet Weinman

middle: Second line up of Surrealists, circa 1995. Photo: Antony Alekna

bottom: Third line up of Surrealists, circa 1995. Photo: Stu Thomas

top: Kim, Bono, Brian. 1993. One of them declared themselves a god. Photo: John Foy

middle: Kim and Iggy, St Kilda, 1993. Photo: Linda Fearon

bottom: Kim in handcuffs with Dave Graney & Clare Moore on the Jimeoin show, circa 1995. Photo: Kim Salmon

top: Kim Salmon and the Business, 1999. Photo: Erick Regnard

bottom: Thurston Moore, Kim Gordon, Kim Salmon, Nick Cave & Mark Arm, 1993. Photo: Tony Mott

top: SALMON. 6 guitars, 2 drums — a 'pretty exciting, confronting social experiment' (Ashley Naylor). Circa 2006. Photo: Jesse Marlow

bottom: Seein' Spots — Kim, Doug and Sam (Worrad) on stage for Salmon for Breakfast in Sydney, 2017. Photo: Lyndal Irons

top: Kim and Michael Stranges — 'I kind of view him now as being my band', 2017. Photo: Ross Johnston

middle: Kim and Leanne (Cowie), 2014. Photo: Kim Salmon

bottom: Kim and Spencer P Jones, circa 2013. Photo: Kim Salmon

top: The Scientists on tour in Europe 2017, with Maxine & tour manager Gary. Photo: Kim Salmon

middle: Current day Scientists — Boris, Kim, Leanne and Tony. Photo: Kim Salmon

bottom: Mark 1 Scientists (Roddy, Kim, Boris & James) reunion tour 2015. Photo: unknown

top: Salmon for Breakfast — a show about writing a book about Kim Salmon. Featuring Brian Nankervis, Kim, Doug & Mike, 2017. Photo: Ross Johnston

middle: Fourth line up of the Surrealists — Kim, Stu & Phil Collings 2018. Photo: Kim Salmon

bottom: A night at the Tote to celebrate Kim's Living Legends night, as part of Leaps and Bounds Festival. Photo: Kim Salmon

top: Kim and Mike as Precious Jules — 'We don't rehearse, but we talk about what we're going to wear' (Mike Stranges). circa 2011. Photo: Elisa Bryant Jones

middle: Kim & Maxine Pryce. Circa 2014. Photo: Kim Salmon

bottom: The front room of Kim and Maxie's house — a relaxed jumble of musical oddments. Photo: Kim Salmon

top: Beasts — still here. Croxton Bandroom, Northcote, 2019. Photo: Ross Johnston

middle: Ron & Kim — Darling Downs. Grandview Hotel, 2016, 'I'm the Ernie Wise to his Eric Morecambe'. Photo: Ross Johnston

bottom: Fucking Shit Up — created by Kim pressing his thumb on his amplified guitar lead to make noise 'just sharp of G'. Photo: Ross Johnston

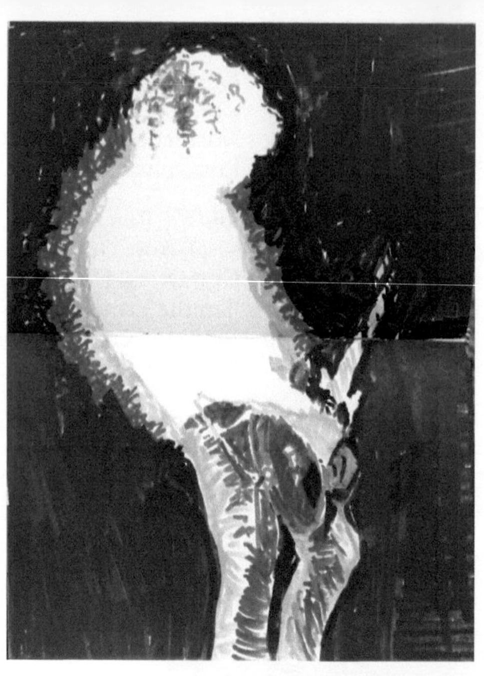

top: Artworks by Kim Salmon. Photo: Ross Johnston

bottom: Kim and Gene at Kim's 60th birthday, 2017. Photo: Barry Doug

Kim and Brian Henry Hooper. Photo: Ninevah Hooper

Kim and Spencer P Jones. Photo: Barry Douglas

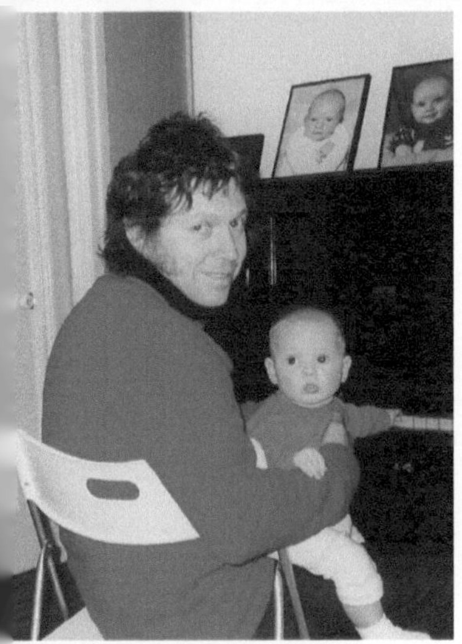

clockwise:

Kim and Emma, 2004

Emma and Gene, 2006

Alex and Jack, 2015

Jack and Kim, 2017

Alex, Kim, Gene and Emma, 2016

Photos: Kim Salmon

www.ingramcontent.com/pod-product-compliance
Ingram Content Group UK Ltd.
Pitfield, Milton Keynes, MK11 3LW, UK
UKHW040603210726
13854UKWH00008B/1883